Wom

WOMEN IN CRIME

The Inside Stories of Life Behind Bars

—

XAVIER WATERKEYN

To everyone that I have ever met. You played your parts.
And to everyone that I never met. You played your parts too.

First published in Australia in 2005 by
New Holland Publishers (Australia) Pty Ltd
Sydney • Auckland • London • Cape Town

14 Aquatic Drive Frenchs Forest NSW 2086 Australia
218 Lake Road Northcote Auckland New Zealand
86 Edgware Road London W2 2EA United Kingdom
80 McKenzie Street Cape Town 8001 South Africa

National Library of Australia Cataloguing-in-Publication Data:
    Waterkeyn, Xavier
    Women in Crime.
    Includes index.
    ISBN 1 74110 313 4.

    1. Female offenders - Australia. I. Title.

    364.374
Publisher: Fiona Schultz
Editor: Jan Hutchinson
Project Editor: Lliane Clarke
Designer: Greg Lamont
Production Manager: Linda Bottari
Printer: McPherson's Printing Group

Cover painting: *Waiting in Vain* by an ex-prisoner, anonymous.

10 9 8 7 6 5 4 3 2 1

Contents

About the author

Xavier Waterkeyn has a wide range of interests. Two of his impulses have resulted in DMHQ, a corporate training business specializing in human relationship and communication problems in the world of work, and Flying Pigs, the manuscript assessment service and literary agency he formed in partnership with book-seller, manager and ABC book reviewer Clare Calvet.

Xavier is the author of several books, including several upcoming New Holland titles, and he is currently mentoring other writers. In no particular order he has also worked as a video director, interviewer, tutor to high school students, teacher of English, tour guide, actor, cook, medical orderly, manager of a Psychic Centre, program coordinator of a Community College, first aid instructor, graphic designer, photographer, marketer and bookseller.

Acknowledgements

First and foremost I would like to thank my unnamed sources—those people who for any number of reasons chose to stay anonymous. Your candour and openness often amazed me. To all of you, I thank you for your trust. I've done my best to preserve your thoughts, feelings and experiences even when sometimes I've had to rearrange your words for the sake of clarity. I've had to protect the innocent from embarrassment and humiliation, and I've had to protect the guilty from giving them the power to exact revenge. As such, I've had to protect people from the consequences of 'lagging' because in jail you can't run away from anything. Even out of jail people can still hurt you or hurt people you care about, just for talking. I hope that I have not betrayed that trust.

To all you others whom I can name, and in no particular order, alphabetical or otherwise, I'd like to thank:

Wolfgang Buschhaus, James Forsyth, Kay Rizzo and all the other staff at Dymocks Sydney for all the ideas and all the help through the years pointing me to the right books. You're a great bunch. Les Drelich for the information about juveniles; David Garland for the historical stuff; Ray Jackson for his insights on Indigenous Australians; Gini Seaton for the psychological insights (and the late Eric Berne for one helluva psychological framework); Neer Korn for some tips; Sara Moeda for the contacts, Lee Rhiannon for her insights into the political process, and Wayne Watson, Jacquelin Giuffre and the team at CRC Sydney for information about the process of community restoration.

Jeremy Angus, Mark Bird, Nick Bird, Dominic Blasonato, Guy Caron, Marianna Grillo, Eric Hanson, Liz Hayden, Sandra McDonald, Annie Neue, Maggie Richardson and Jack Strom for being such great friends and for feeding me—these people know that the way to this boy's heart is through his stomach. James Arkoudis (what a guy!), Suzie Sandrussi, and Ivanka Young (what gals!) for their legal work, Brendan Walsh for the media advice.

Thanks to my mother, Marcelle Waterkeyn, for teaching me what was important, and what wasn't, and for so many other things too, and to my sister, Jacqui Waterkeyn, her partner Tony Esposito, my brother-in-law-to-be, ditto, and to my as yet unborn nephew who will come into the world about the same time as this, my first baby.

Thanks to Susanna Hubarenko, a marvellous friend, and a great proofreader, for so much, and to my agent Clare Calvet at Flying Pigs, a marvellous friend and a great critic (thanks for getting me the gig, Clarushla!). My publisher Fiona Schultz, for being a joy to work with and the team at New Holland, including my editor, Jan Hutchinson. Oh, and to you too, dear reader. Thanks for caring enough about an important issue to pick up this book and read it.

PREFACE   GETTING REAL ABOUT WHAT'S POSSIBLE

This is a book about how innocent little girls become guilty adult criminals, and the sort of lives they have.

It's a book about a process called criminalisation.

It's a book about what it's like to be a woman who gets arrested and who spends time in jail and about what happens to her after getting out.

It's also a little about why, in spite of all the millions of words written about how inadequate 'the system' is, and all the conferences, and all the media attention, and all the experts, and all the do-gooding, and all the hand-wringing, and all the real work being done, the system' isn't changing fast enough.

In this book I raise far more questions than I can possibly answer, but if it makes even one of you think a little bit about the reality beneath the headlines— and the reality that never even makes the headlines in the first place—then it will have served some purpose.

I've chosen to concentrate on the journeys of girls and women. It's not that boys and men are unimportant, but considerably more words have been written about male criminals than female ones. And although there is a substantial body of work comprising government reports, statistical analyses and academic writing on female criminals in Australia there is little in the way of books for the general reader about the life journeys of women who commit crime. Aside from books written by particular women themselves, and tabloid-type books filled with gory details about (extremely rare) violent female criminals there is very little for the general reader about the specific circumstances that lead a woman to crime and what happens after. I embarked on this project to redress that balance, at least partially.

Experts and 'those in the know' about any subject frequently criticise the general public for being ignorant and having ill-informed opinions. You hear things like 'They just don't know what they're talking about' or 'They don't want to know' or 'They don't care' or 'People just don't realise the problems I have to deal with, how under-resourced I am, the sheer scope of the problems'.

As a result, those in the know often find themselves biting their lips in frustration whenever they hear yet another half-baked mishmash of ignorant preconceptions, unexamined prejudices and off-the-cuff criticisms spouting from the lips of those not in the know.

You'd think that those in the know would want you to know as much as you could about female criminals. In that way you'd assume that people could make informed opinions about the subject: that way people might start caring enough to lobby for change where we need it.

When I first started this book I had fantasies that those in the know would see the value of what I was doing. Surely they would seize every opportunity to promote the work that they were doing and understand the importance of getting out the information on a subject that directly affects tens of thousands of Australians every year and that indirectly affects all of us. My fantasies, as it turned out, were a little naive.

Amazingly, I found that the various state Departments of Corrective Services varied tremendously in the scope of cooperation that they were willing to offer. I was unable to secure permission to interview some inmates because waiting three months for an ethics committee to make a decision was simply impractical, given my deadlines. One department implied that they wanted final approval over anything I wrote!

This was completely unreasonable, especially in a democracy that is supposed to pay at least lip service to freedom of speech. I was hardly dealing with classi-fied material, and I was bound by confidentiality agreements already. The upshot is that I can neither confirm nor deny rumours of overcrowding in jails, of inmates sleeping in corridors or of inmates sleeping in transportation vans, because some departments won't even let me ask about such things. I can neither confirm nor deny hearsay reports about the difficulties of working in the system. I can neither confirm nor deny evidence of all the efforts and programs in jails that are making a real positive difference in some women's lives, simply because the people who could confirm or deny whatever there was to confirm or deny wouldn't talk to me.

My experience in corresponding with the various state ministries of justice gave me an insight into one clue as to why you don't hear much about what goes on in prisons. Perhaps the personality of the man at the top (there are so few women at the top) determines the whole culture of the prison system and the decisions that others make? I was given several reasons why the ministries would not co-operate with me. One was that public promotion of particular prisoners can lead other prisoners to target them. However nowhere do I mention any intention to publicly promote individual prisoners or ex-prisoners. In fact, throughout this book I've made it quite clear that I have gone to consid-erable trouble to protect the identities of my sources. So that argument, at least in the case of this book, isn't valid.

Another was that the victims of a crime wouldn't want to relive it by reading about it without some capacity to respond. But again, without identifying the name(s) of the criminal(s) and the details of crime(s), what you read would be unlikely to reopen any wounds unless you were sensitive to generalities that could apply to many cases besides your own. One point was that we need a higher level of responsibility for the stories that we tell, and the stories that we look at. I agree. There is such a thing as exploitative curiosity—just as there is the public good.

My aim isn't to create tabloid journalism in book form. But since the print media is always reporting on cases as they occur I wonder if there is a double standard here. Are there other reasons for Corrective Services Departments not wanting me to speak to prisoners?

'Officialdom' wasn't the only source of silence. Community organisations working with female criminals also varied hugely in their responses. Some staff spent hours with me, but often enough I left messages on answering machines and sent emails galore without ever getting a reply. This is how I explained the project to prospective participants:

> I am currently writing a book called 'Women in Crime' which will be published nationally in 2005. It will be an excellent way to educate the public about issues of female criminals and detainees, and will promote the work of individuals and organisations that are helping, supporting and rehabilitating these women. 'Women in Crime' will provide insights about women who commit offences and the effects of these crimes on their own lives and those of their families.
>
> It's important that the Australian public understands what women experience of the criminal justice system, especially if they spend time in jail or under home detention. I am seeking assistance from organisations that are involved with women who have committed crimes and would like to interview both women who have had dealings with the criminal justice system and professionals who work with current or past female criminals for their unique viewpoints.
>
> I will, of course, treat these enquiries with rigorous attention to any level of confidentiality needed, and I am prepared to provide and sign any confidentiality agreements and interview/photographic releases that may be necessary and acknowledge all assistance.
>
> This book will provide an opportunity for these experiences to be shared with the wider community; the book cannot be published without the assistance of individuals like you or organisations like yours.
>
> Even if you choose not to contribute, I intend to have a 'resources section' in the back of the book as a reference for women and the people who care for them. I would be grateful if you could provide me with whatever contact details you can.
>
> Please let me know if you can help me in any way and feel free to ask me whatever you like for the sake of clarification.

Unfortunately, because some people couldn't, wouldn't or didn't talk to me, there may be organisations that are doing great work with female criminals and ex-prisoners (like helping them to get the life skills they need to make it in the so-called real world) but I can't tell you anything about them, although I can always hope that this situation will change with time.

However, many people, who either currently work in jails or who have worked within the criminal justice system in the past, spoke to me as private citizens with private opinions that they agreed to make public. Nevertheless, they only spoke to me on the understanding that they would not be identified. In order to protect them I omitted any reference that may identify them. And regardless of whether my sources were male or female, I gave them all random female names, and in some cases, professions, in order to protect their identities.

Ex-prisoners themselves are also often reluctant to talk about their experiences. Many just want to get on with things—and who can blame them? They were the people that I thought would be the hardest to track down, and to interview. And I was right. However, the women who did speak to me were incredibly generous with their time and should be commended for being willing to relive their experiences in order to give you an idea of what it is really like to commit a crime, get caught, go to jail, and live with the consequences.

While I chose to highlight three of the women, who I call Angie, Kelli and Rosa, and one of the mothers, who I call Jean, because their stories revealed so much about the journeys of so many others, I'm profoundly grateful to all the women I spoke to.

———

I should make some points about my methodology. I was, first and foremost, interested in a narrative approach. I wanted a little history, a little sociology, a touch of economics and politics and a good dose of psychology to tell you a story about how the innocent become guilty. I didn't want an 'academic' approach, but I did want a framework for asking intelligent questions, even if some of those questions were 'naïve'. I was willing to admit my ignorance.

If you are reading this book it's likely that you are willing to learn something about what makes female criminals tick, and what goes on in their hearts and minds. As a result I have avoided too many statistics. Too much of the dialogue around the issue is framed by statistics, and while people might care about numbers, they can't relate emotionally to them. So since the main story here is how some girls grow up to become criminals, many of the statistics I've drawn on are in the appendices.

Although I did not embark on an academic study I realised that interviewing all of the women (approximately 2000 of them) currently in Australian jails wasn't going to happen, even if they had all been willing to speak to me. And, of course, not all the potential interviewees would have spoken to me. Some had had dealings with 'the media' in the past, and found the experience, shall we say, less than helpful.

For many others their experiences were just too painful to talk about. Others simply didn't want to talk.

Given the nature of the subject, in the end I got the experiences and insights of the most articulate of the women, the ones who, for whatever reason, had acquired enough objectivity to look at their lives with some clarity, and who could then put this into words. For the most part you're only going to read about the strongest survivors here. Every one of these women I spoke to gave me, on average, four to six hours of her time in a series of interviews that sometimes took place over several weeks.

The subject of women in crime is huge. Think of all the people and organisations involved—the women, their families and friends, business associates, the politicians who make law, the police who enforce it, the courts, the magistrates, criminal lawyers, the employees of the Departments of Corrective Services, government support services like the Department of Community Services, funded community services, volunteer organisations, psychologists, psychiatrists, criminologists, journalists. I would have liked to have spoken to them all but, needless to say, I had to get real.

Now about my 'agenda'. I wanted to help people understand and empathise with women who commit crimes. This doesn't mean that you have to agree with what they've said, or what they've done or what they've become. I'm not asking to you to automatically like or respect them, and I'm certainly not stupid enough to suggest that all of you will be able to refrain from judging them. I'm simply asking you to open yourself to the ideas I'm setting forth and to engage with the questions that frame the context for understanding this subject. Listen to what these women were able to tell me about their journeys.

Women in Crime is not an attempt to explain how all women in prisons get there. I have, for the most part, ignored extreme criminal psychopaths.

I have also, for the most part, ignored the role of mental illness and genetics, since the majority of female prisoners are not mentally ill and very few people are born with genetic or chemical imbalances that would predispose them to the behavioural abnormalities that would lead to crime. I have also only lightly touched on the role of psychopathy and personality disorders in crime, because an intelligent discussion of this subject would require a whole book to itself.

Women in Crime is about some realities that don't make the headlines. It's about how someone like you, or someone close to you, given the right, or wrong, set of circumstances, could end up committing crimes or landing in jail.

History, economics and sociology all play their parts, but becoming a criminal is fundamentally, in my view, a psychological and developmental process. Understanding that will mean that the next time the topic of women and crime pops up in the media you will be able to come to a better informed opinion— and no one will be able to accuse you of not knowing, or not caring.

INTRODUCTION CRIMES AND MISDEMEANOURS

People like crime. Police station dramas, police procedurals and lawyer-based programs are among the highest rating of all television shows. Crime fiction and non-fiction are among the highest selling genres in bookstores.

We like crime because it's packed full of drama. Guns blare and cars explode with an exuberance that defies the laws of physics. Lawyers outmanoeuvre each other in courtrooms as they try to extract confessions from people who you know are evil simply because they look evil. You can always tell. You can see it in their eyes. But, like so much else in our society, or as I prefer to think of it, Arsesiety (with thanks to Eric Berne for coining the term), people only like crime as long as it is happening to somebody else. But when it's your house that gets broken into, you are the one who feels violated. When it's you that gets assaulted, you feel the pain. When insurance rates on your car increase because more cars in your area are being stolen, you really feel the pain. As long as you're the observer, not the victim, crime is entertainment.

Of course, how we feel about crime depends on who's doing what to whom. When you get short-changed or overcharged at the supermarket, they're thieves. But when the checkout operator gives you too much change you, well, you just got lucky, and anyway, those 'multi-nationals' can afford it, especially on what they pay their slaves in the Third World.

As you know, nice people who come from nice homes and drive nice cars don't commit crimes. And women, by their very nature, are nicer than men. After all, women are the nurturers; women are the 'gentler' sex; they're soft and feminine and they smell good. Women are mothers, they protect life. They're not like nasty old men, who rape and make war and run organisations with glamourous names like 'the syndicate' or who run billion-dollar companies into the ground (not necessarily in that order). Women don't have their brains basted in testosterone, that amazing chemical that makes mammals territorial and induces them to urinate in corners and go crazy all the time with aggression and rapacious lust. Women's brains float in a warm bath of cerebro-spinal fluid lightly scented in oestrogen. They only go crazy once a month. Even their hormones are gentler. In every way women are the nicer sex. Aren't they?

Women aren't supposed to commit crimes, and when they do they have violated not only the written laws, but also the unwritten ones. They have disappointed us. After all, 'boys will be boys', they're made of 'slugs and snails and puppy dog tails'. You can't really expect much of men in the way of 'good' behaviour, being the natural-born killers that they are. But we do expect a lot from people made of 'sugar and spice and all things nice'. We might expect obedient virgins, nurturing mothers and whores in the bedroom, but we don't expect *criminals*. When women behave badly they are going against their natural instincts. Women who commit offences are not only people who have done nasty things but also people who have become something that they were never meant to be. Or so it goes.

Of course the reality is far more complex than the clichés. Whatever the differences that exist inherently between men and women (and there have been billions of words written and spoken about the subject), our society treats men and women differently and that self-evident fact alone justifies a book like this.

———

Being involved in crime is about being in a state of mind, heart and spirit where you make choices that lead to getting arrested and dealing with the justice system. It's about being in a state of body, relationships and finances that may make all the difference between choosing one path over another. To some extent, the unspoken and frequently unexamined assumption is that a man in crime is embracing his original sin. A woman in crime is a woman who has forsaken her original grace. However you look at it, though, you need to understand how human beings are made, so that you can understand what they can become.

A BASIC PRIMER OF HUMAN PSYCHOLOGY

I began my look into the world of women in crime on the basis of some assumptions. Some of these may have debatable scientific bases, but I had to start somewhere.

For starters, human beings are born with:

- The potential to love and nurture themselves and others
- The potential to grow and to promote the growth of themselves and others
- The potential to make choices and to learn from those choices
- The potential to adapt to their environment, or to change it and innovate, or both.

These are safe assumptions because all of these potentials are functional and adaptive. Properly implemented and exploited, human potentials increase the likelihood of survival. If you survive long enough and well enough in a world where you can be swept away at any moment by an unpredictable tsunami or an earthquake then you may ultimately have children. Those children, in turn, will learn the best of what you have to offer and so the good stuff gets passed down, generation by generation.

Because of this survival orientation I make the further major assumption that everything that humans do has a functional end. That means that there's always a certain logic to people's actions. If someone's logic doesn't make sense to you, it's because you aren't seeing things in the context of their reality. Any individual's reality, of course, can also be pretty screwed up from the point of view of another's reality.

All this leads me to my really big assumption. People commit crimes because, at some level, committing the crime is logical within their frame of reference. Adaptability and innovation are the great strengths of the human animal. That's why humans are at the top of the food chain. That's why there are six billion humans with a population increase of around 236 000 every day. However, adaptability and innovation have always interacted with the forces of conservatism. Novelty works, but so does caution. It's okay to explore, but go too far into the unknown and you wind up taking more risk than you can handle and that usually means ending up as someone else's lunch.

All of human psychology is built around some basic drives, basic hungers, and to some extent all socialisation is about controlling or disciplining those drives. But often, control and discipline become suppression and oppression instead. Control comes first from parents. Parental control may be well intentioned, or it could be a power trip, depending on how far mummy or daddy take it. So what we have are the hungers of children, and the messages that try to curb or modify those hungers or to change them when they are inappropriate for physical, or more often social, survival. You can thwart hungers like the urge to grow and explore for good reasons— 'Don't put that in your mouth! Yuk'. The desire to avoid danger can stop you from having interesting and safe experiences—'Come on, darling. Just try it! It's good for you!' The instinct to procreate may not always be socially appropriate—'Mustn't touch yourself!' Above all, the yearning to become greater can be threatening to losers who can only feel up by putting others down, or to control freaks who are motivated by massive insecurities they won't admit to themselves—'Who do you think you are?'

These fundamental forces, hungers, drives or whatever you want to call them inevitably generate tension. When they are allowed to work properly they generate creative tension. When destructive messages frustrate the drives, you get destructive tension. See how this works? There are messages you get from your parents (or other 'authority' figures) and messages you give to your children (or other people you have 'power' over). These messages may be positive or negative and can arise from love or hate, inspiration or hang-ups, or anything in between. The intention of the messages is to program people: for good or ill.

The other great force is imagination. Reality doesn't always give you all the information at hand and it's safer to be afraid of the unknown than to test it out, just in case it hurts—'No darling, there are no monsters under the bed'. Sure, there are demons out there, but many of them are in your head. Some people even make it their life's mission to put more demons in your head than you would have ever put there on your own. 'You tell anyone about what we just did and they'll take you away!' is one of the classic lines in the paedophile's repertoire. As such, the programming people get depends on the programmer and how easily they can exploit the imaginations of vulnerable minds, no matter how old those minds might be.

So children are born with a variety of different drives that hardwire them for survival. But, because they live in a world which is fundamentally unpredictable, they are also open to learning new tricks based on what works and what doesn't work. Children are therefore born with the ability to respond to carrots and sticks, bouquets and brickbats. The response to experience is highly individual and subjective. No two people have the 'same' experience. No two people share the 'same' responses. People just aren't like that. The genes that control sensation, for example, are hugely variable. One thousand genes control the sense of smell alone. Think what that implies about people's perceptions of and tolerances for different odours.

In particular people vary enormously in the ways they perceive and experience pain. These differences aren't only subjective, they are real and measurable using advanced techniques. What may be nothing to you, may be excruciating to another. In other words, the belief that other people experience the world the same way you do is fundamentally false. It's a failure to understand this that leads a failure of empathy, which always leads to the evil of abuse.

What's normal for you may be a profound violation to another. 'They' may not 'get over it'. Whatever happens, the way that the world sends you messages about what works and doesn't work is known as environmental feedback, and that feedback is filtered through what you as an individual bring to the experience. Feedback can be complex, but a really important point is that it's not just the messages or programming that people get that help make them what they are, it's the way that individuals react to that message. So even the most 'innocent' of messages, the most benign programming, can become corrupted by a mind too immature to handle what it is experiencing, or lead to a personality so warped that even the best treatment is interpreted as abuse. Given enough paranoia, even an ordinary 'Hello, how are you?' can sound like a threat.

WHEN THINGS SCREW UP

Children want to be loved, they want to explore, they want to be safe, they want to 'do it', they want to soar and before they grow wings they fill in the missing pieces any way they can. Just like computers, humans are programmable, and children are rather more programmable than adults. They have to be in order to make it at all.

Anyone who can remember being a child remembers that growing up takes forever. Children are small, weak, vulnerable and utterly dependent. The world is potentially terrifying. For many children, the experience of being alive is actually terrifying. For many people, the years of childhood are not 'the best years of their lives'. For while children are utterly dependant on the adults in their lives, they are also utterly at their mercy.

Initially, children learn from adults. Nature 'figures' that if adults survived long enough to breed they must know something about life and the lessons children learn from their parents (or other primary carers) are the lessons that stick. At a later age, because parents represent the past, children are primed to learn from their peers, who presumably live closer to the 'coal face' of life and have a better grasp of 'where it's at'. Grown-ups know one set of things, but this knowledge can be out of date. Peers know another set of things, mostly about what's happening now, but this knowledge may not have the depth that experience can bring. There is thus an ongoing tension between the old ways and the new ways— in other words, a generation gap. And the faster the rate of social change, the wider the gap. In contemporary Australia, there are also the tensions, along with the delights, that come from exposure to different cultural flavours and values.

But regardless of who they learn from, from the very beginning children, and the adolescents that they become, have a huge vested interest in learning what is possible and what is not possible, what helps and what hurts. Children don't know everything, so when they don't know something they make up stories to explain things to themselves. These stories can last a lifetime.

Do you hear that voice in your head, that constant ongoing commentary that interprets life for you? It's there right now telling you 'This guy's making sense' or 'This bloke's full of shit' or 'What the hell has this got to do with anything?' You are who you are because of this internal monologue, this interior ongoing story.

The power of adults is the power to exploit children's imaginations, and the stories that children tell themselves. The power of adults is to program children for winning or losing, for survival or death.

The power adults have is to nurture or to destroy the potential of children.

The power of peers is to reinforce that programming, to undermine it, or, in rare cases, to liberate the individual.

The power of peers is to allow what's left of any potential to express itself.

The power of the individual is to make choices, regardless of what Mother or Father programmed them to do, or what friends and colleagues encourage them to do or 'let them' get away with. The power of adult human beings, regardless of whatever sort of childhood they had, or whatever life they've chosen for themselves, is to *decide*.

The purpose of this book is therefore to take a fundamental question and attempt to answer it: How do you take a loving child filled with affection and beauty and the potential for greatness and turn her into the sort of person who is likely to end up in jail?

What happened at a personal level? What did the people in this child's life do, and how did she react to it? What happened at a social level?

What acts, what events turned the innocent child into a guilty adult? What was going on in her head and in her heart at the time of 'the moment' when it all changed, when she crossed the line? What decisions did she make and why did she make them? How many lines did she have to cross?

And what keeps happening now that the child is a woman? What keeps her a criminal? What stops her from growing beyond her criminality? What stops her from reinventing herself? What stops her from healing her past? What influences her decisions? What stops her from soaring, no matter how much she wants to?

CRIMINALISATION

The process of criminalisation turns people into criminals. It has two systems. One is socio-criminalisation which turns people into criminals for historical, economic, and legal reasons. This system defines crime. It has its faults but when you get down to it the system by itself can't create criminals on its own unless the system is totally dysfunctional. To use an extreme example, we would all be criminals if breathing oxygen was a crime.

Socio-criminalisation can turn us into criminals simply by deciding to. The results can be tragic, ridiculous or both. For example, in Nazi Germany it was illegal to be Jewish. In Victorian England it was illegal to be a gay male, but legal to be a lesbian. It has often been illegal to be poor—you might even have been transported to a penal colony on the other side of the planet for stealing a loaf of bread. Today it could even be illegal to change a light globe unless you are a qualified electrician.

Socio-criminalisation is the 'big picture stuff'. It's what most people mean when they talk about 'the system'. The main product of the socio-criminalisation process is the body of law, and the institutions formed to generate and enforce those laws. Socio-criminalisation is related to, but separate from the more intimate system of criminalisation, the psychological one that I call psycho-criminalisation. But it pays to take a brief closer look at socio-criminalisation, just so we cover all bases.

SOCIO-CRIMINALISATION—HOW HISTORY SCREWS UP HERSTORY[1]

What exactly is crime? Like every other definition it depends on whom you talk to. The modern legal definition goes something like 'a wrong punishable by the state' but the legal definition also says that before you define a crime you also need both a guilty act and a guilty mind. If I'm driving carefully and soberly along a road at night and there's suddenly an oil slick (that I could not possibly have seen) and I skid and kill a pedestrian I'm not guilty of murder. The hapless pedestrian and I are just the victims of bad luck. It can get more complicated than this (especially if you talk to a lawyer and you go before a judge and a jury) but at least in this simplified case, I may feel guilty, while I'm not really guilty, not in common law anyway.

The legal definition demands another question. What constitutes a guilty act? Our society defines right and wrong, and historically it's usually men who make the rules. Even today you'd be hard pressed to come up with a society or a culture where women set and enforce the legal agenda. You don't need statistics to work out that throughout the world the vast majority of police, military, lawyers, judges, members of Parliament, and heads of State and Government are men. It's been that way for a very long time and because it's men who write the laws and set the legal agenda, laws—and their interpretation and enforcement—have not always been in the best interests of women. History is replete with examples of man's injustice to woman. Just think of the history of witchcraft. Witches, after all, were marginalised women—and marginalisation is still at the core of how you create criminals. Marginalisation is one of the 'big guns' in the arsenal of socio-criminalisation. Even now people can still use archaic and sometimes unconstitutional laws to ruin other people's lives, particularly if they're marginalised.

For instance, in 2003 Olivia Watts tried unsuccessfully to run for a seat on the Council of Casey in Victoria where witchcraft is still technically, though unconstitutionally, illegal. Later she featured in an article about the repeal of this law in which she was described as a witch. As a result of this a Councillor of Casey issued a press release which said in part:

Councillor Rob Wilson is concerned that a Satanic cult is trying to attack or take over Casey Council. The public revelation that one of the recent candidates for the City of Casey elections, Olivia Watts, formally known as Oliver [sic] Watts, has declared herself a which [sic] is a matter of concern for all Casey residents. The recent attacks on Casey Council have all the hallmarks of being linked to the occult and feature links between witchcraft practitioners. Councillor Wilson has asked Casey's Church leaders to consider calling a Day of Prayer.

Soon after, Olivia Watts started getting harassed and physically attacked. Her car and house were vandalised. She took the council and the councillor to court. The issue was finally settled eighteen months later when she was paid an 'undisclosed sum' in an out-of-court settlement. In the meantime though, Olivia Watts lost her business and her home to pay for her legal fees. Even now the law that makes witchcraft illegal in Victoria has not been repealed.[2]

There are glaciers that flow faster than some of the currents of legal reform so I doubt that witchcraft is high on the list of the legal reform agenda, even in the light of the Attorney-General of Victoria's later statement: 'We govern for all Victorians: and that includes witches, magicians and sorcerers.'

As David Garland, president of the Pagan Awareness Network, explained to me:

> We could still spend eighteen months in court, under Victorian law, arguing about a law that is unconstitutional but still stands because it never got to a federal level. This is the way our law works—the undisclosed sealed settlement means that nothing was actually recorded, there was no finding and therefore no precedent was set. ... it probably will [happen all over again]. I'm already dealing with similar cases coming up. The Family First party was last year quoted during the election campaign that all lesbians, witches and Buddhists should be burnt at the stake. These are the same people that said that all Muslims are terrorists. Muslims took them to court and the Muslims won.

———

I'm not saying that a suppressive patriarchy which marginalises women and turns then into 'witches' or the modern equivalent is entirely to blame for the socio-criminalisation of women in today's Australia, but I am saying that it's still worth considering that the social differences between women and men mean that even today, women experience growing up and living differently from men. As a result it's difficult and somewhat artificial to separate socio-criminalisation from psycho-criminalisation. Your experience of life is largely a social experience, and it's your experiences that lead you to make choices that may or may not be criminal as defined by any particular society.

And if you were wondering whether there were any universal, cross-cultural standards of right and wrong, decent and indecent, legal or illegal across all times and places think again. In Carmel, California, women may not drive in a housecoat and women may not wear high heels while in the city limits. In Liverpool, England, it is illegal for a woman to be topless in public—except as a clerk in a tropical fish store! In Mexico, women who work for the government of the city of Guadalajara may not wear miniskirts or any other 'provocative' garment during office hours. In Swaziland in 2003 King Mswati III passed the edict that young girls may not shake hands with men.

These are ridiculous laws, even if they are true. And the point I want to make is that notions of right/wrong, decent/indecent, appropriate/inappropriate, moral/immoral, legal/illegal are culture bound and regardless of how men choose to control the behaviour of women, there are innumerable examples of one set of rules for the boys and another for the girls.

For example, marriage laws throughout the ages have tended to treat women far more unfavourably than men.

To my knowledge, no man was ever forced to commit suttee (that is, throw themselves on a funeral pyre to be burned alive) or was ever forced to wear a brank (a medieval muzzle for women) for the crime of nagging.

DAMNED WHORES

Australia has a history of dealing with crime that springs from its earliest non-Aboriginal foundations. From the European perspective the whole continent was once a prison; from 1788 to the cessation of transportation in 1868 over 160 000 convicts were transported to Australia (the total European population of Australia in 1861 was almost 1.2 million). Although it's difficult to ascertain how many Australians are descended from convicts the number could be in the millions.

Of those 160 000 convicts about 25 000 were women. About 70 per cent of them were aged under 30. Their crimes included 'breaking, pickpocketing, receiving, robbery, shoplifting, stealing, vagrancy, violent crimes and other crimes'.[3] In fact, the list of crimes is much the same as today, with the exception of drug offences, but in an era when continual drunkenness, gin alleys and seamen's grog were part of the culture, the records don't easily separate what we would now call drug-related crimes.

The women were poor—'Many convicts were transported for stealing less than 15 shillings'[4]—but some did not stay that way. The most famous example is Mary Reiby, who was transported to New South Wales in 1790 for horse stealing at the tender age of twelve or thirteen.

The privations of female convicts came not only from being criminals, but also from being women. It's easy to imagine that convict women were nearly always sexually exploited, especially in a situation where men considerably outnumbered women.

The general picture of the lives of convict women is as brutal, humiliating and denigrating as that of many female prisoners today.

Crime and its punishment affected not only the women. Transportation separated families, much as prison still does today, and many women never saw their parents or children again. The punitive cultural dynamic and misplaced parentalism of the British ruling classes that later led to the over-jailing of Aborigines and the stolen generations, was inflicted on British citizens first. 'Inferior' (poor, uneducated) whites found themselves separated from their families just as effectively as 'inferior' (poor, uneducated, at least from the ruler's point of view) blacks.

Today Australians live with many legacies of the convict era and it's interesting to speculate as to how much modern mainstream Australian culture (and perhaps the subculture of law enforcement) owes its flavour to the convict past.

FEMALE CRIME VERSUS MALE CRIME

Helena Kennedy, in the foreword of *Doubly Deviant, Doubly Damned*, makes the following point:

> In the course of my own professional life I have represented many women whose charges have ranged from the most insignificant to the most heinous. At the serious end of the scale they have stabbed, poisoned, shot, garroted, bludgeoned, burned and bombed, proving that women, too, can commit terrible crimes. However, apart from those involved in politically motivated offences nearly all those women had killed someone within their domestic world: their children, their menfolk, their lovers (male and female) relatives, friends, neighbours, people (old or young) for whom they were caretakers. They rarely kill strangers, are hardly ever serial killers and never stalk their prey.[5]

It seems that when women commit serious crimes they tend to stick to their home turf. This fits the pattern of women in most cultures anywhere. Men migrate more than women; men travel, men roam. Even when they garrote and bludgeon, women do so within their smaller, but arguably deeper networks. Some of the people I spoke to had things to say about the differences in the way that men and women relate and I'll return to this later. I'd also like to point out that the vast majority of crimes that women commit are not 'violent' in the sense that many people understand 'violence'. Furthermore, a particular individual woman may not even define what she is about to do as a crime in her own mind, but for better or for worse—and usually for the worse, as far as the law is concerned—this is irrelevant.

You can argue about the 'nature' of women, and the 'styles' of female crime and how the social and psychological motives of women differ from those of men, but whatever other facts you may argue about, there is one indisputable fact: there are far fewer women in jail than men in jail. This is universally true across all cultures and times and no less so here and now. According to the Australian Institute of Criminology:

> The Australian prison population mostly consists of male prisoners (93.2%). Both male and female prisoner numbers have been increasing since 1984, although the

number of female prisoners has been increasing at more that twice the rate than that of their male counterparts. This can be seen with the increase in female prisoners as a percentage of total prisoners since 1984. Between 1984 and 2003, there was a 75% increase in the imprisonment rate per 100 000 male adults (age 17 and over) whereas the equivalent rate for women soared by 209%.[6]

So, in the years 1788 to 1868 about 16% of convicts were women. In 2003 6.8% of inmates were women, but the proportion is increasing and likely to increase further. In spite of this raw data one cannot automatically assume that women commit fewer crimes than men and are now committing more crimes than ever before. Before a woman can end up with the label 'criminal', before a woman ends up with a criminal record, certain conditions have to be in place. Here is a short list of prerequisites and the questions that arise from them. I haven't been able to answer, or even address all the questions in this book, but they're worth asking anyway.

1. Firstly the men (it's usually men) have to create laws that define what is or isn't criminal behaviour. What the law calls criminal supposedly reflects social standards, although, as we have seen, the law is frequently either behind the times, or on another planet altogether. Are the laws in fact double standards masquerading as legitimate legislation? Do they truly reflect our society's standards of all that is 'good' and 'decent'? Do they target particular individuals or groups who have different, but not necessarily 'dangerous' or 'harmful' values? Does the law reveal a gender bias that prejudices women in situations that women are likely to find themselves? And the really big question that arises from what I was to discover: Is the law punishing women for trying to escape their pain?
2. A woman has to have the sort of life that makes crime a real and present possibility. What, if anything, is in a woman's story that will lead her to crime? What kinds of experiences pave the way to crime? Is a criminal woman born or made? How do you make one?
3. A woman has to have the intention of committing a crime, or at least the intention to act in a way that becomes criminal. What motivates that intention? What set of circumstances makes the crime a viable choice? What's in the woman's internal story that makes the choice viable? What is her inner voice telling her?
4. A woman has to have the opportunity to act on that intention. Are there times and places where there are more opportunities to commit crimes than 'normal?' Are the options more limited for women? Are the options for women to choose alternatives to committing crimes more limited too?

5. A woman has to act on that intention. What processes does a woman go through in order to decide to commit or not to commit a crime? What goes through her heart and mind and body? What alternatives is she weighing up? What value system is she using to help her make that decision? What tips the scales? What can you say about her presence of mind at the time? Does she even have the presence of mind at the time of 'the moment' of committing the crime to think: 'This is a crime. I am about to commit a crime.' What does the nature of her crime tell us about everything that happened up to that moment?

6. A woman has to get caught. Is it easier for men to get caught than women? Is it less easy? Is there something in the environment (physical or psychological) that makes getting caught easier or more difficult generally?

7. Once caught the police will deal with her. Are there differences in the way that police treat women as opposed to men? Do different 'types' of women get differential treatment? What are the procedural differences? What are the attitudinal differences? Does it make a difference whether the police officer is male or female? Does it make a difference in which part of the country the police station is? What happens to a woman when she is arrested? What happens to her family and friends?

8. Once caught a whole array of different professionals will deal with a woman. How do the various professionals who deal with the case interact with her? What do they tell themselves? How do they handle the situation?

9. If the crime is serious enough, the woman will go to a hearing. What is court like for women? How are they prepared for it? How are they briefed? How do juries react to women and their crimes? How do magistrates and judges deal with them? What decisions do they make? Do women get an easier or a tougher ride?

10. If the crime warrants it, an accused woman will be on remand or on bail regardless of whether or not she is eventually found guilty or not guilty. What is remand like?

11. If the circumstances warrant it the woman will stand trial. What does the trial experience do to a woman? How does she feel? What is she thinking? If there's a jury involved what are they thinking and feeling?

12. If found guilty a woman will be sentenced. What are the sentencing alternatives? Does being a woman affect the sentence? All things being equal are women likely to get different sentences to men? Are all things ever equal?

13. A convicted woman will serve time. What is prison like in the short term? In the long term? What happens there? What does she do there and what gets done to her? How do her experiences in prison mould her? What does she have to do to survive? How do the survival skills she learns and the adaptive

strategies she makes affect the way she looks at the world? What sort of person does she become then?

14. Some, in fact most, women will eventually leave prison. What's waiting on the outside? How is she prepared to get back to her life? What's the parole process like? What does parole feel like? What will make the difference between 'making it' and 'not making it'?

15. A woman may not make it. What causes a woman to return to prison? Why does she go through the process all over again? What, if anything, does a woman stand to gain by re-offending and going back? Why was going back an option?

16. A woman may make it. If she does make a life for herself again, how does this happen? What new things does she have to deal with? How does she begin and continue the process of healing? Can she ever be whole again? What does 'wholeness' look like?

———

There are so many things that have to happen before a woman ever gets near to committing a crime that you get the impression that there must be some pretty powerful forces at work to compel a woman to commit a crime which will send her to jail. Certainly the comparison of 6.8% women in jail as opposed to 93.2% men raises the question of intent. Maybe women don't want to commit crime. Maybe they do. Or perhaps it's more of a question of opportunity. The very forces that limit a woman's opportunities for creation may also limit her capacity for destruction. Maybe magistrates and judges do treat women differently, for better or for worse. In one study in England, women were found to be more likely than men to undergo psychiatric treatment for their crimes while men were more likely to go to jail for 'punishment'. So sometimes women are more mad than bad and men are more bad than mad.

The sixteen stages of the journey of the female criminal outlined above provided the context in which I conducted my interviews. Were the lives of women-who-are-criminals so different from the women-who-aren't-criminals? Were their lives so aberrant? Our peaceful, crimeless lives could well be illusions. There but for the grace of God, perhaps, go we. Maybe those women were just born at the wrong place and at the wrong time and each step along the road to criminality just got a little easier than the one before, for reasons that only the women themselves, and the men and women who work with them, could fully explain.

No one could possibly have the full story. It's just too big. Whole academic careers and whole professional lives could be—and are—built on just one aspect of the story. In a sense everyone I spoke to was like a blind person, feeling just one small part of a large phenomenon called 'women in crime' and giving contrasting, and often contradictory information about what the problem actually looks like, like the old Buddhist legend of the blind men and the elephant, in which the blind man who is feeling an ear says 'An elephant is thin and flat' while another who is feeling the trunk argues that 'An elephant is long and tubular'—each has only part of the picture and argues that his part represents the whole.

TELLING IT LIKE IT IS OR 'WHO DO YOU HAVE TO BE TO UNDERSTAND'?
Early on in my research for this book a former inmate confronted me. She said:

> You're white, you're middle class, you're male. You're everything I hate. You couldn't possibly tell my story. You have no idea what I have been through and you could never know. The idea that you could is a complete wank. The only way my story is going to be told is if I tell it. If I told it to you, my story, you'd put your own slant, your own meaning and interpretation on it. If you changed even one word I'd cut your balls off and stuff them down your throat.

I happen to agree with her—about not ever knowing completely, not about the balls. Even though I don't perceive myself as she obviously saw me, the truth indeed is that I could not possibly know what she has been through.

It is also irrelevant.

There is a current trend among some, but not all, ex-prisoners that only they are qualified to tell their stories. And it's undeniable that no one tells their own story quite like the person themselves. But I'm not really telling you their stories. I'm telling you my story about their stories. These are my words. However, a lot of what I've written is sourced directly from interviews with ex-offenders, ex-prisoners and the people who have worked, and continue to work with them. While choosing—for their own reasons—to remain anonymous, they've trusted me to be their voice. Their words are often powerful and moving. Still, I've rearranged things, re-worded, cut things out, changed things. Some of the names are actually composites of many different women and their stories. I've done this in order to protect the privacy of these women.

Wherever possible I've double-checked with the women by asking: 'Is this right? Is this true for you?' Many times they replied, 'I couldn't have said it better myself.'

As you read what these women have to say keep your own subjectivity in mind, because understanding subjectivity and the judgments that we make about ourselves and about other people is the key to understanding why women commit crimes. I think the reason that some ex-offenders and prisoners are so protective of their stories is that when you've had everything taken away from you—your freedom, your aspirations, your relationships—the only thing that you have left is your story. You don't want some bozo with a toffy accent and a vocabulary on steroids taking that away too. But some women I spoke to decided that I wasn't 'everything' they 'hated'—and I'm honoured they made that choice.

1   BEHIND THE EIGHT BALL

'Do you know when the bus to Long Bay's comin'?'

I heard the voice from behind me. It was a rough voice. A woman's voice, a little slurred, perhaps drunk.

'No, I don't. Just wait here. It'll come,' I heard another voice say.

The answer was curt. Impatient. I didn't turn around. I figured it was none of my business. She was probably visiting a friend. Long Bay is a men's prison. It wasn't relevant to me. It didn't have my name on it.

'Buses are always fucking late,' said the voice. 'Do you know when the bus to Long Bay's comin'?'

The voice wasn't going to go away. I figured the universe was trying to tell me something. I turned around. People were pointedly ignoring her. I figured I didn't have anything to lose so I approached her.

'Hi,' I said. 'I couldn't help hearing. Are you going to Long Bay?'

'Me brudda's there. You going there too? You wanna come with me? You visitin' someone?' she asked.

'Well I wasn't planning to. But I'm writing a book about women who have been to jail. Do you know anyone like that?'

Her eyes lit up. 'I've been in jail! I've been inside lotsa times! Can I be in your book? You wanna write a book about me?'

'Well, maybe not a whole book. A chapter maybe'.

'Can you buy me a latte? I'm really hungry. I wanna latte. Can I be in your book?'

'You want a latte? Now?'

'Visiting hours don't start until one. We got time. I'm Margie.'

'Well, okay,' I said, wishing I carried around my recording equipment all the time. I wasn't sure about this. She could be a drug addict, a drunk (but she didn't smell drunk). She could be anything. But we were in a public place in broad daylight. There was a limit to how weird things could get, so I took her to a cafe.

'Can I have a strawberry milkshake, please?' she said.

'Okay, no latte?'

We sat down.

'I've been inside lotsa times. Me an' me brudda.'

'Why's your brother inside?'

'There was a woman at a teller machine. He grabbed her handbag and he ran. He didn't get very far. I'm pregnant.'

'Really?' I said, unfazed by the sudden change of topic. I've met lots of eccentric people in my life. I just go with their flow.

'Yeah. Me boyfriend's inside too. Not that I want ta see him again, the cunt. I'm sick of men fuckin' me over. He's inside now too. Reckon he killed someone. Some lady, she only had a few dollars on her. What a prick. I don't want him goin' anywhere near me again. I don't wan' an abortion. I wanna keep this one. This time. Me brudda wants me to get rid of it but I don't wanna.' She looked as if she was about to cry.

'They took me babies, all of them, DoCS took 'em. They never even asked. They just took 'em.'

'That's terrible.'

'Fuck yeah!'

She was silent for a moment then abruptly she started again. She clenched her left fist and rested it on the table between us. Her right hand was still on the straw in the milkshake. She looked down on the table. Oddly, I felt no threat from her at all.

'Please, God, let me brother out so that we can be together again! Please God, me brother's a good kid we just want to be together so that we can have a good life and get away from the Cross. Thank you, God, oh merciful Father.'

Then, just as suddenly, she looked up and spoke to me again. 'When I see me brudda I'm gonna tell him to get rid of that bitch solicitor. She's the one's keepin' 'im inside. She ain't doing no good at all. I'm gonna tell 'im to dump the bitch. We're waiting for the doctor. It takes four weeks to get a psych examination. Me brudda's a good kid, he's just got this thing about Arabs. Hates the bastards. Something in 'is head. He don't like 'em at all. Are you gonna put me in your book? If you put me in your book can I get a copy?'

'Sure,' I said. 'What's your address?' I asked. She told me, but I had to borrow a pen and a piece of paper from the counter. I had been totally unprepared for this. 'Why were you inside?' I asked. I figured if Margie could change the subject abruptly, so could I.

'I was inside in and out for three years, I snatched a handbag. This woman was lookin' at me funny so I just grabbed it. I did somethin' stupid a coupla weeks ago again too. I was in a bank and I just grabbed a woman's bag. Then all these boys started chasin' me. They got me into a corner and surrounded me and called the cops. When I visit me brudda I'm gonna give him some money.' She took out her wallet and put $50 on the table in front of me. It didn't look as if she had much else in her purse. 'They don't give ya nuthin' in jail. What's your book about again?'

'It's about women who commit crimes and get into prison.'

She seemed to think about that for a moment.

'D'ya like books?' she asked. 'I can't even read.'

'You never learned?'

'Nah.'

She reached into her handbag again and took a wallet out. A small bag of something that looked like dried oregano (but that I suspected wasn't) fell out of her bag. She looked at me sheepishly and smiled, like a little girl who had been caught with her hand in Alice B. Toklas' fudge brownie jar. I bit my lips and became incredibly interested in the café ceiling.

'See?' she said. I looked down. She showed me her birth card. I'd never seen one before but I knew that people who didn't have a driver's licence or a passport used them for photo ID. 'You need ID when you visit prison.'

It suddenly occurred to me that I was carrying a lot of shopping. 'Will they let us in with all of this?' I asked.

'They give you a locker,' she said. 'I don't want to have another abortion. I wanna keep this one. I've had three abortions now, it's messing with me head.' Her mobile phone sounded. She got it out of her bag, looked at it for a moment and handed it to me. 'What's it doin'?' she asked.

'Someone's sent you a text message. It's a phone number in Brisbane.'

'Brisbane. It's probably that bastard trying to get in contact with me.'

'Your boyfriend?'

'Nah, his sister. Can you write the phone number down for me?'

She handed me a packet of cigarettes. What was it like going through life being unable to read and write in a country like ours? I wrote the number down on the top of the cigarette packet. Outside the café a Santa Claus was jingling his bells. Margie started singing a Kevin Bloody Wilson song that went something like 'Santa Claus you're a prick!', some song of disappointment over crappy Christmas gifts. I wondered how many times she had heard it to memorise the lines. She stopped. 'I can sing Stevie Nicks too,' she smiled. 'There is no beautyyyyyyyyy, without the beeeeeeeeaaaaaaaasssssssssssst.'

I laughed. 'What was prison like?' I asked.

She looked sombre. 'It's not being in prison so much. It's that our whole lives are fucked. Me ma keeps telling me that I gotta get out of the Cross so that me an' me brudda can start over. Otherwise we just keep doin' the same think year afta year and we keep getting in trouble with the police and we never get anywhere and we never do nuthin' but get in trouble.' Abruptly she started to cry. 'Everyone I know's been in jail. Me cousins, me friends.'

She was wailing, quietly. Tears were streaming down her face and she hunched forward. I patted her on the back.

'I'm sorry,' I said.

She stayed hunched over for about half a minute while I patted her gently. Then she sat up again and looked at me. I withdrew my hand. 'It's so hard, it's just so hard. They don't give you nuthin' in jail, and then you've got nuthin' when you get out. Can you get me a salad roll and some chips?'

'Sure,' I said.

I'd gotten used to the sudden changes of mood and subject by now. I went to the counter and ordered. It didn't take them long to make the roll. When I got back to the table she started eating.

'Dya think they spit in it?' she asked.

'I don't know,' I said. 'I don't think so.'

'The thing about mental illness,' she said suddenly, naming it for the first time, 'is that most of the time I'm all right. But sometimes, I just get paranoid. Like, if I buy something in the prison café, like, they get the inmates to work there, and you know, like, the inmates hate the screws and maybe they spit in the food. Do you think they spit in the food, or is it just me?'

'It might be just you, but I don't know.'

'Please, God,' she said, praying again. 'Let me and me brudda be together again so that we can be all right and smoke a few cones and just have a little fun. Please, Lord Jesus, great loving merciful Father. Amen.'

Then, after a small pause, 'You think maybe they get supervised when they cook? I hope they do.'

As I watched her eat I wondered about what sort of life she had had. She was impulsive. She trusted. The $50 was still there on the table, forgotten. I could have been anyone. Why would she believe me? How many people, how many men had 'fucked her over?' Out of the corner of my eye, I could see that the café proprietor kept looking at us. What was he thinking? He'd been polite enough to me, but how would he have treated her? Would he have suspected that she was just some junkie? Would he have even suspected that she was mentally ill? How could she avoid getting into trouble when she had no real control over her impulses, with a mind that flitted around like a distracted butterfly? What was she doing in the outside world anyway at the mercy of unscrupulous people who could spin her any story and could, and probably had, used her and discarded her? She had no defences; yet somehow she was surviving. I was getting a tiny glimpse of how the mentally ill could be so vulnerable to committing crime but I couldn't have asked for her story. I needed consent, and there was no way I could have argued to myself that this woman with a child's heart could make such an adult decision.

'What's the time?' she asked.

'A quarter past twelve.'

'Shit we gotta go!'

She stood up.

'Look, could we do this some other time?' I said, rising with her.

She looked a little disappointed. 'You know, you're nice. Not like some of them young fellas. I'm sorry we didn't get the time to talk about my crimes.'

'That's okay. Here's my card. You can call me later, if you like.' I didn't want it to look like I was rejecting her.

'Could you do me a favour?' she asked.

'Sure.'

'Could you write me a note, for me brudda?'

We got a piece of paper from the counter. She dictated to me:

'To my brother. I am here and I will always be there for you. I want you to know that I always keep my promises. Love, Margie.'

I handed her the note and she put it in her handbag. She picked up the money from the table. She hadn't forgotten it after all.

'This is the last of my pension,' she said.

'And you're giving it all to your brother?'

'He's all I got.'

As we left the café I gave her a hug. 'Enjoy your visit,' I said.

'Did I cry, before?' she asked.

'Yes you did, a little.'

She nodded. 'If I'm in your book, will you send me a copy? Will you mail it to the address you wrote down? I won't be able to read it, but it would be nice to have. I've never been in a book before.'

'Sure,' I said.

Margie represents only a very small proportion of criminals. Most are not mentally ill. Her story, or rather my brief glimpse into her life, taught me something. Yes, she'd committed crimes. Yes, she'd spent time in prison. I wouldn't have liked to have been one of her victims, but living with mental illness can't be easy. Margie was born this way, behind the eight ball, and she was still there. In many ways she was still so innocent that her decisions to commit crimes weren't really decisions, more whims, as impulsive as those of any child. Drug taking was only making her mind even less discriminating, more confused and so on, in a downward spiral that I would see again and again, although for different reasons.

MAD OR BAD

The 'question of sanity' repeatedly comes up, particularly in regard to violent or bizarre crimes. Commonsense asks questions like, 'What sane person would risk years of prison for stealing a few bucks? What sane person would murder her children?'

The courts grapple with insanity because common law is interested in the issue of responsibility. The idea goes something like this: If the accused is sane then she is able to process reality and is able to distinguish between right and wrong.

Sanity assumes that you are responsible for the choices that you are making. Sanity assumes that if you are making a decision to do wrong you are doing so because you are evil. Therefore you must be punished, you will be deprived of your liberty so that you will not be a danger to the public at large. Also, society demands that you suffer for your evil, because suffering will teach you that nasty things ought to happen to nasty people.

If the accused is insane then she is not in contact with reality. Insanity assumes that you are unable to distinguish between right and wrong, that you are not responsible for the choices that you are making. It assumes that if you are making a decision to do wrong you are doing so because you have no more idea about what you're doing than someone under the influence of a mind-altering substance. If, in these circumstances, you commit a crime then you lack criminal intent and it would be more appropriate to treat you for mental illness than to punish you for being a nasty person. Our society demands that we imprison you not as a punishment, but in order to stop you from hurting yourself or anyone else because you are out of control.

Given this line of reasoning the idea of 'responsibility' becomes closely aligned with the idea of 'blame'. And you can't be 'blamed' if you are not 'responsible'. In order to determine responsibility common law courts use the McNaughton Test, named after Daniel McNaughton, who, on 20 January 1843, after having suffered for some time from delusions that the Minister of England, Robert Peel wanted to kill him, shot and killed the Prime Minister's private secretary, Edward Drummond. McNaughton was found not guilty of murder on account of insanity and he was put into the Bethlehem insane asylum ('Bedlam') until his death 20 years later.

The McNaughton rule established the presumption of sanity. You were sane unless you could prove otherwise. The McNaughton Test requires that you establish that:

> At the time of the committing of the act, the party was labouring under such a defect of reason, from disease of the mind, as to not know the nature or quality of the act he was doing, or, if he did know it, that he did not know what he was doing was wrong. The implication of the McNaughton test is clear: in the context of culpability at trial insanity is a legal concept, not a medical one.[7]

If you're looking for a medical definition of insanity you won't find one. The closest you get to definitions of any mental illness is the *Diagnostic and Statistical*

Manual of Mental Disorders, 4th Edition, Text Revision, published by the American Psychiatric Association in 2000. It is the most widely read handbook for mental health professionals. The DSM-IV-TR lists the diagnostic criteria of most recognised mental illnesses but when I read it I get the impression that I'm reading the equivalent of an alchemist's tract on chemistry before chemists knew anything about atomic theory and before they came up with the periodic table. In other words, we're dealing with a science that is still in its infancy. People with specialist degrees will not only disagree on a particular individual diagnosis but on the definition and symptoms of an illness itself. The patients don't help much either. Their symptoms are often highly individualistic, confusing, and intermittent. It may take months and sometimes years before you 'know' what's wrong with some patients and even then, a treatment that works with one person may be useless or even dangerous to someone else. If even the experts disagree it's an even tougher call for a jury to determine the mental condition of the accused.

The issue is further complicated because there is no clear logical connection between sanity and discriminating between right and wrong.

You can accept that someone may be so mentally ill that there's no way they know what's real and what isn't. In that case 'right and wrong' become irrelevant. That's how I felt about Margie. Her capacity to process 'reality' was impaired.

But even if a person is legally sane, that is, able to distinguish between right and wrong, they may still be suffering from a mental problem. Remember that right and wrong are social concepts—and even people in the same family will disagree over what is meant by them! But even assuming that you establish that someone can distinguish between what 'everybody' thinks is right and wrong they may still make a choice for the wrong.

People like Margie are extremely rare. Most people fail the McNaughton Test. In the vast majority of cases juries find that criminals are sane. They can process reality accurately. Why then do they make the choices that are 'insane' in an everyday sense?

You can find one explanation in that range of ten recognised mental problems known as personality disorders. A personality disorder, as defined by DSM-IV-TR, is:

> an enduring pattern of inner experience and behaviour that deviates markedly from the expectation of the individual's culture, is pervasive and inflexible, has an onset in adolescence or early adulthood, is stable over time, and leads to distress or impairment.

In other words, you have traits that are inflexible and that don't sync with what other people expect is 'normal' or 'healthy', and these traits can and do get you into trouble. Mental illness and personality disorders are diagnosed on an analysis of 'clusters' of traits. Experts may disagree on which traits are important, or symptomatic of pathology. How many traits does it take to make a cluster? The experts may disagree among themselves about this too, but they tend to agree that only they are qualified to make a 'proper' diagnosis.

———

People with personality disorders aren't clinically 'crazy' but they're crazy in the sense that their values or interpretations of events may not coincide with what people generally consider 'normal'. So in that sense, anyone who finds themselves at odds with what other people are thinking and feeling, or who, for whatever reason, is putting an interpretation on events that not everyone else would agree with, is suffering from a personality disorder. This sounds like a no-win situation.

By this definition the only difference between a genius like Isaac Newton (who saw things so differently from everybody else that he copped a lot of ridicule and hostility but also redefined physics) and a nutcase like Isaac Newton (who was so paranoid he felt that everyone was trying to steal all his ideas) is one of degree and of results. In other words, if you think differently from everyone else and people like what you do, you're a genius. If you think differently from everyone else and people don't like what you do, you are a nutcase, or a criminal, or both. Genius and criminality can be defined by usefulness, and by what others are willing to put up with. And geniuses are as rare as the criminally insane.

MAKING CRIMINAL DECISIONS

Right and wrong are moral decisions. They are value judgment calls. In proportion to the majority of criminals hardly any criminals are insane. The vast majority can process reality; even so they still make what many people would consider bad calls.

What makes criminals do this?

The short answer is 'corrupt' values. These could be as sociopathic as 'I don't give a stuff about other people. They're just cattle, waiting for me to slaughter them', to values as self-defeating as 'I'm so worthless I'm lucky to have anyone at all. And he really is nice when he's off the booze and isn't beating me up. Maybe I'll take some drugs to dull the pain.' The people who hold these values aren't insane. But somehow they acquired and integrated some dysfunctional programming into their heads, and the programming leads them to make decisions that may land them in jail. How do people, especially women, acquire such corrupt values without being mentally ill in the clinical sense? Their upbringing and society criminalise them through the process of psycho-criminalisation.

PROGRAMMING FOR CRIME: PSYCHO-CRIMINALISATION

The socio-criminalisation system may be frequently ridiculous and tragic, and even law students are taught from the very beginning that the law does not equal justice. But the law can't, except in extreme cases, make criminals automatically. To create criminals you need the other system of criminalisation, the psychological and developmental system of criminalisation. You need to be 'fucking around with someone's head until you turn them into a crim'.

Mental illness in some ways can be a form of ready-made, inbuilt, hardwired psycho-criminalisation, but for the most part psycho-criminalisation is the process whereby you educate a sane, functional child to become the sort of person who finds it relatively easy to make decisions that will lead them to crime. It's all about programming.

You can program children with values that will lead them to resist crime or embrace it. If you're a parent or an authority figure you can use your power over children to corrupt their programming so that they are more likely to end up in jail because they develop values that predispose them to crime. They can then pass on that program, like a virus, to other children and so on, down the generations, regardless whether or not the children are related to them by 'bad blood' or not.

Criminality, in a healthy democracy, is usually dysfunctional. Commonsense tells me that compared to non-criminals, criminals are more likely to experience more violence, more injury, more emotional disturbance, more drug addiction, more relationship difficulties and more general chaos in their lives. I'd also assume that their mental and physical health is poorer, and their life expectancy is shorter, and that this is true of both women and men. For the most part being a criminal, at least one who ends up in jail, is bad news.

Because of the inbuilt resistance to dysfunction that humans have, children generally resist being programmed to have horrible lives, but children are not indestructible. With enough time and dedication you can corrupt any innocent life, even when you don't intend to. All you need to do is to destroy a child's faith in you.

2   TOXIC NESTS

It all begins with abuse. Here is one startling fact: 85% of women in prisons have been subjected to emotional, mental, physical and/or sexual abuse. Abuse is probably the most powerful tool available to really screw people up. Here is how I define abuse:

If you create an environment where you are responsible for and fail to provide for someone's essential needs, without just cause, then you are committing an act of abuse.

If you create an environment where you are responsible for and actively violate someone's mental, physical, emotional, social or sexual integrity, without just cause, then you are committing an act of abuse.

These definitions, of course, aren't perfect or exhaustive, but the central idea is that anyone who is in a position of power over and has responsibility for the needs and integrity of another and who then violates those needs and that integrity is an abuser. The 'just cause' proviso is a minefield in itself but really only applies to extreme circumstances. 'Just cause' isn't meant to be an escape clause to justify treating someone abominably.

Whatever examples might be going through your mind right now about what is or isn't abuse, there is one group of relationships in which the power/responsibility dynamic and the vulnerability to abuse is undeniable—and that is in the relationship between adults and children, especially small children, say, twelve years old and under.

The child needs to know that she is safe, that the adults in her life are there for her. That adults violate that trust is possibly the worst of all possible betrayals, and for someone to face the fact that the adults in their life betrayed them is possibly the worst, the most painful, of all possible realisations.

———

Angie, a woman who narrowly escaped being put in jail for murder, and whose story continues in Chapter 6, described her early life to me.

Angie: I grew up in an ordinary, middle-class household. I was adopted, but I didn't know I was adopted until I was about eleven from some kid at school. My father was a domineering, authoritarian man. He was never abusive, he never hit me, or anything, but there was only one way, his way. He was out a lot, because of his work as a travelling salesman.

My mother was bedridden while I was very young, so I'd get farmed out to aunties and uncles, and some pretty scary things happened with my uncles. **X:** Like what? **A:** Well, you know, yucky stuff—touchy, feely, kissy, kissy. **X:** Hop on my knee? **A:** And all sloppy kisses and I was really little. My mother died when I was nine and I was really traumatised by that and at about the same time at school the teacher was a total case, really bad. He used to pull your dress up and have his hand down your front—a total cretin. My girlfriend and me told her big sister, who was about twenty. She just freaked and told us that he'd been doing the same thing to her, but she told us 'Don't you dare say anything to anyone because you'll get into trouble.' So we didn't.

X: So this had been going on for years!

A: He was a really old man. He was gross, always asking you these personal questions like whether or not you have a boyfriend. And he was always watching people when they were jumping elastics. He was really creepy. He'd get you in trouble all the time and lift your dress up and whack you in front of the class. Meanwhile, at home dad would be out all the time on business trips and I'd be at home looking after my brother because he was impaired. I used to get these phone calls. I never knew who it was but he used to tell me what I was wearing and where I'd been.

X: You were being stalked! **A:** He knew that my dad was out. He used to call from the phone box across the road. He'd tell me to go to the window and I'd see him there, but I could never tell who it was because he was too far away. It happened nearly every day for about two years. Until about two years ago every time I saw a phone box I would piss myself.

X: Did you tell your father? **A:** He told me not to answer the phone, but he was a salesman. He'd get dozens of calls a day. If I hadn't answered the phone half his orders would have gone. I didn't want to be a burden to him by not answering the phone.

X: That's a big part of you isn't it? You don't want to make trouble. But do you think your father failed to protect you?

A: Some people said, 'How can you leave two kids alone in a house until midnight?' He had no choice, his wife had died, his son was sick; he had to go to work. And I was really capable. I grew up really quickly. I was a really responsible, level-headed kid, but I couldn't deal with all the weirdos on the planet. I was on my own. Still, if I hadn't had this weirdness it wouldn't have prepared me for what happened later, when I kept meeting worse and worse people.

While my mother was dying my father was having an affair with this woman. My mother used to lay in bed crying and we'd ask where dad was and she'd say he was 'at a meeting'. **X:** She knew. **A:** She knew! I didn't. I only worked it out later.

X: How did that feel? **A:** I thought it was disgusting. Later on I thought, 'Oh well, he's a bloke, and his wife's lame and disabled in bed. They're going to go around looking for a piece of, whatever.' And when my mother died she wasn't dead two weeks before this woman moved in. She married my father later. She was a fucked-up unit and she hated me. One day she chopped off all my hair because she thought I was conceited about it. She used to tell me all the time how hopeless I was. How even my real mother didn't want me, which is why I'd been adopted. But she also told me that my father didn't want me either. He was only putting up with me in memory of my mother.

X: Was that true? A: No. She only said that to hurt me. She and my father would be all sloppy-kissy in front of my brother and me and that was just embarrassing because I was thirteen and your father's just not supposed to do that.

X: As far as you're concerned your mother's still warm in the grave. A: Then my brother dies and I run away from home when I'm sixteen and go to stay with another auntie and uncle, because I figure at least if I'm with the family I won't shame the family and my father will still respect me and won't write me off completely. Then my uncle starts cracking on to me. He kept coming into my room and trying to get it on and I'm running around while he's harassing me and touching me.

X: Where was your auntie at this time? A: Pissed on scotch, I'd say. And I'm freaking out because I've left home because I can't stand my stepmother and this is happening. So I tell my cousin, their son, and he starts taking me out to 'rescue me' and he starts intimidating me too. I gave in because if didn't my cousin wouldn't protect me and he'd leave me to his father.

X: It wasn't much of a protection was it? A: His father was scary.

X: But between your cousin and his father your cousin was less scary. It was a choice between two scaries.

A: They're all fucking dead now. I wasn't related to any of them. My real mother was an Aboriginal. I've never met her. She put a stop on any children finding her, so I've never been able to meet her and to tell her that it's okay.

X: How do you feel about your real mother? A: I understand that she's probably a broken woman who's had a lot of pain in her life and that meeting the children that she gave up would be very confronting and painful for her. I can't help feeling that if I had the chance we could get through that pain and mean something to each other, but the law stops that. The law has interfered with the natural process of healing.

X: Did your father know about the way your stepmother was treating you? A: No. I never told him. He wouldn't have believed me. She completely dominated him and I always felt like a disappointment to my father anyway. I've been through so much since I left home but I survived because of what my father taught me. He was consistent. He wouldn't bend for anything. I knew where the lines were. There were no grey areas. I always had my father in my head telling me what was right. There was no 'Why?' it was: 'Because I said so'. To this day I feel hurt about disappointing my father. I didn't want to leave him, but I had to, because of my stepmother.

X: Did things ever get better with her, or with your father? **A:** It was years before I felt strong enough to face her, but she died. They found her dead on her kitchen floor. I felt cheated because I never had it out with her. My father and I made peace, eventually before he died. **X:** But that was long after everything else happened.

A: I left home when I was seventeen. I met this guy, John. I was just this naïve girl from the country and I got pregnant. I wanted to go back home, but I wasn't allowed to because of my stepmother. She wouldn't have me in the house again. So there was no turning back. I married this guy, because I got pregnant, and who was like, from a totally different background to me. John and I ended up having two children. He drank, and when he drank, he got abusive. John had had an outrageous father who abused all his children, physically, sexually: he was a deviate. But I didn't know it at the time I married John. I only found out years later. So all these things were coming up for years, I bore the brunt of it, but I never even knew what the problems were.

X: Did you ask him about it? **A:** He just ignored me. He'd bang tables and hit things. He didn't communicate much. He hit me. First I had a daughter; then I had a son. He totally disregarded our daughter once the boy came along. He did terrible things. He had no patience. Once, the stove caught on fire. Flames up to the ceiling, I'm telling him to grab hold of her so I can put the fire out and he just grabs her and throws her onto the couch. He'd play these mind games. When he got drunk he'd pretend that he was his father and say 'I'm Jaaaaaack' in this really weird voice. I don't know if he was messing with my head, or whether he really meant it. It all got pretty scary. I'm still young at this time. I'm only nineteen or twenty. I didn't know what was going on. I just start throwing myself on the floor and crying and getting really depressed. I was totally isolated. It wasn't until one day I told a neighbour. She said, 'Why don't you leave him?' It never even occurred to me before then. So I did.

X: It never occurred to you until then? **A:** No. I just wasn't in that head space. I was young. I didn't have any experience in life, and he was my husband. I had two children. We had a home, we'd put carpet in. Furniture. This is how you live your life. You do all these things. But once I realised I could leave, it didn't take me long. About a week. I planned it while he was at work.

X: That must have been a tough week, pretending. **A:** Yeah. But I did it. And then, I didn't feel anything. I went to live in a refuge on the other side of town. There was another woman there who had been living in the same street as I had, who had also left her husband. Somehow her husband and my husband got together and found us. Her husband had a gun and came there one day. The refuge transferred us to Sydney. The refuge got me a solicitor and he got me to change my name so I couldn't be traced. Soon after a woman is looking to share the rent on a house for her and her children, and I move in with mine. This woman turned out to be a nutcase. She'd leave her kids for days at a time and go God knows where and I'd be left looking after them and cleaning the house. Other times she'd have these men coming in and out all the time.

One of them threw up in the hall once, I had to clean up the vomit. I'm living on social security, trying to get my life back in order with two young kids. I'm working two night shifts a week at a hospital and getting no sleep. There's all this craziness around me and suddenly I start blacking out. One minute I'm doing something then all of a sudden minutes have gone by. I don't know where. I get really worried and so I call the government and say, 'Help! I don't know what's going wrong with me.' I figured that they'd send someone to help me, say something like, 'Oh, you're not getting enough sleep, you're under too much stress. You can't take all this anymore so your body and mind are shutting down.' I remember calling DoCS, them saying 'Come with us.' I remember grabbing my children and taking them to this old people's house, in fact it was foster care. I remember going to this hospital, falling asleep, waking up and wondering 'How long have I been asleep?' Three months had gone past. They'd kept me sedated for three months. In the meantime, even though I had restraining orders on my husband they'd given him full custody of our kids. He never looked after them anyway. They kept going from sister to sister. Nobody wanted them. They were going to put them in a home. It took a year and a half of legal bullshit to get my kids back.

X: What happened then? **A:** I took the kids and went bush. I just had to get away after all the bullshit I went through. I went to live in a cave near a waterfall. Once a month I went into town to get supplies, but at least I had peace. It was a great way to live. I'm getting some money from the government but I'm growing my own food and we're surviving. After a while the opportunity came to do a little work and we move into a house. That's when Neil came into my life. I was looking for deeper insights into life and this man I meet comes across as really spiritual and I'm strongly attracted to that. He just used all this knowledge that he had to come across as some sort of authority. He wasn't, but I didn't know it at the time. He started taking over my life. He used all those snake-oil tricks—telling me I had to burn all my old photos to 'let go of my past' and that if I don't leave things behind I won't get spiritual knowledge. So I burnt everything. My past is all gone. I figured if that was the Methodology, that was it. I wanted to achieve that goal. All those tricks then cemented me in an emotional bind.

X: So this guy comes to you like some spiritual guru who knows stuff. You haven't learned to discriminate yet.

A: He was extremely intense, and intelligent, and really, really tricky, but I didn't know at the time. And he said all the right things. He said that he always wanted to be with someone who was 'ready made' because I already had my kids. He said it was great that there was no screaming and no nappies. It was all done. I guess I thought he really appreciated who we were. I didn't read anything sinister into it at all. **X:** Why would you?

A: Yeah, well. I should have. So we left. Came back to Sydney, this time with him. So I did what work I could, but whenever things got tough he'd just rack off and leave me. I'd be devastated, because by this time I was really in love with him. He wouldn't work. He just thought he was an artist. I wanted to support his dreams so I'd borrow money and get into debt. I'm mostly living on a pension. He wouldn't get the dole. It was too 'materialistic'—I don't know. It just got really, really hard. So I started to work as an escort. He'd stay home and look after the kids.

Early on, when I was working as an escort, I nearly got killed by a client who tried to strangle me. It doesn't happen very often, but when it does you remember it for the rest of your life. This time one of the other girls just happened to be passing the room and 'felt' something was wrong, which is why they pulled the guy off me. I hated it, that sort of work. But then I got the chance to just do stripping, which was better because I didn't have to do tricks, just take my clothes off and get a few hundred for a few minutes' work. That kept us afloat. **X:** Why did you get into that sort of work?

A: I just got sick of struggling. I didn't want to be struggling anymore. I couldn't live like a dog anymore. Living without money was too debilitating. It wore me down. I was already bankrupt because of this guy. I had no future. He'd leave, then I'd have to stay and look after the kids. I knew no one. I'm on the other side of Australia. I have no family. No one. It just wasn't happening the way it should have. Neil was always pulling the rug from out of me all the time. He kept leaving and coming back, leaving and coming back. I'd sacrificed so much for him. In the end, I just couldn't do it anymore.

X: Did he threaten you? Why did you keep paying for him?

A: He kept saying that he was a 'valuable human being', his time was 'precious too', and if I was earning so much money 'what was the problem?' I'm supposed to be saving up for a house, and never getting anywhere. He never bullied or intimidated me. He always had this intellectual approach to make what he wanted sound reasonable. He just knew how to twist things round. 'You don't expect me to hang around and look after your kids? I've got a life too you know!'

I wanted to just get ahead and escape. I hated living where I was. I just hated it. All I could think about was just earning as much money as I could so that I could escape. I thought he'd come good if we could just go back and buy a little farm and live in the bush. I thought that the pressure of everything was making him be so horrible to me.

X: So you pay for all his mad schemes, and the plan in your head is to do that, while at the same time save up for the farm, then you'd get it, move away, take him with you, and then everything would be all right? **A:** I guess so. But then he left again. So his sister invites me to live with her but she's got six kids, and she's sharing with another woman with a kid and so with us there's like thirteen people in this flat, just kids everywhere. By this time seven years have gone by since I met him. My kids are twelve and eleven. I move into a refuge and he keeps breaking into my van. Hanging around.

Taking my van and getting involved with all these girls. It was really humiliating. All this time he keeps telling me he loves me, trying to get back with me, but he's just fucking around too. He was playing this double game. One version of his life for me: one for his family.

X: Was there any love left at this point? A: I'm thinking, 'I'm not going to let go, after all I've gone through.' I'm paying for his art shows to promote him. In the end he was so horrible I didn't know what was going on. After moving around in and out of refuges I got a government flat, eventually. He moved back in, making out that he was sorry, that he really loved me, even though he'd been with all these women. I didn't really believe him. One part of me wanted to. Then I got pregnant with him. I'd been with him over ten years by then and never gotten pregnant. He was just really violent to me then. Really angry. He abused me badly.

X: What was that abuse like? A: He'd punch me, kick me and throw things at me. I didn't want to know him after that. I just couldn't handle it.

Kelli was the middle of ten children. Her experience was very different to Angie's, but equally damaging.

Kelli: I was crazy about my daddy. He was my happy thought. He was everything to me. He used to take time off work to watch me play sport. I was his number one fan, he was my number one fan. We were always there for each other. I had a near-death experience when I was fifteen. I nearly drowned, and three or four significant events flashed in front of me. My daddy was in every single one. I had been taken by an undertow and I wasn't breathing, and I heard my daddy calling me, and that's what saved me. It was a rough day, no one should have been out there.

X: What were you doing out there? K: I'd run away from home.

X: Why? K: It was because my daddy meant so much to me that I could never tell him that my older brother was sexually abusing me. He had been from the time I was eight years old. He was sixteen; I was eight.

X: You never told him? You never told your father? K: He would have killed my brother. Then he would have gone to jail, so what was the point of telling him? So I had to keep this horrible, dark secret all to myself.

X: How did your brother start abusing you? K: My older sister ran away from home to join the army. I didn't know it at the time but our cousin next door was sexually abusing her. He was a lot older and bigger and there was nothing she could do about it until she was old enough to leave. After she left my brother started abusing me.

X: Did he rape you? K: You know when you're little, and you have older siblings? You trust them. They call you into a room and they lock the door, and you start to panic. And then they start making you do things that you know are totally wrong, because it doesn't matter how young you are, when something's wrong, you know it's wrong. It's an instinct. You just know. Every child knows when they're being abused. He just made me touch him. **X:** What, he said, 'Touch me here'? **K:** He didn't say anything, he just grabbed my hand and made me touch him. **X:** I just wonder how these things happen.

K: They show their strength, their power over you. It's a power thing. They make you fear them as well. When I was eight he made me touch him and then he'd pull himself off in front of me. He said, 'Don't tell anyone, because nobody will ever believe you.' Later when I was eleven or twelve he said, 'If you don't do what I say, I'll get one of the younger ones.' **X:** How often did it happen?

K: Every time my parents went out. My father was a minister and they were away a lot on church stuff. When I was nine I told my parents I could look after the younger ones. That only made it worse because while the younger kids were playing hide and seek he'd just grab me. It affected part of me really badly, but another part of me it didn't, because I blocked it out. Every time it happened I'd just go out of my body. Later, when I was inside, all my friends inside had been abused. They tell you to rise above it, but that's bullshit. Sure we were victims, but you don't remain victims.

X: Because otherwise 'they' win? **K:** Sure. You know, all the paedophiles, the way that we can pick them, they can pick us. You know something else about them. Paedophiles, they have a unique smell—a chemical smell. They can sense me and I can sense them.

X: They have a smell? **K:** I didn't realise they had that smell until when I was thirteen and one of the senior boys trapped me in a corridor and wouldn't let me go. He had the same smell my brother had. Later on, with other paedophiles I've come across, they've had that same smell.

X: What does it smell like? **K:** Really bad. Like an overpowering semen smell. **X:** So the smell of semen but with the volume turned up. **K:** Majorly.

X: And it's on their bodies all the time? **K.** Just when they get aroused. **X:** So your brother is doing all this stuff, and you can't tell your father.

K: He would have broken him in pieces.

X: It wouldn't have been rational. **K:** It wouldn't have been rational at all.

X: There wouldn't even have been anything you could have done to stop him? **K:** I wouldn't even have tried to stop him.

X: Were you protecting your younger siblings? **K:** Definitely. I made the big mistake of running away at fourteen. Then he started targeting them. I didn't even think. I was too busy trying to protect myself.

X: So there was guilt too? **K:** Not at the time, but later when I found out. My younger sister started getting abused. She's dead now. She committed suicide. So when I'm nine years old my parents go out, I'm babysitting the younger ones and once they're all asleep I sneak out, and sneak back in before they got back. I was getting a hiding every day from my mother. Between the sexual abuse from my brother and the physical abuse from my mother it sort of encouraged me to move on. I always loved my mum. No matter how abusive she was to me I always loved her, but I was born between her two pets, and I think she was jealous of my daddy's love for me. At least, that's what I used to tell my friends at school.

X: Do you think that was true? **K:** Yes! Well, in my mind it was true. My daddy had an aura, one word and it was instant discipline. My mother was nag, nag, nag, nag, nag. But my daddy loved my mother and gave her all the money to manage. My daddy was the most perfect human being that God ever put on this earth.

X: But not perfect enough to stop your mother from belting you. **K:** He didn't know. She did it behind his back. And I wasn't a dobber. I'd gotten into that mindset that dobbing was bad. But my mother targeted me because her two pets kept dobbing me in for everything. She didn't believe me when I said it wasn't true, because she said my daddy spoilt me. He never spoilt me.

X: When she belted you what did she do? She'd get out a belt? **K:** And smash me with it. Whip me with it. Whack! Whack! Whack! Every stinking day of my life.

X: How many times? **K:** Oh about a hundred. She used to take a five-minute rest to rest her arm. That's why I'm so strong.

X: How did you take it? **K:** It was nothing compared to the abuse. Nothing. It was only physical pain. I didn't care about her, my daddy was my whole life. But you know every year, on my birthday, was the only day she didn't belt me, and I was allowed to bring at least five of my friends home. That made up for the whole year. My friends usually weren't allowed to come any closer than the mailbox. I used to show the kids at school my whip marks. **X:** But the teachers never saw them? **K:** No way! They used to give me some of their own.

X: This sort of thing doesn't happen now. **K:** No way. But thirty years ago? I never gave them anything.

X: There was this bravado thing. What was that all about? **K:** Just to show them that there was nothing they could do that could hurt me. I'd say 'Huh! My mother can hit harder than you!' **X:** I'm just amazed that you can still feel reasonably positive about people who treated you so badly.

K: I truly believe that they were put into my life to equip me. I have come up against some of the worst kinds of people, and if I hadn't been equipped as a child I'd be a mess now. Much later, my first husband started beating me up. He'd been really nice but he was such a creep after we got married. He turned out to be an arsehole. He told me once to get all dolled up for a Christmas party. So I do. And I wait. He doesn't show up. He finally bashes down the door at one in the morning because he's so drunk. I've been waiting for hours to taken to a party. I'm pregnant. The hormones are going wild. I went ballistic. I got stuck into him, and he turns around and gets stuck into me. Kicking. Punching. I got a lucky kick in. He falls down. I pick up his keys that have fallen on the floor. I run and make it in to the car. He tries to get in, but I just crack a wheely and go. What I didn't realise is that his hand is stuck in the door handle. I race off. I must have dragged him 200 metres before I look through the side window just as he's somersaulting onto the road. I wish I'd had a camera. I'm too scared to look back because he'd already kicked me in the back when I was three and a half months pregnant, so I fetch my brother-in-law and we find him and take him to the hospital.

X: Did you end up having that baby? K: No. I miscarried.

X: Was that the end of the marriage? K: He thought he owned me. We were only married one year and I ran away from him twenty-one times before I left for good. He'd keep chasing after me. But I should have known what he was like. Even at our wedding he went psycho because he thought I was having it off with one of my friends. He starts smashing into him and then one of my cousins starts smashing him. Pretty soon everyone at the wedding's lost the plot. Everyone started fighting. The next minute a splash of blood gets on to my beautiful wedding gown.

X: Wow! That was really symbolic. That was a pretty big sign! K: It was, eh!

X: How did you finally succeed in leaving him? K: I had to leave the country. I came to Australia.

X: But you fell into a pattern, didn't you? K: Four abusive Librans. I had a series of really bad relationships. A psychologist told me that I replaced my mother's abusive love with my boyfriend's abusive love. All the boyfriends I had were obsessive and jealous. Psychos. Even my first boyfriend beat me up. He was so good looking!

X: Was that part of the problem? When you're young you're hung up on looks and you're used to getting beaten up? Were you even thinking at all? K: I don't know. They were all so macho and so loving, but so psycho. Their love was abnormal. They all just wanted to lock me up and put me in a cage and pluck my feathers so that I couldn't fly. That's the sort of people I used to attract.

X: And you were attracted to them. K: No, I wasn't. X: Maybe not consciously, but it's outside of the realm of normal chance that you'll have one abusive relationship after another. Something in you might have been drawing you to these men. You were making bad choices. You weren't fully functional.

K: Obviously not. You know, when you've been an abused child even when you think you're functioning, you're not. I was attracted to these macho men, boxers who used me like a punching bag. The Bulgarian Nazi was really bad. He hated Jews and thought that Hitler had had the right idea. It was crazy; he looked like a Jew, but he hated them. I should have known from that that he was evil. He was no help when my daddy died and everything fell apart.

————

It all begins with abuse. With Angie the abuse was a neglectful father and a witch stepmother who alienated her and forced her into a world she wasn't ready for.

With Kelli the abuse was a predatory brother who put her in an impossible position. Tell daddy and daddy would kill her brother and go to jail. Don't tell and bear it until you have to leave, and leave your younger sisters to be next. And all the while your mother is beating you up because she thinks you're *spoilt*.

Angie and Kelli are just two examples of what can happen to girls in toxic families. They are, in fact relatively mild examples. After all, children die from abuse. The literature on abuse gives innumerable other cases of mistreatment and neglect. If you want to give a grown-up a really crappy life start off with them as a child and give them as much abuse, mental, emotional, physical and sexual as you can. Eventually they'll get the idea that they are worthless (or more valuable than anyone else, as a way of compensating). If you do your job really well they'll get the idea that everyone else is worthless too. Depending on how things go at the extremes you'll get an angry fascist—'I'm great, you're just a piece of meat', a frightened professional victim—'I'm no good, you're right to treat me like shit, and I'll go along with whatever', or a perpetually sad nihilist—'I'm crap, and everyone else is too. I'll just kill myself slowly with drugs or alcohol or anything else I can get my hands on. Or maybe I'll kill myself quickly, but whatever happens I'll make as many people as possible suffer along with me. What do I care? They're just as shitty as I am. We deserve everything we get.' Given these life positions it's almost inevitable that people make maladaptive decisions.

At what point does a little girl begin to believe that she is worthless? How many humiliations, torments and abuses does a child need to have before she decides that she is bad, that she 'deserves' to be treated like dirt, or simply that it's normal to live like this? What does it take?

We all know of people who have seemed strong on the outside, but who 'suddenly' and 'inexplicably' cracked. We all know of people who cracked long ago and keep cracking, both themselves and others. I've heard it said that 'sometimes all it takes is one thing to destroy someone's self-esteem'. I would argue that it always takes only one thing to destroy someone's self-esteem.

It's not in nature's best interest to create dysfunctional people with serious issues. People with 'issues' simply don't play the game of life as well as those who are stable, healthy and happy. People with issues are generally unstable, unhealthy and miserable and they compromise the stability, health and happiness of everyone they come in contact with. So nature creates a defence, an in-built resistance to dysfunction. Destroying a human being is difficult. Humans are tougher than they give themselves credit for. In some environments it's surprising that anyone survives at all. But nature isn't perfect and while the spirit may be strong, it is not indestructible, and the strongest spirit will break, given enough damage.

Think of it this way. Your body has an immune system, but it is not infallible. Although you are exposed to countless potential pathogens every day of your life your natural defence system protects you, and you don't drop dead of bubonic plague every hour, or smallpox every five minutes.

Similarly, our minds live in a place of sensations, messages and ideas that can affect the way you see the world and the way you feel about yourself—a place of voices telling you what to believe. Many of these voices are malign. Most of the time we can ignore the slights, the subtle putdowns, the assaults to our bodies and our spirits. People behave atrociously to each other all the time. We don't all turn to crime.

But what happens if you're living in an environment where everywhere you turn there is something that not only can hurt you, but is actively and maliciously doing so? What happens when the slights become neglect, the put-downs become insults, the assaults become attacks?

How many times does a father or mother have to leave their children without supper to fend for themselves with an empty refrigerator before the children conclude that they aren't worth feeding? How many times does a mother or father have to beat a child until she's bleeding before the child concludes that her pain doesn't matter? How many times does a father have to rape a daughter before the daughter concludes that nothing is safe?

Amazingly, children in toxic families often survive relatively intact if someone reaches them before too much harm is done. However, more often than not no one comes to their aid and they are left to themselves. They become people who think that being beaten to within an inch of your life is normal. They become people who think that everyone's mum or dad gets drunk every night, and that you'd better stay out of the way then, because that's when mum or dad gets mean. They become people who think that everyone lives in a world where only the slyest or the most vicious make it.

How many slaps, punches or beatings, both verbal and physical, does it take? How many straws does it take to break the camel's back? How many assaults does it take to crush a human spirit? Only one.

The one that counts is the one that breaks you. It just happens to be the one where your natural defences fail.

What does it take to get to that point of the one message, the one abuse that breaks the girl's spirit? The short answer is: quite a lot. The human spirit is remarkably robust; it's had to survive sabre tooth cats, plagues, volcanoes, earthquakes and tidal waves. It's also had to survive wars, tortures and famine. We are the descendents of the strong, and the lucky. It's natural selection working on the strongest.

Now before some redneck fundamentalist of the 'spare the rod, spoil the child' school thinks that it actually might be a good idea to abuse children to 'make them stronger', let me remind you of one thing. If you subject a sapling to storms and stress, or droughts and starvation during its tender years, you'll either kill it, or the tree will grow twisted and gnarled, and it will never reach its full height. Abuse a child enough and the adult grows up twisted too.

At some point the abuse will get to you, and from that point on you take a stand. You reach a decision. That decision can take many forms but they are all variations on the one theme—'The world isn't safe and it will kill me if I don't do something about it.' You can then spend the rest of your life fighting back, or you can find a slow or fast way to die. The door then opens on a universe of possibilities, a universe where you will do whatever it takes to survive, or whatever it takes to kill yourself. And who teaches you how to survive, emotionally and physically or how to kill yourself, emotionally and physically? Who else, but the very people around you? After all, they're all you've ever known.

———

Abuse is not the only way a kid ends up in detention. Sometimes madness is hereditary—you get it from your children. Jean brought up her daughters in Los Angeles. The story of one daughter gives you an inkling of what happens to women in crime elsewhere, and what it's like for the family.

Jean: My daughter Sophie was a heroin addict who had been committing crimes to support her habit—no violence, according to her.

X: How did she become a heroin addict? **J:** She'd caused me nothing but grief since she was born, basically. It wasn't her fault but she was uncontrollable and hyperactive. It wasn't until she was twelve that she was diagnosed with ADD. She was one of the first. They put her on Dexedrine, which acts as a tranquilliser. She was seeing a psychiatrist, the whole family was, to try to figure out what was going on. She couldn't concentrate, couldn't sit still, wild at school, demanding—nothing ever satisfied her. I remember when she was three years old she was at a birthday party. All the kids had oranges and she was complaining that her orange wasn't as big as the others. But she was so bright! She was walking and talking at eight months old, which was very rare. I thought I had a genius on my hands. It was really difficult. I had no support from my family or from my husband.

X: Why not? **J:** My mother was an alcoholic. My father was just useless. My husband just wasn't a supportive guy. That's why I separated from him. Even when I did he'd follow me around. Steal my car. Threaten to shoot any man that went near me. I'm sure a lot of women go through the same stuff. My other daughter, Hailey, who was fifteen months younger than Sophie, was never a problem. Sophie claims now that the Dexedrine led her to drugs. But she was on Dexedrine for a few years. She was perfectly normal and had mellowed out, she was concentrating, she got her stuff done. Then when she was fifteen she says, 'I'm not taking these pills anymore. I'm not crazy.' With that, the trouble really began. She started running away from home, stealing. It was back and forth with shrinks and social workers.

X: So she decided for herself that she wasn't crazy. But the minute she stopped? When was the first time she got in trouble with the police?

J: She was impulsive. I used to buy groceries for a month and while I was out she'd go to the park and give all the groceries away. Then she got caught stealing cigarettes out of a stranger's car. The social worker and the police agreed that she should spend the night in juvenile hall. They felt that she needed to learn the consequences of her actions. It didn't help.

She started running away from home. I'd be getting fired from jobs because instead of doing my work I'd be on the phone all the time to the police. I'd be in tears. Other times I'd spend my lunch hour just looking for her. I kept losing jobs. You wonder how you live through it. These sorts of things just kept happening. **X:** What sort of things? **J:** I don't know the full story. **X:** Why not? **J:** I was just too busy trying to make ends meet. I could never get any child support from my husband. I had to work all the time. I also think I've blocked out a lot of the stuff now, so it's hard to remember.

Eventually Sophie just ran away one day when she was seventeen. But she'd keep coming back. She started to gravitate towards particular people and about this time she was hanging around with a heroin dealer. I reported it to the police but they said they couldn't do anything unless they caught him in the act of dealing. It just went on and on. It was really unfair on Hailey because Sophie got so much more attention. All the attention was going on the negative. It's always the negative that gets all the power. The whole house was in Sophie's power.

X: There is a limit to parental love?

J: According to some people, no. Unconditional love is the only way that you're supposed to live. I don't agree with that. It all came to a head when, for the first time in my life, I had an opportunity to leave Los Angeles and go on holiday for a week. At this point Hailey is sixteen and she'd be okay for a week. I told her that under no circumstances could Sophie come in while I was away. But she forced her way in anyway. She and her boyfriend had stolen a whole bunch of stuff and was using our house to hide it. I came home the next day to a door that the police had kicked when they raided the place. The police had been there with guns. Hailey had to watch all that. I told Sophie I never wanted to see her again. It wasn't easy to detach myself from my child but I had to do it, for my sake and for the sake of my other child.

X: It was a survival skill. **J:** And still is. **X:** This helps to balance out the picture for me. So many of the stories I hear are about bad parenting, but there are also cases of impossible children.

J: I can't even sort it out anymore! Maybe I was a terrible mother. I don't even know! I never beat them; I never abused them. There were a couple of long relationships with men in my life but they were wholesome people. Except one, I got into a relationship with a sociopath, and that just about did me in.

X: How does a woman, who is intelligent and reasonable, find herself getting involved in a destructive relationship? J: You don't know at the time. Sociopaths are the best actors.

X: They have no conscience. They'll say anything to anyone just to do whatever they want to do. J: And they fool you.

X: So when you combine that with an ex that's stalking you, an alcoholic mother, a sociopathic boyfriend, a disturbed child? J: And LA, which is just a crazy place anyway. It's a place where you feel lonely and alone and displaced. It's hard to describe unless you've been there. It's bizarre. It has no heart. By a miracle I got the opportunity to go to Australia. I discussed it with Hailey and it was okay because she's eighteen now and she got an opportunity to live with a friend. Her family had money, so they were okay.

X: Hailey came later though.

J: It was always my intention to bring her. Meanwhile, Sophie was committing burglaries, minor thefts. Her father was bailing her out all the time. Somehow, for a long time, she never got incarcerated. X: This is interesting. Your husband had been totally unsupportive of you, but he was supporting Sophie's dysfunction by bailing her out.

J: She had no one else. I'd been dealing with it for twenty years, but now he had to deal with it. He got her to work for him a few times and she embezzled money from his business for her drugs. This had been her pattern all her life. My brother was a schoolteacher and he offered to look after her and see what he could do with her. She was really chuffed but the first night she was with him she stole a toothbrush from the supermarket. My God! My brother would have bought it for her. It was a no-win situation. She was constantly self-destructive. X: She had ADD though. She was mentally ill. And she wasn't getting any treatment.

J: I'd tried. I took her to therapists.

X: But you can't talk your way out of bad brain chemistry.

J: A cousin of mine, a psychologist, explained the chemistry. He said, 'It's not you, it's her.' He told me that there was no correlation between Dexedrine and heroin. That's just bullshit. But the guilt is always there. As time went on and she was getting crazier maybe I was getting crazier too. Mothers always have guilt unless they're sociopaths with no conscience.

I had no contact with Sophie, but Hailey did. Hailey didn't want to tell me anything. She was protecting me from what happened later.

Angie's story gives you some inkling of what happens to some people of Indigenous background and I would be committing a crime myself if I did not devote some time to the position of Aboriginal women in the criminal justice system.

If you're an Aboriginal woman in Australia then nationally you're about eighteen times more likely to end up behind bars than your 'white' counterparts. Why? Aboriginal activist and President of the Indigenous Social Justice Association, Ray Jackson, made me aware of some of the realities of being an indigenous Australian. If it takes you a while to see how what Ray is saying applies to Aboriginal women in crime, it's because the issue doesn't lend itself to a five-second sound bite.

It occurred to me that a lot of the reasons that proportionally more Aboriginals end up in detention was because of profound misunderstandings between the cultures. 'Mainstream' Australian society doesn't even seem to know how to talk to Indigenous Australians. It doesn't even know how to engage with them. I realised I didn't have a clue, and it was from this position of cluelessness that I began. For example, what's the best name to refer to the original inhabitants of Australia. Do you call them Aboriginals, Kooris, what? Ray and I finally decided on 'Indigenous Australians' as the term that would probably offend the fewest people. According to Ray, at the last count about 2% of Australians are Indigenous, roughly 418 000.

R: We are not a united people and never have been. There were hundreds of languages. We were fractured but pretty much peaceful. That's part of the problem. Governments can't pick people to represent us all because that's just the way it is. Try taking ten suburbs from Melbourne to represent all of Melbourne.

X: Suburbs as different as Toorak and Werribee.

R: Yes. X: And the non-Indigenous population tends to lump you all together.

R: No matter where you come from, you're all Australian. But that doesn't work with the Aborigines. We're not homogenous.

X: From the point of view of the Indigenous Australians there was, just over 200 years ago, an invasion of a continent populated by different nations.

R: So if you want a treaty you don't talk to just ten people, you've got to talk to the elders of each area. Take culture. If, by culture, you mean singing, dancing etcetera, there is a generic culture in that sense, but one of our continuing arguments is that if you're looking for an eastern seaboard 'style' it's just not there. X: Is that because the cultures have been eliminated? The people eliminated?

R: Yes. X: So from the very beginning we're not dealing with one culture, but many, not one people, but many. So it's a gross oversimplification to talk about 'Aboriginal Culture'.

R: And because of the invasion although there's 400 000 of us, less than half of us would be connected to our culture, and our land in a daily sense. X: And it's hard to have a connection to the land that is occupied by an invader.

R: And our connection to the land is not just as hunter-gatherers. The land has, for us, as it has worldwide for most indigenous groups, a deep spiritual significance.

So when you remove Indigenous Australians from the land of their ancestors you are not only displacing them physically, you are displacing them spiritually.

R: For the more remote mobs, who still live on the land, there is still that active spirituality with that land. For example, from 1918 the Queensland government took about forty distinct groups and dumped them on Palm Island. That's where you get those sorts of problems.

X: So even if you got some prize hunter-gatherer real estate back, it wouldn't be your traditional land, and you couldn't go back to living like that, no matter what you thought of our culture. R: We could no longer go back to our traditional ways than you could to yours. We don't even talk our own languages. They've been taken away. The land isn't there so that we can go back to living in caves! The land is there for the spirituality of it, especially for our young people, so we can say that this is your land. We know we have to live in the 21st century, not the 18th century. But when we do exploit the land with mining and pastoral leases the sacred sites must remain untouched, not with bulldozers running over everything.

R: And there's still a lot of anger about the invasion and all the things that have been done to the Aboriginal people since then. My land is the Wiradjuri land, but I, as an Aboriginal, would not go into Badjalang country and say 'this is my land' because it isn't. My history isn't there. My cultural roots and religion are not there. That's why we didn't make war.

X: There was no point in claiming land that you didn't have any spiritual connection to. But you're at war with the invaders. They're taking prisoners.

R: Governments and authorities refuse to engage us on our terms. We're not in your boxes. We have our own identifiers. In the early days of the invasion the invaders would identify 'chiefs' among us who would speak for 'all of us'. We didn't have chiefs; we had elders.

X: They projected their identifiers onto you.

R: Which is what invaders do all the time. This has been happening in Europe for thousands of years. But we are very much involved in the struggle to keep ourselves, our culture intact. So there's a total breakdown of culture. If you're old and you have the opportunity to go back to your ancestral lands you do because you still have that connection. But the young who don't have that connection don't want to live in the Bush Way. They want the City Way.

And it's this cultural and economic breakdown of Aboriginal people, that has cast them adrift in places they have no connection to.

X: The City Way has its appeal. R: Certainly! The pubs are there. Alcohol is a major problem for our people.

X: I've heard that you don't have the enzymes to cope with alcohol— alcohol dehydrogenase in particular. As a result alcohol is even more toxic to you than to Europeans.

R: I have never been able to find any alcohol in the traditional history of the Aboriginal people. Betel nut came from New Guinea. I read an article once that said that we, the Aboriginal people never had any drugs.

X: No narcotics? No hallucinogens? R: Nothing.[8]

X: So you suddenly have a group of people who have been living for tens of thousands of years without drugs. R: It's like setting off a time bomb. So the invader ploy was to give the men the alcohol so that you'd have access to the women. They'd even set off fights between groups of men, fuelled by alcohol. Gladiator stuff. We don't own the pubs or the breweries. Non-Aborigines are still the suppliers. In the north a carton of beer can cost $80 to $100.

X: So in terms of the expense, proportional to the income, alcohol is the cocaine of the more remote Aborigines.

R: It keeps them poor. It keeps them subdued. You finish up with nothing. X: There's always this breakage. Indigenous people are torn from their land. Torn from their cultural roots. Torn from their families. It's all about 'divide and conquer'.

R: There's no guarantee that reunions will turn out well, either. Not all of the reunions work. Some are very soul destroying. I've read reports. It's in the stolen generations report as well. Sons and daughters would return to their mother, only to have their mother reject them, through her own problems.

X: So finding your natural birth parents is not a guaranteed path to happiness, wholeness and intimacy? R: Not at all. My mother was Indigenous. I was adopted at the age of three. I'm sixty-three now. My birth mother would be up in the eighties or something. Why would I do that? To what end? What do you say after you say 'Hello?' 'How have you been? What have you been doing over the last sixty odd years?' To me it would be such a stupidity, and be hurtful to all.

X: You don't think it would create healing? R: If I were ever going to have done anything, it would have been in my thirties. I've missed the boat, but it was the boat I pushed away. X: Given the upheavals that Aborigines have experienced it's not surprising that the families have broken down and with them, whatever stability that could keep kids out of trouble.

R: If it hadn't been for the strength of the women we would certainly have not survived.

X: Because so many of the men were killed? **R:** So many men simply fell to pieces when their cultural role was taken away from them. If it had not been for the women staying strong then we would not be here today. I think we owe a tremendous debt to our mothers, aunts, grandmothers and sisters, all those who struggled since the days of the invasion to maintain the connections. Now we're living more in the white world and we've lost the links, the respect for our elders. We owe the women a huge debt. That's not to say that some of our younger women don't have problems. Alcohol and drugs have torn the families to pieces—along with the stolen generations. When you take an Aboriginal child from their fractured family do you give them to a white family or to another Aboriginal family?

X: Do you take a Polish child and give it to a Chinese family or a Tongan family?

R: That sort of thing. But because the stolen generations have been going on for so long you now have families with no family skills whatsoever. They've never had an intact family. If the fathers were even there they were struggling with poverty, some were drunks. Once you lose the links of culture you have genocide, people falling to pieces who have no way of getting back onto that track.

X: We're really looking at cultural genocide, aside from the well-documented fact that Aborigines were frequently hunted for sport. So you have an ongoing situation of a dysfunctional Aboriginal family, some well-meaning but misguided whitefella takes them away and puts them in a white family, but a lot of the adoptive families were dysfunctional too.

R: My earliest memories of my mother's first husband was that he wasn't around much. She eventually divorced him. She then met her second husband.

X: How did you get along with him? **R:** Not well at all. I was just something that happened to come along with his new wife.

X: Did he ever hit you? **R:** Oh, God yes.

X: Why did your mother put up with this? **R:** I assume she knew that there were tensions and that she assumed these tensions were normal.

X: If your case was not uncommon it means that the whole stolen generations thing was completely misguided. If the presumption was that being in a white family was going to mean a better, more stable, more nurturing, more caring and sharing and loving life for the child then?

R: Well he was an alcoholic as well ... It started from the very beginning. Even during the early invasion children were being taken away from their parents. It officially began in the 1890s but it had been unofficially going on since the beginning.

X: Fucked-up cultures, disconnection, discontinuity—fragmentation. In the post-2000 world what forces conspire to send an Aboriginal woman to prison? What forces conspire to ensure that Aborigines are so over-represented in jails?

R: The relationship between the police and our young people. You've got to remember that the role of the police started with troopers who went out shooting the people, 'clearing the land' as they used to call it.

X: So you're arguing a sub-cultural continuity. Troopers evolve into police and it gets reinforced in the sub-culture of the police force that 'you've really got to watch them darkies'. Are you saying that even with modern police training that's still around?

R: One only has to look at the current spate of deaths in custodies. The police have this innate culture of absolute disinterest in how Aboriginal people can live their bloody lives. As far as the police are concerned we are all thieves, we are all rapists, we are all drug addicts, prostitutes. X: You are the Gypsies? R: We are the Gypsies of Australia. The American Indians are the same, the Canadian Indians. X: Maoris.

R: The police have this culture against the Indigenous populations around the world because to invade a country, you've got to get rid of the original people. In South Africa there were too many for them, but they managed to subjugate them for a long, long time. If we had had the numbers the history of this country would have been totally different.

X: But the fact of the matter is that you are 2% of the population. R: And lucky to be there at all. X: You are not going to win this. So how do you survive?

R: Sheer bloody grit, basically. Guts, cunning.

X: Have you ever met a good policeman? R: Of course! Not all coppers are feral. There's good coppers in Redfern! But the trouble with the police is that they have this culture, drilled into them by the old sergeants who had it drilled into them by the old sergeants before them. It's a historical thing.

X: You're saying that their elders are corrupt, and they are passing down a corrupt dreaming?

R: And we are all the products of other people's dreams. And the police harass our youth especially. I have seen instances, I have represented families at police stations where young Jack, or Jill, who is seven or eight years old is being looked at because they swore at the police. Now they swear at the police because the police swear at them. 'I'm gonna fuck your sister'—all this sort of crap. And they point their fingers like guns and say, 'You're next.' Our kids grow with this.

X: So you're saying that the police have a culture of mistrust. The kids react with a culture of mistrust and disrespect of their own, and it never gets any better? R: It only gets worse. And the drugs and alcohol don't help our youth as they don't help anyone's youth.

X: The Middle Australia argument will be that if the youth takes drugs it's the youth's fault.

R: It's like the argument that if the youth comes into contact with the police it's their fault, more than any other group. Not all coppers, but a fair percentage of police, go out of their way to pick out a black kid and ask, 'Where did you get that bike?'

X: What percentage?

R: Of absolute corrupt coppers I'd put it at about a quarter. Our problem is that the large amount of non-corrupt cops, because of the police culture, cover up for the corrupt ones. And that comes from the Police Commissioner down and we saw it in the case of that boy who died in Redfern impaled on a metal fence and we'll see it in the Palm Island deaths in custody.

X: Are girls more vulnerable? What conspires to send girls through the justice system?

R: I don't know that the girls are more vulnerable. But girls and boys are targeted from a very young age well over and above any other youth. So that by the time that they are of an age to be charged they are well known to the police and to welfare groups. And because you can't be charged before the age of ten drug dealers target young kids to run the drugs for them.

X: Who are the 'they' who get Aboriginal children into drugs?

R: Like the alcohol providers up north, the big drug runners are all non-Aboriginal. The Block is an area of Redfern that has a community centre and a housing cooperative surrounding a square. There've been numerous riots at The Block. The Block is the most over policed area in Australia. Some reports I've read have stated that there are sixty incursions by police into The Block daily. Sixty.

X: Does all that policing stop anything?

R: It doesn't stop the drugs, the paedophiles, the pornographers? X: Why not? R: Because the police don't want to remove the crime, they want to remove the people that live there. The government wants the land back.

X: Your argument is that The Block is now valuable real estate, let's get the blackies out of there? R: As one report said, if we can get the blacks out of Redfern, land and housing values will rise by at least 30%. We're talking money.

———

The story of the Indigenous peoples of Australia has it all. Genocide, cultural, social and individual rape, drugs (and a genetic predisposition to be vulnerable to their effects), chronic health issues, deaths in custody, an erosion of the basic skills to live a viable life, cover ups, whitewashes, hidden agendas. You name it, it's there.

Ray's story is a story of violation and abuse—not just on an individual level, but at the level of entire groups of people. The story of Indigenous Australians is where social-criminalisation and psycho-criminalisation merge so that it becomes impossible—and pointless—to distinguish between the two. This is where the dreaming is so corrupt as to have become a nightmare. Given the social circumstances that many Indigenous Australians are born into and grow up in it, is surprising that there are not even more Indigenous Australians in jail.

The situation in New Zealand is even worse. Maoris comprise 13% of the New Zealand population but over 50% of inmates in jail. In many cases, being Indigenous is like playing poker where the odds are really stacked against you. None of the above historical realities constituted an excuse. The last thing I want to do is to give any criminal—black, white, yellow, brown or whatever—the opportunity to say: 'I'm justified in stealing your car because of what happened to my ancestors.' You could say that about anybody. We're all programmable computers. If your family programming has been so corrupted by history and circumstance that your options and opportunities are severely compromised it doesn't matter what colour you are. Nevertheless we, as a society, frequently find ourselves in the position where the black computers are more likely to get the viruses than the cream-coloured ones, and the response is to kick the black computers to 'make them work' and when that doesn't work (as it wouldn't work with the cream ones either) we put the black computers into the store-room—with bars—in the hopes that the viruses will magically disappear. And all the while the computers continue to infect each other with each other's viruses. To the extent that humans can be seen as programmable computers I think this analogy is sound, albeit oversimplified.

More than anything the story of many Indigenous Australians is one of fracture, broken histories and broken lives. It's this breakage that ultimately creates broken people, or a broken people. And at times it seems that once broken everything conspires to keep you that way. The Aboriginal and Torres Strait Islander Social Justice Commissioner report of 2002 devoted an entire chapter to Indigenous women in prisons. Chapter 5, 'Indigenous Women and Corrections, a Landscape of Risk' revealed that in 2001 in New South Wales Indigenous women were over twenty-five times more likely than non-Indigenous women to be in jail: 'In New South Wales, Indigenous women represented 30% of the total female population in custody in October 2002 despite constituting only 2% of the female population of the state.'[9] In Western Australia the figure of over-representation was over twenty-four times, and in South Australia over twenty-one times.

To give you an idea of what the situation was like only recently here is a table from the report cited above, reproduced in full.

When it comes to Indigenous women the top five places for most serious offences for which they were incarcerated in 2001 were Assault and Related, Robbery, Break and Enter, Justice Procedures (meaning parole violations etcetera) and Theft and Related tying with Homicide.

Table 1: Most Serious Offence, Indigenous Women Prisoners, Australia 1994-2001

	1994	1995	1996	1997	1998	1999	2000	2001	1994-2001
	No	No	No	No	No	No	No	No	% change
Homicide	18	17	17	25	28	30	33	36	100
Assault and related	40	39	42	53	48	91	69	91	127
Sex offences	1			1		2	3	1	
Robbery	10	16	29	25	27	29	43	54	440
Extortion				1	1	1	4	4	
Break and enter	32	24	28	39	45	43	42	51	59
Fraud	8	9	9	12	18	18	9	12	50
Theft and related	16	20	32	30	32	28	37	36	125
Property damage	4	7	4	7	3	2	4	9	125
Justice procedures	16	18	25	23	35	49	30	38	137
Weapons				1				1	
Good order	2	1	2	3	5	11	6	4	
Drugs	5	7	6	3	3	7	6	11	120
Driving and related	3	5	10	10	16	20	22	14	366
Other	3	1	2		1	1	3	8	166
Total	158	164	206	233	261	332	308	370	134

Source: Aboriginal and Torres Strait Islander Social Justice Commission, 2002.

Note though that: 'census data records the most serious crime for which an inmate is convicted. Therefore, other offences which might contextualise the criminal behaviour are generally not recorded'. In other words the statistics don't give the full picture. Finally, from M. Cameron's article 'Women Prisoners and Correctional Programs' in the February 2001 issue of *Australian Institute of Criminology*, which is referred to towards the end of 'A Landscape of Risk', here is the most damning observation of all:

As the recent study by NSW AJAC into the needs of incarcerated Indigenous women in NSW stated: The most significant findings of this study are the level of serious drug addiction among women in prison and the causal role that addiction has played in their current imprisonment. Fundamentally significant is the levels of abuse that has [sic] been suffered by the women and the clear link those women have drawn between that abuse and their drug use, their drug use and their current imprisonment. It is clear from this study that unless the abuse experienced by Aboriginal women is effectively addressed they will continue with their drug habit and continue to offend.

Does anyone else ever wonder why so many jails have Aboriginal names?

Black, white, yellow, male, female, whatever—people who feel that they have nurturing, caring homes with regular meals and regular hugs tend not to leave those homes.

Having said that, I don't know of any families that are perfect. In fact, many of the families I've observed are at least a little dysfunctional, and if a dysfunctional family is one in which the individuals are subjected to regular abuse then I would say that dysfunctional families make up a substantial minority, with barely functional families making up the majority. For many people though, barely functional is adequate enough not to want to leave. It all depends what you're used to.

Even though I have said that it is not in nature's best interests to create families with programming that leads them away from survival, that doesn't mean that a family can't continue to limp along, generation after generation, never truly fulfilling the potential of its individual members—a seemingly endless cycle of thwarted destinies. When things get really bad though, the only real alternative for many young people is to leave. I wondered how these kids make it. Kelli was able to help me understand.

X: How did you survive on the streets, once you ran away from home? **K:** I lived with my boyfriend's parents. **X:** You were fourteen and you had a boyfriend? **K:** He didn't know I was fourteen. I was a tall girl and I looked older. I fixed myself up.

X: He never knew? **K:** No. Not even his parents. When I was twelve I had wanted to run away but I realised that there was no way at the time that I could survive on my own. But as soon as I could get away with it I put on make-up, and stuffed my bra and pretended I was sixteen so that I could work. What was happening to me at home forced me to think outside the square. I loved my daddy and I loved my other brothers and sisters, but what my older brother was doing to me, it was sending me bonkers. I was becoming schizo.

X: You were already having out of body experiences every time he sexually abused you.

K: I used to literally block my eyes, so that I couldn't see what was happening, so that it didn't affect me later on. And it worked. **X:** What specifically led to your decision to run away from home? **K:** My older brother's abuse just escalated. It was happening three times a week. **X:** He was getting used to it? **K:** He was getting addicted to it. The older I was getting the more beautiful I was getting. I was so stunning as a kid.

X: You're still a good-looking woman now. **K:** But then!

X: You were glamourous.

K: So I waited until I was fourteen because I knew I wouldn't survive until then. The first time was for exactly one week. I ran away with an older girl, who was already a high school dropout, her elder brother and her boyfriend. They were going up the coast. I just decided to go with them. It was a spontaneous decision. When you become a street kid you always find a place to party. There's always one kid, with a solo parent who's not there.

X: So the kid says, 'Come on over!'

K: And there are always a couple of kids that are old enough to get the alcohol. It's just networking. I even met this boy. He didn't become my boyfriend, but we kissed a lot.

X: You didn't waste any time did you?

K: Noooo! It's all about survival. But the stupid friends I went up with were high school dropouts—losers and thieves. The police caught up with them. I happened to be there. The police sent me home. I was terrified, but my parents were so glad to see me, I didn't even get a hiding. I stayed for three months, but the creep just kept getting worse. He forced himself into my room. Trying to get into bed with me. I used to sleep in between my two younger sisters in a big double bed, so I was safe, but then we changed to bunk beds. I slept on the top bunk and he'd just come straight at me in the top bunk. I started freaking because I wanted to scream. This is while my parents were at home, in the next room. I wanted to scream but I couldn't because that would have been it. My father would have come in and snapped his neck in half.

X: And your poor younger sister is in the bunk below, witnessing this.

K: I'm pretty sure. He was getting worse. He was a good-looking kid, he didn't need to do this. Why hassle me?

X: It must have been some sort of addiction.

K: He was a psycho!

X: And then you ran away for another month.

K: When I first started sneaking out it was to go to the disco with my friends. All my other friends were allowed out—not me. Like my older sister, the first time she went out was when she was eighteen to join the army! That day, when my sister ran away, was the first time I saw my mother cry. I felt so sorry for my mum that day.

X: And the boys were treated differently from the girls.

K: The boys were allowed to do anything. It was a lot of things, why I ran away. But for me being a street kid was exciting! I've always liked to live close to the edge. I've always crossed boundaries.

X: You had an adventurous attitude.

K: I could look after myself. That's why I waited until I was fourteen.

X : How did you find a bed every night?

K: We'd just gatecrash a party.

X: Who feeds you?

K: Back in those days we'd empty out the milk bottle money and buy stuff. It was a good rort.

Broken homes frequently create broken people and the people, the children break out. If they have nowhere else to turn, they end up on the streets. Eve, a former child prostitute who left home because 'my stepfather couldn't stay out of my skirt and my mother was too drunk to care' and who spent time in prison on drugs charges, told me much more about this way of life.

Eve: Living on the streets makes you hard. Depending on where you're living, if you've learned how to look after yourself from an early age you're rougher and tougher than girls who've come from mum and dad and who are just on the street for kicks.

X: When you're young it's usually not at home that you become a criminal it's usually something that happens on the streets.

E: Especially when you're living on the streets. Not just visiting.

X: How do girls get on the streets? How does that happen? Does she end up there because she's being abused by her father, stepfather or mother's boyfriend? Is she there because she has issues of growing up that nobody's dealing with properly? How does it happen?

E: In lots of ways. It can be the ways that you've just described or it could be because she's on drugs.

X: I can understand how she could be on drugs if she's living on the streets but how does it happen if she's got loving parents at home?

E: Taking them at school.

X: School and the streets. That's where the drugs are.

E: Yeah, well, I don't know too many drug pushers that make house calls.

X: Not unless you live in Hollywood, anyway. So it always comes down to, at some point, the girl is being exposed to an environment that is not protective or nurturing.

E: Yes. And she's on the streets and things happen there. The streets are a place where things can go bad pretty quickly. And you've got to learn to stand up for yourself. If you're gonna let every bloke that comes by take advantage of you, you're gonna cop whatever they throw at you. But if you stand up for yourself word gets round that you don't touch 'that one there'.

X: So what sort of things happen on streets? Stealing? Shoplifting? Drugs? What else can happen on streets?

E: Prostitution.

X: I once heard a prostitute say that prostitution is really easy to get into but really hard to get out of.

E: You get these people come up to you and they say what about getting a real job. Well, what sort of job could you offer me? Something in a shop, probably. And how much do you get? Well you look into that when you're sixteen and you probably only get about $200. Well that's junk. I don't even want that crap. I get $1500 a week. Easy.

X: And what have you got to show for it?

E: Nothing.

X: So what do you do with it?

E: I go live in a hotel. I don't have to clean up after myself. And all I've got to do is put my stuff in an overnight bag and I can go wherever, whenever I like.

X: So it makes sense. You do the sums in your head and where you're coming from, you're better off being a prostitute. But that's where you can get into bigger trouble because the life you lead opens up opportunities for trouble. So you're on the streets, but you discover the easiest way to make money is to put out. You're in a hotel and you make enough money that you can pay other people to do what most of us have to do for ourselves. So you don't learn how to cook, or how to do your laundry?

E: You don't have to do anything. So you don't learn self-pride, or self-respect. You live on takeaways. You get up when you want to and do whatever you feel like doing. You don't have to make a bed or anything because the maid does it all.

X: It works for you. And you have no shortage of clients.

E: The younger the better.

X: How young?

E: Twelve. You can look older. Or younger. There's lots of guys get off on girls that look, or are ten. Or younger.

X: Is that the only way that girls can survive on the streets?

E: You can deal drugs. You can steal. You can fence. Or you can live just going from one refuge to another.

X: And nobody's looking after these girls.

E: They're looking after themselves.

X: Is that because they won't let anyone look after them?

E: They don't trust anyone. They can't.

X: So the classic scenario of this young girl is that she's left home because of abuse, neglect or drugs. She makes a living stealing, dealing or selling her body.

E: And that same young girl is now at Yasmar or Emu Plains.

5   THE KIDDIE CLINK—JUVENILE DETENTION

Little girls who end up on streets often end up in Juvenile Detention. Some, a very few, manage to get into trouble without ever leaving home. Even with the best intentions and in the 'best' families, some young people just have a tough time growing up. What specific circumstances lead young girls to end up in the 'kiddie clink'? Kelli filled me in.

Kelli: The skirts were supposed to be three inches below the knee. Mine were always three inches below my crotch. I was an abused child so I used to have my entertainment at school. Do you understanding what I'm saying? **X:** You were getting so much crap at home that ... **K:** I needed some relief. As much as I hated school there were three teachers who loved me and that was great.

———

Les Drelich, from the Department of Health and Human Services Tasmania, was able to tell me more about some of the other early warning signs of possible future female criminals.

Les: The girls that we see end up in juvenile detention generally come from a single parent family generally with a series of men coming in and out of the mother's life. They don't report abuse as a factor.

X: It might be they're just not telling you.

L: We can only know what they report. Fairly early on in their history they present with problems at school.

X: How early?

L: Usually early high school. Disciplinary problems that escalate to violence. This leads to detentions, suspensions and often you have to resort to alternative education strategies and programs outside the school.

X: What exactly are the warning signs?

L: They start to miss a lot of school. They become bullies. Verbal abuse to teachers. Some early experimentation with drugs. In Tasmania it's usually marijuana and amphetamines. Kids show up in the classroom with erratic behaviour, slurred speech, significant changes in their normal behaviour. Kids even tell teachers that they're smoking dope. They're quite open about it. They minimise the extent of it. A lot of the kids don't see it as a big deal. They don't see it as illegal or bad.

X: What sort of behaviour leads to the suspensions?

L: Aggression, threats to students and staff, openly defiant behaviour and school refusal.

Sometimes you get theft from other kids or teachers as well.

X: Are they stealing for kicks?

L: Yes, but often for survival. Survival can mean getting more drugs but often the kids have been kicked out of home because their behaviour has become unacceptable, or they leave and stay with older friends.

X: Couch surfing.

L: Yes. Some end up in shelters, but if they break the rules of those shelters and get thrown out they'll end up squatting or on a downward spiral that lands them in detention.

X: How do they fill their days, if they're not at school?

L: They don't do a lot. They hang out at the mall. A lot of focus is on getting drugs and using drugs. Drifting. Watching television. They don't read at all. Chilling out. The reason I'm so vague about this is that they themselves are vague about it. When we try to get a handle on what's going on they really don't tell you much more than what I've told you. A lot of them say they're bored but they choose not to go back to school.

X: What are the young girls doing to come to your notice?

L: Mostly it's stealing from shops and to a lesser extent 'civil disobedience'—abusive language to police, refusing to leave a public place and so forth. If they damage property it's usually in the company of boys.

———

There's a lot of 'give' in the juvenile justice system. Our society will do almost anything to keep minors out of detention, as Les was able to expand on.

Les: We'd generally start with a formal caution. We have special youth police that deal only with young people. A police officer sits down with the child and the parent and they address the issues and see what can be done. Then there's community conferences which include teachers, social workers, the victims. If that doesn't work it's usually court. Youth Justice has to provide a report and again the presumption is that detention in a last resort. There are reprimands and Release and Adjourn orders where if the offence doesn't recur in six or twelve months the matter just disappears.

X: So you don't even get a criminal record?

L: That's right. Then there are fines and probation orders and suspended detention orders which is like a suspended sentence and then there's community service. But even at the level of community conferences the outcomes are that the offender submits a formal apology to the victims and agreed outcomes like counselling and community service if the offences are serious enough.

X: So there is some sense of accountability.

L: A major theme of community conferences is how the offender can repair the harm

X: So they get to feel valuable, that they're making a difference.

L: Young people today are no different to young people at any other time. What they struggle with is the availability of drugs and the way that drugs alter their behaviour.

X: The drugs alter their minds. They become different people?

L: Exactly. I've been doing this work for thirty years and we're beginning to see now the beginnings of mental illness as a result of long-term drug use. It's normal for young people to experiment with behaviour, and if they do wrong they feel sorry about it and the process of coming together with the victims is a very powerful process.

X: But when even that fails?

L: It's detention, which for some young people means stability, good nutrition and a forced opportunity to go cold turkey. Detention is not supposed to be positive, for some it's not a deterrent, in a sense, but some will also refuse to return to detention because they don't want to lose their liberty.

X: What straws break the camels' backs and finally land the girls in detention?

L: Breach of parole, usually. With women it's usually stealing. Car theft usually with boys. In fact, I don't recall a girl involved in car theft without a boy being present.

X: So they get charged with aiding and abetting?

L: No. Under the act, if you get into a car that you know is stolen you are charged with stealing the car. If it gets trashed you get charged with destruction, regardless of whether or not you do it directly. There's this package of drugs, possession, or theft, disobedience. It's the package that lands you in detention.

X: It's seldom just one act.

L: Murder or armed robbery. Armed robbery has happened once. We only have a handful of girls in detention in Tasmania. It's a fair call that it's easier to manage down here than in a larger jurisdiction.

Some girls make the wrong choice so often that they exhaust their parents' patience, the police's patience, and the courts' patience. What happens next? Vera used to work in Yasmar, the only facility exclusively for juvenile females in New South Wales, which is located in the pleasant and very middle-class suburb of Haberfield in Sydney's inner west.

X: What's a day in the life like for a girl at Yasmar?

V: They have to be up at six for muster. They have to set up for breakfast. They'd divide the work up like you do at camp. There'd be a breakfast, lunch and dinner roster. Breakfast was cereals, fruit juice, toast. They shower and get ready for school at nine. There's a special school on the premises, just for them. Then lunch, sandwiches etcetera. Then school and then they get locked down at two for the change-over of staff. You didn't want one escaping while you were changing over the officers.

Accommodation at Yasmar is a lot like an adult jail. Girls are housed in wings, comprising a courtyard and main room. Leading off the main room are individual cells. Girls can either get locked in to their wing or locked down into their individual cells. The individual cells are only a bed (sometimes two beds) a three-drawer chest and a toilet. Vera provided me with lots of details.

V: Depending on what was going on during the day they might be allowed in the pool for a couple of hours. They could have a basketball game or watch some videos. There's a lot they can do. They don't always agree to do it.

X: Why wouldn't they? Out of sheer bloody-mindedness?

V: Yeah. If they've behaved badly they don't get to do anything. Or they may be too depressed to worry about doing anything. Dinner's about six. Then they go to their rooms about seven o'clock.

Sandra worked on and off at Yasmar for some years.

X: Tell me about the first time you went to Yasmar.

S: I will never ever, ever, ever, ever, forget my first week at Yasmar. It was terrible. All I heard was the clanging of the gate and the locking of the bolt behind me. And there were these fourteen girls swearing and carrying on and I'm thinking 'What have I gotten myself into? I don't know how to handle this!' They're all in greens.

X: They're like normal, unruly teens but with the volume really turned up?

S: And every second word was 'fuck'. Actually I think they said the f-word more than any other word.

X: Were you ever assaulted?

S: In my role I don't think I would ever have been assaulted unless I had instigated the assault. We got respect, even when they called us 'fucking rotten moles' they still knew not to lay a hand on us.

Penny also worked at Yasmar:

X: What was it like, working with juvenile girls? P: Hell on earth. X: Why?

P: They, the girls, 'didn't do no wrong'. They had no respect for anyone or anything, and because they didn't see that they had done anything wrong it was too hard to get through to them. They played tough. Don't get me wrong. I simply called it hell on earth because I was stressed to the max. I couldn't find anyone who I could talk to. I had my own issues, but I was doing all right until that girl killed that teacher. I almost chucked it all in then. I wanted to leave and just go home for good.

In late July 1999, Yasmar Juvenile Justice Centre inmate Debbie Marie Adams (then sixteen years old) stabbed and killed TAFE assistant teacher Scott Bremner, 32, in the back during a cooking class at Yasmar. In 2004 the courts found her to be a continuing danger both to herself and the community and ordered her to imprisonment until 2014.

Liz had a different take on the girls:

L: Sometimes a teenager is still a child. If you look at her handwriting it doesn't look like that of a sixteen-year-old—seven or eight but not sixteen. Some girls do anything for a dare. Other girls put her up to stuff and they get off scott-free. One girl, she's at Mulawa now. Segregated. And you know, she only has an hour of sun each day. You wonder if she's losing the ability to walk because she doesn't get enough chances to?

––––––

Terry tended to agree with Penny:

T: Yasmar is not an easy place for anyone. X: What makes it so hard?
T: Watching what happens to the girls. Even if you're innocent you're exposed to some really bad girls. Some of these girls are hardened criminals, and even if they're inno-cent being at Yasmar can turn some girls into crims. Maybe you've had mum and dad to protect you right up until this particular night when you got drunk and you've been accused of something you did when you were drunk and you've gone home and you didn't know anything about it until the police come to your door and mum and dad say 'Hey! What's going on here?' And you don't know anything because you were drunk and you end up going to Yasmar. It's a matter of time. How long you're there determines whether or not you get scarred for life.
X: So you could be a hardened crim by the time you get into Yasmar, or you could be a girl who got into trouble one too many times. But if you put in a 'relatively innocent' girl or maybe just a confused, immature girl into a place with a group of hardened, streetwise, street kids? T: They're going to make or break her.
X: What does that mean? T: That means they'll either turn the girl to their way, or they'll break her, so that she'll have a breakdown, and have to be on medication for quite some time. X: So to break her means to put her into a place where she can't cope anymore. She'll withdraw, she'll go nuts and she'll do what she can just to escape. Or she'll become just as hard as the others.
T: Or there are the odd few that have a strong family support and they've gone back to

mum and dad after they've gotten over that hurdle, that horrible period between thirteen and seventeen when some kids just go feral. I think of some kids at that age as just wild. They don't respond to anything—not love, not discipline. The majority of the young girls I saw at that time were feral, but these odd few kids who came through, who had good family support, survived.

X: Did you ever see a case where somebody survived without that support? T: No.

X: It's a crucial difference.

T: They've got to have something to go back to. When they don't have anything to go back to, that's what breaks them. You picture a family that is going through sheer hell. There comes a time when you get to the straw that breaks the camel's back. They've had to put up with their child going to court, just about every three months. The kids go to Yasmar for six months, a year, and then they go out. And the parents say, 'Yes, you can come home.' But there comes a time where: 'Now listen. Enough is enough. We can't take this no more. You're draining our finances. You're draining us physically and mentally. Your brothers and sisters are losing out because we're spending so much time with you. Enough!'

So what makes some children go feral? Remember it's not just the messages or programming that people get that help make them what they are. It's the way that individuals react to that message.

Lots of people are under the illusion that in 'fair' families everyone gets treated the same. But the fact is that children are never treated the same. Each child is different. Parents program children differently for two main reasons. The parent's programming may say something like 'turn Peta into an economic rationalist and turn Tamara into a humanitarian socialist'. But the children themselves can make different demands on the parents who then respond to the demands of the moment. Cumulatively, the effects over years are huge. Sometimes you wonder how some very different siblings even come from the same families. Even in some hypothetical fantasyland where all children are dealt with identically, the children themselves would interpret things differently. It's these different ways of interpreting reality that make up a large part of what is commonly called a person's character, nature or personality, as Vera made clear.

V: Some kids just can't take discipline. And when all the hormones kick in, they can't handle it, and that's when they become destructive. They rebel against anything that mum or dad say. But the worst family that I've seen was one where there has been no discipline whatsoever. And there was no boundary, no line you couldn't walk over.

X: And when the line is there?

V: You may lose one child, but you won't lose all of them. Some girls I asked, 'Do you miss your brothers and sisters?' and if they didn't care I knew I've had to get to those girls as quickly as possible. What churns me up is that after I stopped working in Juvenile Justice these girls would end up at Mulawa, Emu Plains or Dillwynia. The women were broken but we couldn't break the cycle.

X: What happens to a girl at Yasmar to make her break?

V: The worse thing is the other girls picking on her. Some of the girls there are not the sort of girls you'd take home to have tea with mum and dad. You take say, ten girls, living in the same wing and the only freedom they have is when they're locked in their cell. It gives them all day, to do whatever they want to do. And take them at that certain time of the month when all the hormones are raging and they'd all be either crying or emotionally upset anyway. That's a horrible time. I've seen it when there have been thirteen girls and nine of them were going and I tell you, it's worse than sheer hell. Hell could not have been worse than what I was seeing in front of me that particular day.

X: So imagine the worse possible bullying that you can get. Imagine the most inventive petty tortures that a malevolent teenager can think of. There's a lot in popular literature about how nasty kids can be to each other. And anyone who's ever been bullied, or belittled, or insulted as a child would know what that felt like.

V: It doesn't happen all the time, but it does happen and it happens long enough to eventually get to the victim and depending on whether the supervisors even see it.

X: And the girls can be sneaky about it.

V: And that's the killer.

X: There could be threats. **V:** It's how you go about it. Another thing that happens is that if even one of the girls goes too far everyone gets locked up for that one girl's behaviour.

X: Why does that happen? **V:** Sometimes that's the only way you can deal with it. If the officers sense that something's about to erupt then everyone gets locked in. You know, I debated with myself about whether or not I should tell you all this, because I can imagine parents who have girls at Yasmar reading this and getting upset because they're getting an idea of what it's really like.

X: I know, but I think that there's a greater good involved here. People have to know the truth, even if it's just your version of it. You were there. You were at the coalface. There will be kids reading this too and if they have any sense left at all they'll realise that going into juvenile detention isn't a holiday camp.

V: It's not a good place to be. Things can get pretty bad in there.

X: And things can often only get worse. What can be done?

V: Short of pulling these places down and starting over, not much.

X: Why do we put up with this, as a society?

V: You see it's very hard to bring something in. When teachers come in with a program they've got to make sure that what they've got is not a weapon. They have to make

sure that there's no glue, scissors, needles or whatever. They have to count everything that they've come in with, and they have to come out with the same number
of things. Not many people want to do that, and the ones that do are qualified for
the job, but not necessarily qualified to handle the situation that they're coming in
to. Yasmar used to get some beautiful people as teachers. The girls destroyed them
by not using them. Girls would come into class but they wouldn't persevere. You'd
get maybe one or two. And a teacher would have to go to all this trouble for just one
or two. Some people would say that that's all they need to keep coming. Others would
say, 'I can't keep doing it' and they leave.

X: So you get a reinforcement of that sort of punctuated life where nothing ever really
gets finished and you can never get to dedicate yourself to anything because people
are always leaving you. At this point the girls are beginning to become their own
worst enemies because they're refusing whatever breaks well-meaning people are
wanting to give them. So what is a hardened criminal? What does it mean to turn
into a teenage girl who's a hardened criminal?

V: The majority of the girls don't want you. There's nothing much you can do with that.
They're not ready to accept anything. They're so 'tough' and they know everything,
they don't think they need a helping hand. The odd few that you help, you remember
for the rest of your life. It's their language, it's all the 'fucks' and the 'cunts' and
words that you've never even heard and you're copping that day in day out. And it's
walking from the parking lot to the court, stepping over globs of spit. I didn't want
to hear it all but there would come a day that you would be just that little bit more
sensitive and then you'd hear everything. And it was those days ... It was just that
offensive behaviour.

———

Collette told me a story that told of how isolating the experience of incarcera-
tion can be for a young girl.

C: There was this poor girl at Yasmar who just wandered around. She did whatever the
officers asked her to do, but she had nothing to do with anyone else that was there.
She was completely isolated. When I met her, she had already been at Yasmar for a
few months. So I used to come up to her every day and say, 'Hi! How are you?' It took
me two months solid of just going up to her and just saying, 'I hope you're feeling
okay today.' And then I'd walk away and leave her. I wouldn't push her for anything.
In the third month you could see her gradually moving towards me. It was about a
month before she went to court that the breakthrough came with her. She then
started meeting me at the door and say, 'Come, I need to talk to you.' From that point
on it got better. We used to meet under the tree in the courtyard of her wing, in a
place where the officers could see us. Whenever I saw her under the tree I knew that

she wanted to talk to me. We just sat on the ground and talked. It was huge with her. She'd been accused of killing her mother. There was nobody else in the house at the time they found her mother's body so the police thought she was lying. She was taken to Yasmar. She was only fourteen when she came in. She did not go to her mother's funeral. She wasn't allowed to.

X: That was tough. She wasn't even allowed closure.

C: Not only that, a year down the track she had to go back to the house where it all happened and she hadn't been back since.

X: Was she in remand for a year?

C: Yes.

X: That's a long time for a fourteen-year-old.

C: That's normal! There are women at Emu Plains who have already done a year, eighteen months, and they haven't been sentenced yet.

X: But when you're thirteen or fourteen a year is a long time. A lot of things can happen in a year.

C: The girl started mutilating herself. She couldn't cope with what was going on. Sometimes the girls would talk about their lives. We're not allowed to ask them why they're in there, but if they want to, that's different. They usually kick off, and you just let them talk. When you can acknowledge what they've gone through then they often come back with 'How can I keep going?'

X: Somehow the girl who'd been accused of killing her mother found a way to keep going?

C: She always told me that she was innocent and for some unknown reason I believed her, and I think she knew that. Once I told her 'Even though I believe what you're saying and you believe what you're telling me, it's not altering the fact that you're here. We have to find a way of getting you the strength to get through each day. The only thing I can think of is God.' Two weeks later she made a decision and you saw the difference. She said 'Lord, I want you in my heart and I'm sorry for all the things I've done and I know, Father, I have not killed my mother.' When she finally went to court she was fourteen and they found her not guilty, and she'd gone through hell, sheer hell. Yasmar is not nice. You know, you always have in the back of your mind that it only takes someone, somewhere, sometime, somehow to reach them.

X: And you felt you had, on several occasions?

C: A handful. I'd like to know what happened to that girl. How she went back to having a normal life. I can't imagine how.

X: Well, if she's reading this and she recognises herself or if someone thinks they know something maybe they can contact me. Would you like that?

C: Yes.

X: I hope she's all right. I hope she made it.

C: So do I.

Eve had more to say on the subject.

X: What happens when the girls leave if they have no home to go to?

E: They're back on the streets. Or if they're lucky the Ted Noffs Foundation runs a residential program for up to three months. But if Ted Noffs is full they have nowhere
else to go. The Salvation Army, who do such great work, have nothing for juveniles.

X: Many girls then have nothing. They can't even get a flat.

E: How can they get a flat when most of the flats want a bond? Juveniles used to have
more refuges to go to. They've closed a lot of them down.

X: So the pragmatic choice for young women is to go back to prostitution or drug
dealing or whatever. So the cycle, once begun, is extremely difficult to break?

E: It's familiar territory. No matter what it is, it's what they know.

X: The choices that they then have are extremely limited. But even at these tender ages
these girls, these women, are often their own worst enemy, because they seldom
allow anyone to help them. They leave classes. They abandon responsibility. So there's
some responsibility on their parts.

E: If they say to their case worker, or whoever, that they are getting out in a month's
time and they have nowhere to go, the case worker, if they're a good one, will generally find something. But often that doesn't happen because the girl simply doesn't
open her mouth and say 'I've got nowhere to go'.

X: And why don't they?

E: Because they still don't trust anybody. Everything in their lives has taught them:
'Don't trust no one'.

X: You mentioned refuges before. How many refuges are there then?

E: I think there are about fourteen in Sydney that can take women for up to two months
or so.

X: But they don't always go.

E: Sometimes they don't like them. If you've got a girl who's been around they'll know
the ones that they want to go back to. And some of them just aren't nice. Some kick
you out the door at 10:00 am at the latest and you've got to be out until they let you
back in at 5:00 or 6:00 pm. Some of the better ones let you stay the full twenty-four
hours. Those ones have case workers but even the case workers will tell you that
there's only one girl in twenty finds a way out of that life.

X: So these girls are really up shit creek without a paddle.

E: And some of them want it that way. Whatever they can get just might be enough to
get them to the first motel, which means, 'Hey, I'm back in business'.

6   THE MOMENT

Given enough provocation any woman, or any man, in my opinion, would become what we label a criminal. Particularly tragic are the cases where women kill their partners or husbands after having been the victims of the man's violence, often for many, many years.

Fiction often gives the impression that it's just one act, one moment that can land you in jail—the shot in the dark, the stab in the back. Reality isn't that clear cut, but there is always a moment, a crucial point when you make a decision to go down one path, rather than another. Some paths leading down are gentle descents, a long series of steps that take a while before you find yourself neck deep in shit, though by now you're used to the smell. Some paths are more like sudden drops. With women, landing in jail is often the end of a long journey of shallow steps that then lead to sudden drops. It's not straightforward, but it is understandable, if you take the time to understand it.

I asked Angie what led her to 'the moment'. We started by talking about her abusive partner, Neil. Here is the rest of Angie's story, and the choice that she made.

X: Couldn't you just get rid of him? A: I didn't know how. I got a loan from a friend. I got another flat. I started going out. I had friends and everything. Then he'd just show up and started intimidating people and they just wouldn't come back.

X: So he isolated you? He'd alienate people from you. He wanted to control you?

A: Yes, but he'd make out that it was me who wanted to control him. He'd always twist things around. He'd say, 'I don't want to be here. You're making me be here because I feel sorry for the kids.' He slept with someone I knew really well. He'd pick my daughter up from school with this woman. Then one day he came around and wanted to take my van. I just snapped. I'd lost everything. In the last move he'd 'helped' by putting all the stuff we needed in one set of boxes and all the rubbish in another set. He took all our valuables to sell, came back with $20 saying that that's all he'd gotten for it. And then he shipped all the boxes of rubbish to store at our new place and he dumped all the boxes of our precious things in a dumpster—all the kids' things, every-thing. I didn't know until I'd picked up the boxes from storage. I'd been paying storage for garbage. Just too many things got on top of me. I couldn't believe it; I just hated him. I wasn't able to keep up the payments of my loan. I was being accused of fraud and they wanted to put me in jail. I'm having to go back to doing tricks. Everything.

It just got too much. So here he is—in this new flat that someone had lent me the money for. He's trying to take the car, trying to pull another scam. Smoking all my grass. He was just such a liar. It was that moment when he wanted to take my van.

X: And that's when something snapped in you.

A: Yeah. I got a big knife and put it under a cushion. See, it wasn't one thing. It was no big deal. It was the lead up. It was years of all of that. He put me down all the time, all the time, all the time. And I really didn't think I could manage without him.

X: Even though he abused you.

A: Yeah, because he was really nice to me too.

X: So you got this knife.

A: And I put it under this cushion in the lounge room. And I was really pumped. I was berserk—on the inside.

X: What was it like on the inside? What were you feeling? What were you thinking?

A: Just that he'd put me through so much pain. At the time I wasn't taking responsibility for myself so at the time I'm thinking: 'He's wrecked my life. He's just made me go through all this garbage that nobody should have to go through.' And I just hated him for it. I was a good person. Why should this happen to me? And I? I just wanted to kill him.

X: How were you going to do it?

A: I was just going to stab him. He'd gone to the bathroom. He was going to go out and I was just going to stab him, as many times as I could, really quickly.

X: And that was it?

A: That was it.

X: Simple.

A: Easy—with fury.

X: Absolute fury? The angriest you'd ever been? A: It was a quiet anger. I wasn't screaming or anything.

X: Cold? A: It was, really contained—quiet and calm. I wasn't out of control, I was really still. And my heart was beating, but I wasn't erratic or anything. I was very, very calculating.

X: What were you calculating?

A: The precise moment that I would actually plunge the knife into him the first time so that he wouldn't stop me or I would get cut or something. I had to do this right. He was much bigger than me.

X: And you're a small, slight woman.

A: I didn't want to stuff it up.

X: So you're thinking, 'I've got to get it right, because otherwise I'm not going to survive this.'

A: He'd kill me.

X: It had to be calculating, didn't it? It really couldn't have been any other way.

A: I was really raging inside and I really meant to do it. I really meant this, from every part of me. But something made me look at the photo of the kids that was on the TV. And I started going through all these details, like there's going to be blood everywhere and I'm going to have to drag the body into the bathroom. And then I'm going to have to tell the kids that I've killed Neil: that I've stabbed him. He's in the bathroom, and we're going to have to hide the body and all of that.

X: So it wasn't until you saw the photograph of your children that you thought about the consequences of what might happen. But for some reason, you don't know why, you looked at that photograph.

A: I pictured it. I pictured that I'd done it. I'd killed him and there was blood everywhere. And I'd have to get the kids to help me hide the body. And where was I going to put it? How were we going to get it out? There was a possibility that I could get caught. And then I thought: 'Man. I can't. And what if I go to jail, and my poor kids won't have a mum? I can't do that to the kids.' And I couldn't kill him then. If I didn't have the kids, maybe I could have. But the kids were coming home from school in maybe like, half an hour. I just had to let it go and that made me feel useless as well.

So I leave. I lose that place and I get another housing flat. He beats me. There are stitches on my face. I'm pregnant with his child. The doctor says that if anything happens to the baby he's gonna charge him. So I have the baby, and I didn't have to see him much. But I'd finally had enough. You know, even through all those years when he was humiliating me I kept saying to him, 'Why are you saying this? You don't really mean it. You talk like that. It's not true.' I was just in total denial. I believed 'He HAS to love me.' Otherwise everything I'd been through has been for what?

X: I'm sorry. Until that moment I didn't get it. And now I get it.

A: I had hard lessons. I didn't know shit and life just gave me some hard lessons to know stuff. I can help a lot of people with what I know now, but it was, tricky, going through that. I thought he was my soul mate, forever and ever. He used to hang around and I told him to go. I didn't want to know him anymore. And I started to get on with my life. And then the kids told me, when they got to eighteen, that all those years he'd been molesting them.

X: How did that feel?

A: Well. It was really strange. It was like ... I never understood why everything wasn't all right. I'd tried so hard to make everything all right for everyone. There was always a question mark. The kids were always more aloof with me, and friendlier with him. And I used to think, 'Why? He's such a pig. Why are the kids always so supportive of him, and they make fun of me?' Nothing really made any sense. I was the one doing everything—caring for everyone and loving everyone. It wasn't the way it was supposed to be. So when I found out it sort of had a domino effect, it was like 'Ahhh-hhhh!'. And then all the stuff that didn't make sense, made sense. And then you could see signs, right back to the beginning. Things I'd never noticed.

X: Like what?

A: Counsellors tell you that when they have reports of child abuse the counsellors go to that place where the abuse is alleged to have happened and they find that the kids will be physically close to one adult and not close to another. It's the one that they're close to that's the one that's abusing them. The one they're distant to is the one that's not saving them.

X: Saving?

A: Saving them from what's happening to them.

X: Why then do kids get closer to the abuser? What are they looking for?

A: I don't know.

———

Maybe they were looking for the same thing that drives a woman to stay with an abusive man. Maybe it was all about appeasement—'If I'm nice to him, maybe he won't hurt me anymore.' People who are abused often deal with it with child logic—'He's abusing me but the real meanie is my mother who isn't saving me from him.' However most people deal with abuse, appeasement probably never works. Only later did Angie begin to get some insight as to what might have been going on in Neil's mind.

A: Neil got angry when I got pregnant because he was with my daughter: how dare I get pregnant! He was treating me like shit in front of my kids, and he was with them. That didn't look right to him. In his head he was having a 'love affair' with my daughter. I'm not sure what he did to my son. He even wrote this long letter, this weird shit, saying that he loved the kids, that they were 'his life' and he was protecting them from me. It was really awful. I really misappropriated my affections. Big time. I'd really love to have killed him but, damn, I didn't even know what he'd done at the time I wanted to. The abuse. I've left so much stuff out.

X: But it's pretty difficult to remember isn't it? A: You can't just, on call, remember it all. But he did alienate me from everyone.

X: So suddenly everything made sense.

A: And then I got really sick. I had to go into counselling for over a year. I was in shock. I was a mess. I was a total mess. I went through all different stages, feeling that I didn't deserve to live because I was so stupid. I can't get anything right. How could somebody be that blind? How could somebody be that pathetic? To let their own little children go through something like that? You know, maybe the world would be better without me, because I was faulty. Depression's crazy. You cry every time you open your eyes in the morning and you wonder how you're going to make it through the day. Everything you do feels like your pretending. Nothing's real. Food doesn't have any taste. There's no joy in anything. You're going through the motions, pretending to be alive.

X: It's sounds as if sometimes it's really hard just to get rid of people.

A: I just had to learn about barriers. I mean, nothing like that's ever happened to you.

X: True. Other things have happened though.

A: But it's hard when you have kids.

X: Sure! I don't doubt that.

A: Where are you going to run to, you know? And the crime just goes on and on. My son's all fucked up now with children of his own. He doesn't look after them properly. Those kids, what's gonna happen to them? And I can't do a thing about it. Because my kids are now over eighteen it's up to them to do something about it. Why can't I? They're still my children! They're fucked up because of what he did to them! My kids are paying for that. What the hell's that law? How come when your kids are over eighteen a mother can't charge the paedophile?

X: Unless the kids charge him. And they won't do it. Why?

A: I don't know. My daughter won't talk about it at all. What do you teach your kids? Falling in love is not forever? Don't believe the fairy tale? I carried that victim mentality for a long while, until I could identify it, and let it go. You know there are so many people out there that are struggling with poverty, and it just forces you into so many places you'd rather not be. I had the kids. I wanted to keep it all together. I didn't want to fail, but all my parents are dead now and I don't have to answer to anyone but myself. I needed the husband, family, car—everything to be okay about myself, but I don't need that anymore.

X: What a strange place to be. You went through all that because you were damned if you were going to fail.

A: I'm always more effective when I'm on my own.

X: So why does it take some people so long to realise that? A: You're trapped. You're in denial and girls have to put up a good front.

X: And putting up the front exhausts you to the point where you're not thinking straight, and then you've got to 'kill the bastard'.

A: And to this day he got away with it. And I've got to learn to get my head around that too. But if I didn't have the kids, I'd be dead. I would have probably killed myself. Or I would have become a really nasty criminal with a terrible attitude—because if I had had to have gone to jail for killing the bastard I would have been soooooo angry, after what he'd put me through.

———

But of course a lot of women end up in jail after what 'he' has put them through. Angie's story shows us what goes on in the heart and mind of a woman at the point where she is about to commit murder. But not all women are saved at that hair's breadth point. Not all women find the photo of the children that makes them stop to think. They go through with it. And we put them through the ordeal of court and prison and then leave them to deal with their stuff behind bars, as became obvious from some of the things Vera told me.

X: Many women in jail have had to deal with extraordinary provocation, not only in their adult relationships but in their childhood as well. Years of abuse. They then have to deal with anger, as a result of that abuse. Who wouldn't be angry?

V: But how you control the anger is going to determine the quality of life that you have.

X: To that extent it is an issue of responsibility. You can't escape the issue of responsibility?

V: No. X: Regardless of what you've done, regardless of what you've suffered?

V: No, because there are other people around, who will take the time to sit and talk them through their past, and into their present. Not everyone will do that.

X: But there are women out there who are so trapped they can't even imagine that there's someone out there who can help them.

V: But until they try they'll never know.

X: Do you believe that anyone asking for help will always get it? V: Depending on the help, yes.

X: If I'm a woman in an abusive situation will I find someone who will help me leave?

V: Not help you to leave, but who will empower you so that you can make the decision to leave on your own and who can open a door for you so that you can go from one open door to another.

X: Can a woman in some situations be protected from particularly abusive, violent or destructive men?

V: With all my heart I'd have to say no.

X: In that case what options do some women have?

V: Money is the initial factor. If a woman can walk out with only the clothes on her back and enough money to see her through for about a month, she could go into a refuge. She'd probably have to change her name and get a new flat in her new name. There's a lot of stuff they'd have to go through to protect themselves.

X: This would require a lot of planning.

V: A lot of guts and planning with someone else. It would be very hard to do on your own. The reason so many women stay in abusive situations is that starting from nothing is what overwhelms them.

X: Even if these women leave there are some men who are so crazy that they do anything to find them.

V: And some women spend the rest of their lives looking over their shoulders.

X: What's then to stop a woman killing a man just so that she won't have to spend the rest of her life looking over her shoulder? Think of it. It's a rational decision. V: In sheer desperation that would be the only solution for her.

X: Do you believe that such situations happen.

V: Yes.

X: Do you believe that such things happen more often than people are willing to admit?

V: Yes.

X: Do you believe that we're not doing the best by these women by putting them in jail?

V: Yes. But the only thing going for them in jail is to give them a chance to collect their thinking again, to come to terms with themselves and get a better understanding of themselves.

Some, if not most women come to crime because of rational decisions. They're not mad. They're not crazy. They may, as Liz explained, make violent choices but they are not insane.

X: If you're in an environment that limits your options?

L: Sheer desperation, whether it's financial, physical, emotional,

X: Sheer desperation will drive the vast majority of the human race to crime, to some act of desperation that could be interpreted as criminal.

L: Sometimes you're so stewed up and mentally drained that you can't think of any other way out.

X: Do the women ever talk about the moment when they're committing their crime?

L: No, never. They'll talk about the moment leading up to it and what they felt afterward, yes.

X: But not the moment they do it.

L: No. Only once.

X: Why is that, do you think? Didn't you hear those stories?

L: It's not something I look for. I deal with the now. When the past comes into the now that's the only time I deal with the past.

X: When that person talked to you about it that one time what did they say?

L: They said that there was a lot going on, a lot of confusion. They told themselves, 'If you do this, you will be released. But if you don't do it you'll have hell all the time.'

X: And this was a case of a woman who killed someone who was abusing her.

L: Yes.

X: Even in that moment, with all that confusion there is a moment of decision. She's thinking, 'If I do this, this will happen. But if I don't do this, that will happen, and if I don't do this what will happen is so much worse. So I'd better do this, even if it means going to jail.'

L: Women who make these decisions see jail as the easy way out.

X: No rational person—and for the most part we're dealing with rational people here— would choose, for example, murder and jail unless it was the lesser of two evils. For all the horror that jail might be, whether it's projected horror because you think that's what jail is, or real horror because that's what jail really is, for all the inconvenience, for all of the pain, the restrictions, the prison that is prison, for all of that people are aware of the consequences of their actions and that if they make that decision knowing that they'll end up there jail then that must be a much lesser hell than the hell that they are living in.

L: Yes—to everything you've said.

The almost classic story of the woman who kills her husband or partner after years of abuse doesn't always end in the tragedy of a living hell for the woman and her children, or a dead and unredeemed husband. The Buddhist monk Ajahn Brahm tells the following story of what he calls positive forgiveness:

> Some ten years ago, at the end of one of our Friday night talks in Perth, a woman came up to speak with me. She had begun coming to our temple seven years previously. Her main reason for attending was as an excuse to get out of her house. She was the victim of horrendous domestic violence. In those days, support structures just weren't available to help such a victim. In such a cauldron of boiling emotions she couldn't see clearly enough to walk out forever. She came to our Buddhist centre, with the idea that two hours in the temple were two hours she wouldn't be bashed. She decided to try it (positive forgiveness) out on her husband. She told me that every time he hit her she would forgive him and let it go. How she did that, only she knows. Then every time he did, or said, anything kind, no matter how trifling, she would hug him or cover him with kisses or use any other gesture to let him know how much that kindness meant to her. She took nothing for granted.
>
> 'Seven long years', she told me, 'and now you wouldn't recognise the man. We have such a precious, loving relationship now, and two wonderful children.' Her face radiated the glow of a saint. I felt like getting on my knees and bowing to her. 'See that stool', she said, stopping me, 'he made that wooden meditation stool for me this week as a surprise. If it had been seven years ago, he would have used it to hit me with!'
>
> She changed a monster into a caring man. That was an extreme example of positive forgiveness, recommended only for those heading for sainthood.[10]

The woman's approach has a sound psychological foundation. She 'ignored' her husband's brutal provocation, thus depriving him of feedback of her suffering, which at some level would turn him on and 'reward' him.

Instead she reinforced his positive side. This feedback let him know that his pay-off for being a decent loving human being was always going to be greater than his pay-off for being a bastard. The fact that it took her seven years tells us how damaged he was, and how strong she was. Truly the woman is a saint.

Unfortunately hardly anyone is a saint, or heading for sainthood. Whatever this woman had, and I can only guess at this, she must have had a wealth of positive strength to draw on. No doubt a lot of that strength came from her religion, and her relationship with the monks. This too would have helped. Positive role models of maleness surrounded her—men who would never even say an unkind thing, men who would never hurt her. Saint or no saint, I doubt that the woman would have been able to go on if she hadn't had that support. Many women don't have any strong positive men in their lives. Many women don't even have strong positive women in their lives. Many women are isolated. Many are too damaged even to leave. Many remain trapped in the 'cauldron of boiling emotions' that clouds vision, much to the dismay of their friends and the people who try to help them.

This story shows that love isn't enough; you need a powerful tool, and the power to use it—and help, lots of help. But what happens when there's not enough love or help to go around?

At best, our society has an inconsistent attitude toward drugs. Tobacco is legal, marijuana isn't. Maybe it's because tobacco doesn't alter consciousness and give you 'reefer madness'. Tobacco just kills you and costs millions of dollars in hospital bills and lost productivity. I guess that's okay. But wait, alcohol is legal, and it alters consciousness; it kills you too in car accidents and cirrhosis. Why is alcohol legal? Shouldn't they ban that too? Ooops! They tried that in the United States. It didn't work. So why are all the other drugs that alter consciousness and that can kill you illegal? Prohibition didn't work for alcohol, why should it work for cocaine and heroin?

Drugs certainly have a lot going for them. They're a possible answer for everything. They make you feel good—at least until your body adjusts to them and you build up a resistance. And they do all sorts of neat things. There are uppers (stimulants), downers (depressants), hypnotics (inducers of sleep), tranquillisers (inducers of calm), narcotics (inducers of calm, sleep and painlessness), inebriants to make you drunk, and hallucinogens to take you to another place altogether.[11] Maybe the problem is in the addiction thing—which is certainly a big issue; ask anyone who's ever tried giving up—like Evie.

Evie is representative of a great many 'working girls' who have gotten into trouble over drugs. I wonder how many people who've 'worked the streets' have had to deal with substance use or abuse issues in their lives?

Evie: I could give up the grog. That wasn't so bad, but giving up the cigarettes nearly killed me. But the only time I ever came close to going on the grog again was the day my husband died. That night I got as far as the gate, I undid the latch and I realised that my kids needed me. They were younger, they weren't coping and they needed me to be strong. I turned back and I never touched the grog again.

When you're an alcoholic you learn a lot of the tricks of the trade, and one of them is to hide how you're really feeling.

X: Even from yourself?

E: Especially from yourself. And to put up a good front.

Maybe it's not the drugs themselves, but that the drugs don't exist in isolation from any other part of a person's life. Kelli talked about her own relationship with recreational chemistry, and the reasons why she needed that sort of recreation.

Kelli: I have tremendous willpower. The same instinct that told me not to breathe in when I was underwater and nearly dead. Well, I've given up cigarettes; hard drugs, heroin, coke; I've given up anti-depressants, sleeping pills—you name it, the works. No matter how addictive a personality I have, I've gotten over it. I was being abused at eight, I started smoking cigarettes at nine. My best friend and I would have a big reefer of tobacco when her mother was out. There we were, two little nine-year-olds doing this before school.

X: So you acquired your first addiction because you were doing anything you could to stay out of the house as long as possible.

K: I couldn't stay outside forever because I was babysitting. I wasn't generally allowed out anyway.

X: It's ironic. Your parents weren't letting you out because they were trying to protect you?

K: When all the while the monster was in the house.

One monster in the house—another monster in the body. Or several. New monsters for old.

I'm not saying anything new here. But I think a really a big clue is that we use the same word—drugs—to describe both medicines and 'recreational chemicals'—although I have serious doubts about the quality of the recreation. What sort of person are you 're-creating' or re-making yourself into when you start taking recreational chemicals, chemicals that were once mostly medicines, and in fact, still are?

Most women in jail have histories of drug addiction and physical, psychological and sexual abuse. Might there be a connection? Is a lot of drug taking simply a clumsy attempt to self-medicate, the prescriptions written by amateur quacks who really don't know what they're doing but have to do something, anything?

Drugs as a clumsy attempt at self-medication. Drugs as medicine to mend a broken life. Is there anything to this idea at all?

Drug offences are the number one reason why, nominally, women are in jail. Rosa's story shows us just how far you can take the drug thing.

Rosa: I come from South America. I come from a broken home. When I was about six and my brother was five we were playing in our apartment building and this man invited us into his flat. Something happened. I don't know what. I remember flashes, like my brother being locked in the bathroom. Somehow we ended up in a police station. All I remember was these legs and me not wanting to look up. Anyway we left Uruguay and came to live in Australia when I was ten. My mother had to work all the time, so I guess we were neglected, in a way. When we first got to Australia we stayed with an auntie. She had a schizophrenic son who sexually molested me. I never said a word to anybody. I think I started getting depressed at that age. I remember sitting in Ashfield Park and really wanting to die. **X:** Is this because of the molestation?

R: I believe so.

X: Did the molestation go on for a long while? **R:** The whole year we were there.

X: How old was he? **R:** About twenty-four, twenty-five.

X: So a twenty-five year old man is molesting a ten or eleven-year-old girl. He's your cousin. **R:** Yes.

X: But it stopped the minute you moved.

R: Yes. But I was still there, wishing that I wasn't existing.

X: You were isolated a little because of your language, weren't you?

R: It took me a year to learn to communicate. I struggled through year seven, eight and nine. It wasn't perfect. I kept getting into trouble at school because I didn't understand what the teachers were telling me.

X: So your mother's busy, you're brother's busy, you can't speak the language, you were really left on your own quite a bit.

R: But I did have one friend, this Arab girl. We're still friends.

X: She's been a constant in your life? **R:** Yes.

X: But she wasn't enough to stop you from doing all this other stuff.

R: She came from a Muslim background—very strict. Her family wanted to convert me, but it never happened. During this time, between say eleven and fourteen, I grew up with her. I was happy.

X: But with this underlying depression.

R: Yeah. My mother was trying to finish her degree in nursing, my older brother was in year twelve. My younger brother was getting into trouble spray-painting trains. I had a lot of responsibilities at that age— cleaning the house, doing the washing. Feeding my brothers. Fighting with my brothers. They didn't take responsibility for anything. I had to be the mother. Especially when my mother was diagnosed with a bone-marrow disorder and we didn't know if she was going to live. That put a lot of pressure on me.

X: You had to grow up really quickly, in that sense. No one was helping you through this.

R: My mother was involved in a long-term relationship with Tim. He eventually became my stepfather. Tim and my mum bought a house and we all moved in. But I never really felt at home there. I always felt like it was his house.

X: So even at home you weren't feeling welcome.

R: I remember later leaving home early, getting home late and spending very little time at home. And it was easy to take drugs. I started cutting myself with a razor—cutting letters in my arm. Later, in jail the psychologist told me that it was to get rid of the pain. Years pass, I'm fourteen, I'm going to school, I've got a job working three days a week. I'm doing okay.

X: Aside from the occasional bits of depression and self-mutilation.

R: To me that was normal. That was me. That was my life. I didn't know any better. I felt that all fourteen-year-olds felt like that. Then there was a boy who was interested in me. He took me to his house. He had some pot. He asked me if I wanted to try it. I thought 'Why not?' We had a few cones and I remember just passing out. Peer pressure, same as the cigarettes. So through that circle I started meeting other girls around my age that smoked pot. So I decided to hang around with them. We all smoked together. It became a weekend thing. We'd get a twenty-dollar deal and catch trains and buses for hours and hours and hours to get the stuff. Then we'd smoke it and then go home. With that came alcohol. All this before I'm eighteen.

X: It was a way of passing time.

R: I didn't know any better. I didn't have any other friends that knew any different.

X: It's normal.

R: And it's fun, because with all the smoking and the drinking I'm blocking the pain, brewing inside me, because of what happened. X: And because you never told anyone?

R: I wasn't dealing with it. So to me it was fine to go out with my friends and spend my money on drugs.

X: Was it affecting your studies?

R: Yes, because I used to go to school stoned and by the end of year eleven and twelve I had no motivation left. I only went to school because I had to. I didn't really like going to school stoned but if I had any pot left over from the weekend I'd smoke it on Monday morning. But even though I wasn't paying attention, I was still passing.

X: You didn't have much incentive to do better.

R: Passing was good enough for me. Why want more? So anyway a group of us would also occasionally hire a hotel room with fake ID and just go there and drink and smoke and pass out. I was on a twelve o'clock curfew but I used to push it till two because my mother wouldn't know.

X: She was too busy working and studying and trying to keep the family together. Did she succeed in the end?

R: Yeah. She got her degree. She's okay.

X: What about your education?

R: About the time I graduated from high school I met a girl who worked in an electronics shop. She introduced me to an Ecuadorian who owned it. Up until that time I hadn't had much to do with the South American community. At this time I was really depressed because a cousin of mine in South America had committed suicide, so I was doing a lot more smoking and drinking and passing out—this time at home. This had never happened before; I'd always done everything outside. So everything was just getting bigger and bigger. So when this guy, Pablo, offers me a job in the store I just take it. I'm really good at my job and because I get commissions I'm earning well too. Pablo's impressed and starts giving me gifts. One night at a company function for franchisees he makes a pass. He's forty; I'm eighteen. I'm really uncomfortable. The next day I tell him I'm quitting so he apologises and I stay. But the gifts keep coming and I keep accepting and then I start feeling as if I owe him something.

X: It's all very confusing for you.

R: Yeah, and he starts taking me to all these company functions and business meetings like he wants me to be the face of the company or something. Anyway there's free booze wherever we go so it's very convenient for me.

X: Do you think at this time that you were an alcoholic?

R: Depends what you mean by an alcoholic.

X: In your terms were you an alcoholic?

R: In my terms, yes. Someone who binge drinks every Friday and Saturday—that's a pattern.

X: Free drinks? Saving you money? Drives you there and back? It's pretty easy. It's working for you.

R: But the more and more I went out with him, the more and more I worked with him, the more he started controlling my life. There were times when friends called me at work and he'd answer and say I wasn't there. I'd ask who it was and he'd say 'Nobody'.

X: Control games.

R: I'd find out later, then we'd start having conflict. Then he sells the business and suggests that I become a partner in a new business. I don't know about this but he says it'll all be done properly and we'll 'set boundaries'. So I go for it and the business is very successful. But I find out later that he's paying himself $2000 a week to my $550. Even though I'm a director of this company he's calling all the shots. I ask him about the money and he tells me his wife has a drinking and a gambling problem.

X: This was true?

R: Yes. I'd go to his house for dinner, his wife would go out for twenty minutes to 'buy bread'. She'd drink a lot so I felt at home there.

X: They made it easy.

R: They 'enabled'. This all happened in the space of about a year. Throughout all this time we're meeting all these people in the South American community including this Bolivian, Alfredo and his girlfriend, Leona. Alfredo tells Pablo and me that he has a 'business proposition'. He can import 'translator boxes'. Satellite TV is becoming big business because of all the new channels and these translator boxes are supposed to interpret the signals. 'What do we have to do?' we ask. He says we have to send money overseas to get the receivers. Fine. Alfredo says that we have to send the money in lots of $9999 because if the amount is $10 000 or over you have to report it to the tax office. So Pablo gives us the money to buy the translator boxes. The translators cost about $200 000 at a time, so we're sending twenty lots of almost

$10 000. I do this about five times. It all came together for me a few weeks later when Alfredo and Leona want to get married and I help them because Leona can't speak a word of English. I'm also questioning the whole deal in my head because I never see any of these 'translators'. While we're organizing the wedding one night I start getting narky and refuse to send any more money. Pablo comes up to me and says 'Look what Alfredo gave me'. It was cocaine. I'd never seen it before; I'd never had it before. So I tried it. Up my nose went a gram in the matter of a night.

X: How much is a gram?

R: A lot, and it was good stuff. Pure. What they call 'Mother of Pearl'.

X: What did it feel like?

R: Great. It was the best feeling I'd ever had in my entire life. It gave me confidence. I felt like talking. I just loved it. It made me feel fantastic. All my worries were gone. I was just the happiest person in the world.

X: All due to this marvellous ...

R: White powder. But because it makes you very hyperactive and awake, I had to smoke pot to calm down, to get to sleep. Otherwise I'd just be 'on'. It's very frustrating because it takes a while to slow down.

X: The first time you tried it, how long did the effects last.

R: I was awake until the next day. I didn't sleep for, like, forty-eight hours. I was feeling great and the funny thing is, no matter how much I drank, I could not get drunk, but even though I was mentally alert when I tried to stand up I could feel the alcohol in my body, and I couldn't get up.

X: So your body could get drunk, but your mind couldn't because it was stoned on the coke?

R: So I'm in love with cocaine so I want to know how I can keep getting it. I asked my dealers, the people I used to buy the pot from, how much one gram of cocaine costs. They said $200. And I figured it would be cut, whereas Alfredo's getting the real stuff for Pablo. So I'm thinking: how should I play it to get the real stuff? After he gave me that, of course I asked for more. Pablo says: 'If you want more, this is what you have to do'. Then Pablo shows me what's really going on. He showed me a translator box. It was completely destroyed. They'd been putting about a kilo of cocaine in the box. So Pablo asks me whether I'm with them, or not. I tell him I'll think about it. And I thought of my family, and I'm thinking, 'If this goes bad, I am breaking the law. And if this goes bad, I could end up in jail'. And then I thought about it and I thought: 'Who cares?'

I couldn't see anything in front of me. I couldn't see the damage I might do. I was very selfish. I blame that on the depression. I couldn't see any good in my life so I didn't have anything to lose. 'Who cares? I have nothing better to live for'.

X: You couldn't see past your nose.

R: So I said. Okay, but I'm not sending all this money for nothing. So Pablo says that for every $10 000 I send, I'd get a thousand. I say okay, so I keep sending the money. Trouble is I send the money—I keep getting the cocaine but no money. Pablo keeps making excuses, 'Oh, I'll pay you next week'. I ended up sending another $300 000 and I didn't see one dollar. Once they sent me to the bank with about $100 000 in CASH and I'm sending it on, using all my ID.

X: But they keep giving you cocaine, and you're feeling so good?

R: I figure, 'What the hell, I'll get it later'.

X: It was a good deal for Pablo. He got a gram of cocaine that he used to get for free he keeps you happy and gets your services.

R: I got more. I started sharing it with my friends. We had a great time. Later on I learned in jail that he was getting the money to give to me, he was just ripping me off, helping his wife with her gambling habit, just to keep her quiet. But I'm sending a packet a week and I'm pretty much hooked on coke.

X: How long did it take to get hooked?

R: Oh, the first time.

X: Because it was just so good?

R: You could have it every day if you wanted to. Another strange thing happened then. Alfredo gave Pablo a leather jacket. He showed it to me. It was padded, but the padding was all stiff. I said to Pablo, 'I think it's got something in it.' Pablo says, 'I know, but I don't think he knows because he just gave it to me.' So I say 'Why don't you let me take it home? I'll empty it and give you what's inside.' I'm thinking that if its full of coke I can give him half, keep half and I wouldn't have to ask him for anymore or do any favours for him. I'd have my own stash. He said, 'Okay' So I took it home and emptied the linings. I tried some. I put it on my tongue. It wasn't coke. Coke makes your tongue go numb instantly. This was just a sour taste, like paracetamol. It was something that I'd never had before. I came to realise it was heroin. I didn't want to have anything to do with it because two years before someone I knew was smoking a cone and he decided to sprinkle some heroin on it. He died. So I hated the stuff. I thought, 'This stuff will kill me.' I put it in a plastic bag. I didn't want to carry it on a bus so I rang Pablo to pick it up. He never did. He always made excuses. I hid it in my room and tried to forget about it.

X: What happened then?

R: The wedding happens. They're even passing around glasses with coke in them—Cola and coke.

X: Ah! Going back to the original recipe.

R: Everybody's having a great time. At the time of the wedding we're waiting for another receiver. It was late.

X: How much money had gone by now?

R: All in all we ended up sending about $1 million. The police told us that three got through. One was at customs and another was in Bolivia, waiting to be sent.

X: Let's do the sums. Each translator box is costing about $200 000? **R:** I was told that the street value of the uncut stuff was $600 a gram.

X: So it was costing the 'wholesaler-importers' $200 a gram. They were selling it to their 'retailers' for about $400 a gram. The 'retailers' were selling it on the streets at $600 a gram. What you would have been getting on the street would only have been only about a quarter cocaine, because there was no way you could've gotten the pure stuff for $200 a gram. If you're a retailer you divide your $400 gram into quarters, add 'filler' and sell it for $200 a gram. It was probably three-quarters baking soda.

R: Glucose.

X: So you were getting 'Mother of Pearl' wholesale.

R: And at the wedding they're worried because the next lot is late.

X: Little do you know that at the time the receiver is in the hands of ...

R: Customs. You know this is how stupid the Bolivians were. They got greedy. You can't have a package that says, 'Weight: 2 kilos' and when you pick it up it's obviously heavier. So customs got suspicious. They got the dogs around. They looked inside. Then they took the cocaine out of the translator and replaced it with salt. Pablo sends a friend, we called him the mad Turk, to investigate. The Turk was also sending money, but I didn't know it at the time.

X: Pablo was keeping you in the dark about a lot of things.

R: That's what controlling people do. The Turk picks up the package. Pablo tells Alfredo that 'the lady's arrived'. Alfredo had rented a separate flat for the receipt of the 'ladies'. Little did they know that the police had planted bugs all over the 'lady' and the police could hear everything they said. Alfredo realised that the lady is filled with salt. Immediately he suspects Pablo's done the dirty.

X: That doesn't sound smart. If Pablo had wanted to rip him off he would've been cleverer about it.

R: Alfredo was a loser. He'd just done a few years in the states for smuggling. He was on parole in the States when he was doing this in Australia.

X: How did Australia let him in? **R:** He came in on a Bolivian passport. False name.

X: So Alfredo's blaming Pablo. **R:** And Pablo's blaming the people in Bolivia. But the people who were supplying the money were other Bolivians and Pablo was worried that they'd blame him and when you screw the Bolivians they screw you and your family. While this is happening the Federal Police are moving in on the flat, and they're also making the way to the store, where the Turk and I are sitting down having lunch.

Drugs aren't only about pain. While they remain illegal and fetch huge prices they will also be about greed. Although I've chosen to focus on abuse as the primary mechanism of psycho-criminalisation, no understanding of the complete process would be complete without understanding the crucial role of drugs in our society. Drugs connect both the system of socio-criminalisation—in that most of them are illegal, expensive, addictive and make some people do crazy, illegal and damaging things to get the money to pay for them—and the process of psycho-criminalisation—in that abused people take them to dull the pain. And then there are the just plain, bored people who use them to take the lazy route to joy and fulfilment. Then the drugs addle their brains and make some people do crazy, illegal and damaging things for their own sake. People commit crimes to get the money to buy their illegal 'medicines', but other people can also exploit their addictions and pain and profit from the black economy. Terry offered some further insights into this and related issues.

X: Greed? T: Maybe it wasn't greed in their eyes. They knew what they wanted but they could never see any other way of getting what they wanted. Depending on how desperate they were. Some of them just wanted a house. Is that wrong? A house is a place to live in. Everybody needs a place to live in.

X: But not everybody needs the sort of house that kilos of heroin or cocaine will buy.

T: That's right.

X: So there's desperation, or there's greed and greed born of feeling that there's no option. But it could also be laziness. It's quicker, faster, easier to sell a lot of drugs than to build a life or a business that will enhance people and all that messy stuff.

T: What was wrong with renting a house? Maybe you're a 'classy' person who finds yourself 'financially embarrassed' and you can't face the thought of living below your means. You could only afford a 'less than immaculate' house? One woman came from overseas and imported drugs to buy a house in Lebanon. Her family came to visit her in jail. When she met them the first thing they said to her was 'You have shamed us.'

Kelli's journey into crime also involved drugs. Her background and experience led her down a different path to Rosa's. One that was even more chaotic.

Kelli: I had a premonition that my daddy was going to die. I had this dream. It was sooooo real. I'm walking in a building and there are these four corridors. One corridor has four doors and I walk past them into another room. And I froze. My daddy was in a casket in the centre of the room. And this room is full of my family. My mother and brothers and sisters are on the left, my aunts, uncles and cousins on the right. They're all quiet. I say 'Can't you see that daddy's lying in a coffin?' I thought it was real. I was going mental. The next minute, I'm getting slapped about. The Nazi wanker is punching me. That's what woke me up.
'What are you doing?' I said. 'You were asleep and crying and I tried shaking you awake and it was like you were in a trance, so I had to backhand you to wake you up.'

So I realised I'd had a bad dream. Somebody once told me that if you have a bad dream and you tell someone it won't come true, so I tell this creep about my dream and he says to me, 'You make me sick. You think you're the only person in this whole wide world who loves your daddy. You know what? You're nothing but a little girl from a little village.' I told him he was a creep. I ran downstairs to call my daddy. He was okay. He was going to visit me in four weeks and wanted to come sooner but I told him to wait until mum could come too. It was only four weeks, I said. Then what happens is that my sister gets caught in bed with a cousin, the son of my daddy's brother. My uncle went ballistic and ran to our house calling my sister a slut and a whore. My daddy just wasted his brother. My daddy came from a long line of chiefs. He was so proud of our name. A week later my sister calls me and tells me that daddy had been in hospital since last night and was now in a coma. I went nuts. 'You're only telling me now!' I screamed.

'We didn't think it was that serious,' she said. 'He's in hospital and you don't think it's serious!' He had high blood pressure and he had had a stroke, over this thing my sister did.

X: You think that did it?

K: I know that did it. But I only found this out later. But you can see why I never told my daddy about my brother. I fly back home. My brother-in-law meets me at the airport, I ask him 'Where's my daddy?' and he starts answering me but I don't hear a word because I start acting like a nut. I plug my ears and start singing so as not to hear him.

X: You were hysterical.

K: Obviously. We get to our house and as I go in I realise that it's exactly like my dream, except this time my family is all crying and I'm completely okay because I think I'm dreaming. I really believe that I'm in a dream, so I didn't freak out. I just went with it. The only difference was the soundtrack. They were all crying and I was quiet. Everyone knew that my daddy was my life, they were waiting for an explosion, but instead I start talking to my daddy as he's in the coffin, showing him some photos while another part of me thinks he's asleep.

My mother takes me aside and says, 'You've been drinking.' She says, 'Why you no cry for your daddy?' 'Because he's sleeping!' He'd died the morning I arrived and I was in total denial.

X: Nobody at this point is getting through their thick skulls that you are in deep, psychotic shock. You have no grasp of reality at this point, because the pain is just too huge.

K: I am pinching myself trying to wake up. I've got blood dripping from my thigh. I am ripping flesh from myself to wake myself up. But I wouldn't wake up. I went through a whole week like this. And every day, while I'm going through this the Nazi is ringing me up and saying. 'Are you okay over there? Are you having fun over there while I'm slaving my guts out over here?' I cannot describe what that creep put me through. I'm in this nightmare and I want to wake up but I don't want him to wake me up. Him ringing up each time would bring me back to reality and I didn't want to know about it.

X: While you were 'in the dream' you could still pretend that you would wake up and everything would be all right.

K: And I didn't want him waking me. At the end of the week they're ready to take my daddy to the cemetery. They start closing the casket and that's when all the clouds started closing in on me. It was like that casket was the end of my life. I'm trying to get into the coffin. They keep pulling me off. I must've been strong because it took four or five of them to hold me down. Then I just blacked out. That had never happened to me before. I'd been crow-barred by my first husband across the head and that hadn't even knocked me out.

And you know, while I was out, they tried, but they couldn't lift the casket. It was like my daddy wouldn't leave until his baby had woken up. Then I woke up from the abyss and I start it all again. There was no way my daddy was going to leave this earth without me. Then I passed out again. They carry me to the bus going to the cemetery and I was in a trance crying, 'daddy, daddy, daddy.' It was the only thing coming out of my mouth and it was like I was watching myself being this other person crying out, 'daddy, daddy, daddy.' And when they started lowering the casket into the ground I blacked out again. They left me in the bus alone, while I was passing in and out of consciousness. Later again they were eating ice-cream and I was furious. There was no way anything was ever going to pass through my lips and into this body again. I swore at God because he had no right to take my daddy away. I was so angry.

When I got back home I went to the doctor to get some anti-depressants, tranquillisers, anything so that I wouldn't feel this pain anymore. I just kept myself in this zombie state. I left the Nazi a week later. Then I met another ex-boxer who beat me up. He was a total nutcase. He nearly started a war between the Greeks and the Arabs. And then I met Tom. It was instant attraction. I was in love and I wanted to be here now. I thought it was love. Later I decided that I fell in lust.

I moved in with Tom after a few weeks. He's a mechanic and he and his brothers lived with his mother and she was a total nutter. She used to take off her clothes in front of her children and dress in front of them. We were so in love and she made our life hell because she was a Muslim and I was a Christian. And here's another pattern of mine. I stayed in that situation for a year and then I said 'I'm out of here, your mother is driving me nuts.'

So Tom and I leave the house and set up on our own. Tom starts hanging out with his other Lebo mates. His mates come to our house and spend an unusually long time in the bathroom. This happens all the time and after a few weeks I get fed up and say, 'Whatever they're doing in the bathroom they can do out here.' Big mistake. They start shooting up heroin in the lounge room and because it's out in the open Tom decides to try some. I don't like what I'm seeing but then I get stroppy and on the third day of this I say to him, 'You're not putting any more of that into you unless I get some into me.' I have this tiny amount and I get off my face.

X: What does it feel like? **K:** Heroin? It numbs everything. It just numbs everything and I like the feeling.

X: It dulls the pain. **K:** It's warm. It warms you all over.

X: Is it like being drunk?

K: No. When you're drunk your brain's not aligned with your body, but this is like the zombie feeling you get from anti-depressants only faster—it got you there instantly.

X: It's like falling asleep on a summer afternoon? **K:** But still being awake, still being in that state. That's what it's like, in the beginning, and for a long time.

X: Were you addicted from the first time? **K:** No. I didn't think that at all. It went on like this for three days and then I said 'Enough! I don't want these people in my life anymore.' But Tom was already addicted. I couldn't believe that he was that weak, that he could get addicted so fast! So I didn't have any that day. I thought I was stronger but when I didn't get any I started to feel like I was getting the flu. I was going through withdrawal. I couldn't believe this stuff could take control so quickly. Then we started taking it every day, then, after a few weeks, twice a day.

X: Isn't this expensive?

K: Yeah!

X: How did you pay for it all?

K: We started dealing, and Tom and his friends would go out and do B and Es—break and enters—and sell the stuff to pay for the gear. They'd been doing this for years. Tom used the money for cars, until he started using it for the gear.

X: So how did you get arrested?

K: Tom used to like to speed and he had a whole page full of warrants. One night the police caught up with him, I was in the car with him and taken as an accomplice. It was the first time ever I had ever had my freedom taken away from me.

A DIET OF BAD IDEAS

The first thing that prisoners ask each other is: 'What are you in for?' For whose benefit is that question? Would the answer alter the way you felt about someone? Would it change the way you spoke to them?

As humans, we are tellers of stories. We create and consume stories—and the juicier the story, the better. A hunger for stories has a survival advantage. You never know when a particular piece of information will increase your chances for a meal or give you an advantage over a rival, and advantages can add up to the point where you may get more food, make more babies, leave more descendants who will carry and reinforce the hunger for stories.

People look down on gossip, but gossip gives you a survival advantage. Just think of how uncomfortable some people get when they're 'out of the loop'.

But an undiscriminating desire for stories is a little like an undiscriminating desire for fatty and sugary foods. It's fine to be a cave dweller and have a genetic predisposition to like fats when fatty and sugary meals are rare, but when the supermarket shelves are full of fats then indulging a hunger for easily available fats and sugars will clog your arteries and give you diabetes, and who knows what effects a bad diet might have on behaviour, even 'criminal' behaviour.

In the same way an indiscriminate hunger for information is fine if you're a cave dweller with only five or six senses and fifty other people in your life, and life or death depends on knowing when the macadamias ripen. But in a world of billions of books, radios, television sets, recordings, computers and magazines, rubbishy information can clog your brain with some counter-productive ideas. You can end up programming yourself and embracing a value system that tells you that you are totally inadequate unless you look like a supermodel, live like a supermodel and are as blissfully happy as you are told a supermodel ought to be with such good looks and so much money and attention.

The attraction of drugs is that they appeal for all sorts of reasons. This makes the issue 'complex', but it's not really complex at all. People take drugs because, at some level, they feel that their lives are inadequate—whatever they have it just doesn't measure up, it's not enough.

If you're really hung up on the beautiful/rich/centre of attention trip but are lazy, why not take the white powder road to instant happiness? After all those magic white powders will, for a while at least, make you feel so good that you won't care how you look, how much money you have or how much attention you get because, for a while at least, you could swim in diamonds and pearls before you'd feel anywhere near as good as those white powders make you feel.

Even if you don't care about driving expensive foreign cars and living in penthouse apartments those white powders can, for a while at least, help you forget the pain of being buggered by your uncle or being beaten up by mum, or the grief of a life without the daddy you adore. They can also help you forget that you have no education, no prospects for a better life and no hope. They can help you forget that life is unfair and some people have it all, and are going to keep it all, while no one's ever given you a free ride or even a break in a life you think of as worthless, pointless, miserable or so boring that you'll take whatever kick you can get.

Even if you come from a 'privileged' background those white powders can help you forget that Mother treats you like a fashion accessory and that Father is too busy carving out his corporate empire and banging his secretary to pay much attention to you. Those magic little powders can also help you bond with other vapid, spoilt brats who are also under the illusion that they are part of an indestructible elite who will live forever. And if you don't mind dealing with ruthless people, because all you've ever known are ruthless people, you can get all the white powders you'll ever want.

8 GETTING CAUGHT, STANDING TRIAL, GETTING SENTENCED

Rosa's account of her arrest for drug importing and what happened after is not typical, but when it comes to arrest there is no 'typical'. Her story though, gives you a taste of what it's like to go through the process, the issues that come up, and how what went on in her mind at the time affected the decisions she was making.

Rosa: The store is on a main street. It's busy and it's very public. About fifteen Federal Police officers just storm into the place. The leader pulls out his badge and says 'Rosa _____ and Turk _____ you are under arrest for the importation of cocaine'. I say, 'This is a joke, right?' He says, 'Hands up against the wall.' But the wall is the glass shopfront window, facing the street, and everyone walking by can see me while the police frisk me.

X: How did that feel?

R: Shocking. I was too stunned to think. They frisk me. They handcuff me and sit me behind my desk. A customer tries to come in and one of the officers says, 'You'll have to leave. This shop is in the hands of the Federal Police.' And she slams the door in his face. I'm thinking, 'What am I going to do? What am I going to do? What am I going to tell my mum?' Then my hands were going tingly. I looked at my hands and they were turning purple because they'd done the handcuffs so tight. I ask them, 'Is this really necessary?' showing them my hands. One of them said, 'Yes.' But another one took them off. There's always one smart-arse in a group of police—I wasn't a threat. They were waiting for a search warrant to be typed up and faxed, so that they could search my room at home. Then I remember the heroin I've hidden at home. Later on I discovered that it was about 230 grams of pure heroin, worth about $50 000. They wouldn't let me go anywhere. They wouldn't let me call anyone.

X: Did they caution you?

R: Yes. I didn't want to say anything. The search warrant came at about six o'clock so between two thirty and six I was sitting in the shop with all those people. Just sitting. Then they gave us the option of joining them as they searched our places. The Turk chose to go to his house. I chose to go straight to the Federal Police headquarters because I didn't want to face my family. They hardly ever saw me. My mother had no idea what was going on. She just assumed that I was working all the time. So I'm at the Federal Police. They photograph me, they take my fingerprints, all fingers and my whole hand. They're videotaping me and they're playing all these games saying things like, 'Pablo's given you up. He's already told us everything. Why don't you tell us what he's been doing and it'll go easier on you.'

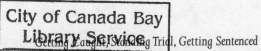

They always play 'good cop, bad cop'. There's always the abusive one and the nice one. All I kept saying was,: 'I have nothing to say to you, if I did, I wouldn't.' They said: 'We found the big bag of powder in your room.' I said: 'I don't know what you're talking about.' They said: 'Oh. Now you're trying to be smart. You're in big trouble now. You're looking at doing about five years.' I just kept saying: 'I don't know what you're talking about.' I was thinking maybe that something else had happened, you know, wishful thinking. All these things go through your mind.

X: What time was it now?

R: We didn't get to the Federal Police headquarters until about nine.

X: You were arrested at two thirty? What took so long?

R: They were looking for evidence to make the charge stick. They had to hold me while they looked for evidence.

X: The suspicion was enough. The bank records? R: They didn't even know about them yet.

X: So why did they come and get you?

R: Because I was in the shop. They arrested Pablo.

X: So they could arrest you even by association.

R: And while they're questioning me they go to my house, but somebody must have said something because they only searched my room. It must have been Pablo.

X: So the police might have been telling the truth when they said that Pablo had blabbed. You just assumed they were playing games. No lawyer yet? R: It's nine at night. No lawyer's going to come, and for what? They got me. It really doesn't matter if you've got a lawyer or not, because if you commit an offence, and you get arrested, they will take you to court the next day.

X: But in the meantime they can interview you all you like. You were reasonably together.

R: They found $6000 in my bag that I was supposed to deposit. They asked me about it. 'We're going to charge you with the possession of drug money.' 'That's not drug money.' 'Where did this come from?' 'I don't know.' 'It just walked there?' 'Maybe.'
That was how I was answering their questions. It was that battle. They brought in the money and an officer started counting it on the table in front of me. 'Fifty. One hundred.' One pile. 'Fifty. One hundred.' Another pile. 'Fifty. One hundred.' Another pile. It went on and on like this. At the trial, when they showed the tape everybody had a big laugh about it. But when they counted it, there was only four thousand. Not six thousand.

X: What happened to the other two thousand?

R: In the pockets of one of the Federal agents. Unbelievable, but it's true. I know that there was six thousand there and they're the only ones who touched it. They asked me on tape. 'Is there four thousand there?' I said, 'Yes, but there should be six thousand.' 'But is there four thousand there?' 'Yes,' I said. And they let it go at that.

Then they took me to the cells. Everybody else was already there— Alfredo, Leona, Pablo, the Turk. Leona always pretended she knew nothing but she was just as involved as Alfredo. She actually had more control. You know how women often control the money?

X: If the men are weaker than the women, the women will take over. They have to.

R: Sometimes men let the women take control so that the men can go and take care of other things. You know what I mean? Anyway, I was put in a huge cell with the light on twenty-four hours a day—a camera watching me all the time. They gave me blankets. They tell you to take a lot of blankets because there's no mattress and they have the airconditioning on really high. There were only four blankets though because I was the last one in. No sheets. No pillows just these grey blankets, like they were in the war or something. There was an open stainless steel toilet. No toilet seat. The bed was just a concrete platform where you could put your blankets.

They asked me for my boots, my belt. I didn't want to give them my boots because the floor was so disgusting. 'Why do you want my boots?' I asked.

'In case you try to commit suicide'.

'With my boots?'

'You'd be surprised what people can get up to when they're desperate.'

The floor was disgusting with spit. They pick up drunks from the road. By this time it was one o'clock in the morning. I slept. I don't know how. I was mentally and emotionally exhausted.

The next morning they woke me up. Early. About five o'clock. An officer throws me a paper bag with two slices of white bread, honey, butter and a plastic knife. He puts a small carton of milk on the floor. They asked me if I wanted tea or coffee. I said coffee. That was my breakfast. They took us all in a van to court. Back then they handcuffed women and shackled the men. I was in the van with the others. We were put in these very, very old cells at the court. I'm still in my socks. My socks were atrocious; I couldn't even look at them. Leona and I are sharing a cell. Waiting for our hearing. The actual cells are underground. Sandstone. Very cold. The floor is filthy with cigarette butts and spit. It smells like an old, wet ashtray—fungus, and unwashed body. We wait while the police present their evidence to the magistrate to determine whether the case should go to trial. There's a little window on top of the steel door of the cell.

The Salvation Army person peeks through. 'Is your family here? Do you want me to tell them that you're okay?' she asks. I ask her to tell them that I'm okay. She didn't come back. So we're in these cells from about nine o'clock. Our case was heard just before five. I get taken through these underground passages. I'm in the courtroom. I see my family. They all look very, very disappointed and sad. My solicitor asked for bail. They wanted $50 000 dollars bail. It's five o'clock on a Wednesday. My family couldn't organise the paperwork because it meant putting their house on the line so the authorities decided to send me to Mulawa correctional centre. I got to Mulawa at about seven o'clock at night. I was the last one in. They photographed me with my MIN number. They took my fingerprints again. Then I finally got my shower. I was so grateful for that shower. I was given new underwear, because you weren't allowed g-strings. I put all my clothes in a bag. And they gave me my first green clothes. Bottle green. They asked me about any medical conditions I had.

They put me in a room with Leona. The next day we're woken up. The guard just throws us another bag of bread, a sachet of coffee, sugar, whitener. 'Muster!' we hear. With my ethnic background I don't know what 'Muster!' means.

X: Nobody told you anything? R: No. So we just show up outside our room in our pyjamas. Everyone else is dressed and showered. Everyone else knew what they were doing. We're confused. Then the officers are screaming at us: 'When muster's called your meant to be blah, blah, blah?!' So. OooooooKaaaaayyyy. We're then just left in this big house with all these different rooms where there were two girls in every room. There's a common room and we see the big window leading to an office. We can see the officers. It's like a psych ward in the movies. There's a kitchen sink with plastic cups, plastic, knives, forks, plastic everything. Outside there's a patio with a roof, covered in bars. I'm translating everything to Leona. She won't stop crying. She'd had a face peel the month before and her tears were irritating her skin. Other girls ask me why I'm there. I say, 'Possession.' They ask me why Leona's there and I have to pretend that I don't know her because I respect her right to not say anything because she doesn't want anyone to know. Leona's constantly nagging me. 'Ask them if I can make a phone call. I want to talk to Alfredo.' I keep telling her ,'You're not allowed, so don't ask!' 'But what's going to happen with Alfredo?' 'I don't know!' 'When are they going to come? When are we going to go?' 'I don't know!' She just went on and on.

X: There was nothing in your experience that even remotely resembled an induction process? R: I just got chucked in the lion's cage.

X: What were the lions like? R: There they were okay. We were the most serious case there. We were the biggest crims in that little area. They let me call my mother; she said not to worry. They were doing the paperwork. I washed sheets just to have some-thing to do and to get away from Leona, who was driving me crazy. Later that night they told me I was going. I got to change into my clothes. My property got returned and I was told basically to go. An officer joked to me, 'Don't look back, because if you look back, you'll come back.' So I'm walking along this path. My mother's there getting all emotional and I'm getting all emotional. The officer screams, 'Don't look back?' And I go, 'What?' And I turn around and look back. I did go back.

Rosa spent eight months on bail, before her case went to trial.

R: I go out on bail and I start reporting to the police every morning and every afternoon for eight months. Every day I have to physically go there and sign. Before nine o'clock in the morning and before nine o'clock at night. I tried innumerable times during those eight months to get my bail conditions changed but the police kept objecting. I never came up with a good enough reason why they should change the conditions.

X: So you're in limbo for eight months. How was your relationship with your family while you were on bail?

R: I was very humble. I did whatever they wanted me to. My stepfather used to hassle me about signing on because it was his half of the house that was up as guarantee for the bail. My parents were really anxious about me stuffing up.

X: It would have only taken one screw up for them to lose their house?

R: Yes. So I was very obedient but I was still hooked on cocaine because I kept buying it.

X: With what money?

R: I got a job cleaning floors. I got about three fifty a week. Most of it went up my nose. I got into debt. Borrowed off friends. **X:** Did you ever pay it back?

R: No, not a cent. I had to leave my job because my trial started. I decided to plead 'not guilty' to take a chance.

X: On whose advice?

R: My solicitor. He said, 'You're charged with 'Possession without a Reasonable Excuse'. I said: 'But I've got an excuse! Pablo gave it to me. I was just holding it for him! I wasn't doing anything wrong with it. That is an excuse!' I started making myself believe that I did have a chance. He said: 'Well, we're here to represent you so we'll just represent you.' Legal Aid had given me money to get a private solicitor. Pablo got Legal Aid before any of us, so all of us who got in after got some subsidy to avoid a 'conflict of interest'. While I was on bail I visited Pablo and the Turk in jail. I was supporting them as a friend. I was visiting Pablo's kids, putting money into his account and getting into debt because of it. I was closing down the shop because I was a director. I had to get rid of the stock. I was in debt because we had to pay to get out of the lease. Pablo told me that he would say at the trial that the drugs were his, not mine. My solicitor subpoenaed Pablo at my trial but Pablo said nothing like that. Pablo denied knowing anything about the heroin in my possession. I thought,: 'Oh my God! How could he do this to me after all I've done for him, selling everything, getting myself into debt so that they could have money for solicitors?' **X:** He just completely washed his hands of you? **R:** Exactly!

X: He had gotten what he wanted out of you.

R: Eventually he did. He wasn't going to put himself into a deeper mess by getting me out. Later, in jail, I learned that when you're drowning, you've just got to save yourself.

X: You hadn't learned that lesson yet.

R: I believed that we were 'a team' and that we were going to help each other. We'd discussed that there wasn't a point in having everybody locked up. There was going to have to be somebody outside who would look after the people on the inside.

X: You felt that as the 'least guilty' of the lot it should have been you.

R: My charges were minimal. They weren't even grouped with their charges. My solicitor arranged to separate my case completely so that they wouldn't compare my sentence with theirs. If they had gotten ten years, they would have given me seven, because of the scale of the crime within the group. My charges were 'Possession of a Prohibited Import Being Heroin' and 'Possession of Money: Being the Proceeds of Crime'. As for the money I sent away, they said that if I pleaded guilty to that one charge they would drop it, because otherwise that would have implicated me in trafficking.

X: Which was a much more serious offence. What guarantee did you have that they would live up to their part of the plea bargain?

R: No guarantee at all. Just word of mouth.

X: Who were the 'they' who were telling you these things? The lawyers?

R: The lawyers know because they're criminal lawyers and they've been through all this before and it's just like a system.

X: They know how the game works. Did you choose to plead guilty to the third count?

R: Yes, but I stuck to my guns on the others. My trial lasted five days. The actual judge said that even if I didn't know what the stuff was I must have assumed that it was something bad because it was in a plastic bag, wrapped up in a shirt and hidden in a wardrobe from the rest of my family. Then the judge explained to the jury that if it had been a can of coke, sealed, and you didn't know what was in it, you couldn't be charged with possession because ...

X: No reasonable person would have assumed? How did you find the process of the trial itself?

R: It was very nerve wracking. My mother had to take the stand. She'd seen the bag and to her the bag was empty. She said she'd seen the bag and the shirt, but she never saw any drugs. My mother had probably seen the bag and the shirt before I put the drugs in them. My brother made necklaces out of beads and he had all these small bags for the beads, so the police thought we were selling drugs because of all of the little plastic bags. He was a slob. There were little bags everywhere. They called him to the stand to say that the bags were for his beads. My stepfather, Tim, was called to the stand as a character witness, to speak on my behalf.

X: Your entire family was put through this experience.

R: The trial finished on Friday at lunchtime. The jury left and they didn't get back to me until eight o'clock. It took them that long to decide.

X: Five days of hearings. Eight hours of deliberation.

R: While the jury were out I told my mother not to worry. If they found me guilty I'd be all right. I took off all my jewellery and gave it to her. We waited and waited. I just couldn't eat, I was so nervous. My mother and brother who were with me, kept saying, 'Whatever happens, we're with you. We'll deal with it.' And I said, 'Look, it's all right. I've been there before, it's not that bad.' But, you know, I was really just trying my luck by pleading 'Not Guilty'. If you plead 'Not Guilty' and you are, it's worse. You get a higher sentence. If you just say 'I'm guilty, sentence me and let me get on with my life' it costs less money.

X: So you get extra punishment for wasting the taxpayers' money and the court's time on a bullshit trial. But you felt it was worth the gamble?

R: Yeah! So, at eight o'clock I was back in court. They told me to stand up. I stood up. They read the charges and they went through a summary of the whole case. They judge asked the jury for their verdict. They found me guilty on both charges.

X: How did that feel?

R: I was numb. It was strange. Everything got really still. I guess part of me was ready for it. In your life you got things inside you that help you sustain shock.

X: It's not like the movies where the guilty starts yelling and screaming.

R: Not for me. There was just emptiness. It's such a long process that there's even this 'Oh finally, finally, I know where I stand now'.

X: So it's like relief?

R: It's like 'Well just let me get my sentence over and done with now after all I've been through'. Like bail for instance and everything that happened with my father and mother and not being able to do anything. There were officers waiting to take me to Mulawa. They took me downstairs to a holding cell that looked as if it was made of thick chicken wire. A transport truck came. They handcuffed me. I got to Mulawa. I went through the whole process again. I got a mug shot taken of me with my MIN number. Then, because of a stuff-up, I was put into a room in the annex of a medical wing.

———

So Rosa found herself at the beginning of her sentence. The actual sentence had not yet been set. That would come later, but for now she was in jail along with about 500 other women in New South Wales, and about another 1000 nationally, most of whom were between the ages of eighteen and thirty-five. So what exactly are 'they' in for? [12]

The female top five crimes are: drug offences, fraud, assault and robbery at equal third, homicide and other theft equal fourth and justice procedures in fifth place.

Table 2:
Sentenced prisoners by most serious offence, by gender, number and percent, 2003

Offence	Male		Female	
	Number	Percent	Number	Percent
Homicide	1 807	10	134	11
Assault	2 325	13	138	12
Sex offences	1 904	11	13	1
Robbery	2 310	13	138	12
Unlawful entry with intent	2 260	13	131	11
Other theft*	1 157	7	134	11
Fraud**	507	3	140	12
GSJ***	1 249	7	109	9
Drug offences	1 674	10	167	14
Other****	2 347	13	94	8
Total	17 540	100	1198	100

Source: Australian Bureau of Statistics, 2004.

*   Includes motor vehicle theft

**   Deception and related offences

***   Government security and justice procedures, includes offences such as: breach of court order, breach of parole, escape custody, offences against justice procedures, treason, sedition and resisting customs officials.

**** Includes other offences against the person and property, public order offences and driving offences.

The Australian Institute of Criminology has this to say about these figures:

> The main offences for which male offenders were sentenced included break and enter, robbery and assault. For female offenders the main offences included drug offences, assault, fraud and robbery.
>
> Male prisoners sentenced for the violent offences of homicide, assault, sex offences and robbery accounted for 45% of all sentenced male prisoners in 2003, whereas only 36% of female sentenced prisoners were incarcerated for violent offences.

These figures are only for the most serious offences. The raw statistics deny us the context. The fraud might be to get money for drugs, or in one case I heard of, to pay off a blackmailing boyfriend who was threatening to kill the woman. The assaults may well be as part of an attempt to rob someone for drug money. The thefts might take place to fence the goods for drug money. The homicides might well be the result of self-defence or the last straw from years of abuse. The statistics don't tell us these details.

Including her eight months on bail Rosa served ten months before going back to court for sentencing.

Rosa: When I was getting sentenced the judge asked me to stand up and I could barely stand up because I was so nervous. He started talking but automatically, it was like a shutdown. I just kept staring at the floor and I couldn't understand anything that he was saying and all I could hear was blah, blah, blah, blah, blah, and at the end all I heard was 'and you can do the rest inside'. I walked past my family and all I saw in their faces was 'How could you?' It probably wasn't what they were thinking at all but it was what I saw. I'm in the holding cell and I ask the officer what my sentence was and she said, 'Four years and nine months.' I couldn't believe it. I knew that there were people who'd trafficked 5 kilos and had only gotten three years. I knew something was wrong. My solicitors told me later, 'Don't worry, we'll appeal.' I said, 'Why do I have to appeal? Why do I have to go through all this again? Why can't the judge get it right in the first place?'

X: All this just ended up costing the taxpayer even more money.

R: When I got back to Mulawa the mental health nurse gave me two sleeping tablets and they just knocked me out. It was great, not having to deal with all this shit. The next day I went back to the nurse for some more but she said, 'I think you've got a pretty strong head on your shoulders, you don't need anymore.' And I thought 'Damn!' It was just so much easier to take the pills. That drug was so comforting to me, at that time, with that shocking news. It's pretty easy to get a habit when you're in a state of mind where you've got something you don't want to deal with.

Eight months later Rosa was in court again appealing her sentence.

R: First I got sentenced to four years and nine months, plus two years parole. That's six years and nine months. After I'd been in prison for eighteen months I appealed and I got resentenced because the original judge had made an error. He calculated my sentence compared to people who had been trafficking. But I was never trafficking, I just had it in my possession, I wasn't even selling it. So I got resentenced to three years. I got twenty-two months knocked off my sentence. I'd already served eighteen months so when I was resentenced I only had another eighteen months to go.

X: That was good news.

R: It was like I had kicked a goal! I had to go to the Supreme Court for my appeal and the three judges almost reduced the sentence to just eighteen months which meant I could've gone free, but the Department of Public Prosecution reminded them that if they'd done that I would've walked from that courtroom that day. So one of the judges said, 'We can't have that' and started counting down from twenty-five years. That's how they do it. They start at the maximum sentence and deduct. They say things like 'I take it into consideration that this is her first offence. Okay fifteen years. I take into consideration she has a good record, ten years.' And so on. I ended up with eighteen months left to serve.

Regardless of what you think of Rosa or her crimes, the fact is that she spent a year and a half in limbo before knowing what 'price' she was going to pay for her sins. The situation isn't even any better if you're innocent. Someone can be in jail for eighteen months and then be found innocent, because they are. In the meantime they lose their jobs, their relationships go into a tailspin and when they're released they receive no compensation, no counselling, no support. Innocent people can be framed, or just be in the wrong place at the wrong time. That person could be you.

One woman recently spent almost two years waiting for her trial.

She was found innocent.

In the meantime her relationship with her partner (who was also put on remand and also acquitted) went down the toilet.

Her children were put into care.

She lost her house.

On release she received no counselling or support services, so she turned to drugs instead.

9   INSIDE—PRISON AND IMPRISONMENT

Here are Rosa's first impressions of being on the inside:

Rosa: I'm in Mulawa, carrying my bag with the extra clothes they've given me. I walk
    down this short corridor with doors everywhere. I go into this common room. All the
    women are dressed the same in this bottle green with white volleys (white-soled
    shoes made by Dunlop); they're disgusting shoes but they've all got them. All the
    women are piled up in a corner of this room, looking up at this little TV that doesn't
    even have an aerial. It was all squiggly lines but they were looking at it because there
    was nothing else to do. They looked at me for a second like 'Oh no, not another one',
    as if I were invading their space because it was already pretty crowded in there. It
    was like looking into a tin of sardines. There were so many people there. I was sharing
    a room with three other girls and there were at least three or four people in each
    room and there were eight rooms and a little skinny corridor about the width of two
    doors. That was maximum security.
X: You were in maximum security? You hadn't ever been violent or anything!
R: It was automatic because of the nature of my crimes. There was a place to make
    toast, but breakfast, lunch and dinner were given to us, pre-cooked and everything
    plastic. I was there for five days.

More women are in New South Wales prisons now than ever before. In the
1990s Lee Rhiannon was on the NSW Parliament's Select Committee on the
Increase in Prison Population. The Interim Report: Issues Relating to Women
was published in July 2000.

X: When you were part of that committee was that the first time you'd ever been in a
    prison?
Lee: Yes, and I must say it was one of the most shocking experiences of my life. I found
    all of them deeply disturbing and I was only going to be there for a few hours. What
    was it like for people who were going to be there for a very long time? I remember
    some of the older jails, big sandstone buildings. It was like going back to the 19th
    century. What was shocking was that I saw more young Aboriginal men inside jail
    than at any other time in my life. There weren't huge differences between the men's
    and women's prisons but when you've got a lot of women together it's a different
    energy. Women's prisons seemed calmer, and not as overcrowded.

Overcrowding is an issue you hear about time and time again in regard to prisons. It's just one of a number of general impressions that the public gathers from the media and the entertainment industries. These collective impressions form a whole that supposedly tell us what prisons are supposed to be really like. I thought it would make sense to track down several people who had worked in both male and female prisons and challenge them on the public's perception of jail.

X: The image of male prisons is that they are horrible, violent pressure cookers of psychosis and madness and nasty, terrible, sadistic behaviour with a lot of psychological abuse, physical abuse and sexual abuse only just barely under control.

Sandra: You've just described Silverwater and Long Bay. Mulawa, is almost as bad as what you've just described. Almost, I said. There are parts of Mulawa that are not that bad.

X: So jails are complex institutions. Even within a jail there are different parts, where things are different? There are sub-cultures within the larger jails?

S: Yes.

X: What makes some parts of Mulawa so bad? Is it the inmates themselves? If it is, why? Why perpetuate hell?

S: You can't just look at what the inmates are doing to each other. Mulawa was over-crowded for a long time.

X: Where do you put people when there's no room for them?

S: Every woman that has to go to jail has to go to Mulawa first. So even someone who ends up in a minimum security jail like Emu Plains will be exposed to maximum security at least at first.

X: Maximum security implies the most serious of crimes and the most serious criminals. So all women prisoners get exposed to serious criminals regardless of what they've done? Even those on remand, who may later be found not guilty, with remand lasting up to eighteen months?

S: Mulawa will hold them for one or two weeks and then they'll be classified and depending on their classification they'll then go to Dillwynia, Emu Plains, Berrima or Kempsey, way up north.

X: What happens to women in prison?

S: Women's prisons are filled with women who are struggling. They don't want to be there. Some of them have lost their units because the rent was due the week they were picked up and they can't pay the rent because they're in jail and they lose their flats and they don't know what happens to everything that was in the flat.

X: What happens to their stuff?

S: Who knows? They don't know, I don't know and unless they can ring someone who can check out their flat and get their stuff and hang on to it for them they don't know what happens to it.

X: If a woman has no one on the outside that they can trust, which is not an uncommon thing, then they lose everything? **S:** There is Prisoners' Aid. If she had no one that can help, Prisoners' Aid can go as long as the place isn't locked up because there was money owing on rent. Prisoners' Aid will store their personal stuff, but not their furniture.

Rachel talked about having to do 'that little bit extra' to help out.

Rachel: I've taken women to Prisoners' Aid to fetch their stuff and then driven them to their accommodation because they haven't had any transport. When you're arrested, you don't get a chance to go back. You don't even get a chance to pick up anything. When the police knock on your door you get about ten minutes before you're out the door.

X: And if there's nobody there with you?

R: The ones on their own are not as common as ones with boyfriends, de factos or husbands, or someone. But I get women coming up to me in this position and I have to get Prisoners' Aid to help. If they're in public housing the department takes all their stuff away, stores it, charges them for the storage and they won't get a thing back until they've paid their back rent. So sometimes when women get out they have nothing.

Michelle had a surprisingly different attitude to her work and demonstrates that it's not just the job, but the person who fills it that can make all the difference:

X: What was it like? Your first women's prison?

M: I felt like every Christmas had come at once.

X: Really? How extraordinary!

M: I felt loved, wanted, appreciated. I went out of there bawling my eyes out for about half an hour in the car before I drove home. When I went there that particular morning I had no idea what to expect. The first cup of coffee that I got I didn't know whether to trust the woman but I thought, 'No. You've got to show her that you trust her.' But at Mulawa I felt loved, needed and cared for.

X: What do the women need you for?

M: Sometimes people coming into prison, it's the first time, their first words to me are usually 'What can you do for me?'

X: And what can you do for them?

M: We can tell them who the people are they need to speak to and where the places are that they've got to attend. We can supply them with wool if they knit or crochet and, depending on their classification, we can also supply them with knitting needles and crochet hooks. We usually have to suss that out first. If they want to read the chapel usually has a library, so we lend books. Not all prisoners can read. Maybe they're so alone in the place, being new, they haven't struck up a conversation with anyone else and they just want to talk. Maybe they want a cry and they can't cry in front of someone for fear of being pulled to pieces?

X: How real is that fear? That they'll be pulled to pieces?

M: There is a fear there. It depends on whether or not they can stand up for themselves. There is a pecking order in jail. And if you come in thinking that there's not then you're in for a rude awakening. A woman came up to me once and said, 'I might as well kill myself.' I said, 'Whoah! Hold on a minute. Let's talk about this. Don't just throw this onto me!' And she said, 'Well I've got to throw it on to somebody.' I can't picture being in a place and not being able to get away. These women can't. They don't have the pleasure of going for a walk in the park or watching a movie. It can be quite hard to come from living on your own, or with a boyfriend, to living in a sort of dorm situation— one or two-to-a-room. There's no effort made to try to put you in with someone you'll get along with. You get what you're given and you just have to lump it. You wouldn't be put in a house of smokers if you don't smoke, but you're not allowed to smoke in the house anyway. They'll only separate people if they know there are fights. What's surprising is the number of elderly people who are coming in. The young ones look up to the old ones. They see them like their grandmothers.

X: What do you call elderly?

M: Over seventy.

X: What are they in for? Pension fraud? M: I don't know. You're not supposed to ask. I didn't notice it so much in 2003 but I definitely noticed it in 2004.

X: You've got blue-collar crime, white-collar crime, young and old. Is there anything that any of these women have in common? Anything we can point to and say, 'Avoid this, and you won't go to jail?'

M: No. Nothing. Anybody can end up in jail—more so now. More judges are saying that you've got to do your time. You see Corrective Services have no control over how many get put in.

X: Corrective Services just has to deal with what they get.

M: It's the judges and the magistrates that control who gets put in jail.

———

This is an important point. You hear rumours all the time about jail over-crowding. If they're true, where do you put people when you've run out of room for them? Do you put them in corridors or on floors? What happens when you run out of floors? Transport vans (the so-called 'meat wagons') are supposed to transfer prisoners between Prison A and Prison B but you could use them instead as temporary mobile prison cells that park somewhere overnight with the prisoners still in them. A van is, after all, just another room on wheels. If you were in charge, and desperate because there just isn't any more room anywhere, you might do that. You might even put the prisoners up in a hotel. And if you had to resort to such extreme measures it's not something that any Department of Corrective Services is responsible for. A prison is, when all is said and done, just a building. And a building is of a finite size. There's only so much room. When you run out of room where do you put the extra prisoners that magistrates and judges keep sending you? After all, magistrates and judges and that great, impersonal thing called 'the law' set the 'agenda' of who goes into jail and when (aside, of course, from the criminals themselves).

Who sets the judges' agenda? Well, public opinion, or the perception of public opinion, which also encourages governments with a law-and-order agenda to set punitive policies. The media may or may not go along with this and either reinforce or discourage the growth of such a punitive climate. As Marilyn Manson in the film *Bowling for Columbine* said about American culture, the US runs on 'fear and consumption'. I wonder if we're far behind. Is it possible that a punitive climate may encourage more sentencing? If so, then if the public insists on more punishment there is a greater likelihood that you also could find yourself arrested and before the courts on some minor offence. In such a climate, you too could end up in jail, rubbing shoulders with rapists and murderers. Then you wouldn't have to read books like this one—you could live the experience for yourselves.

———

Kelli's experience of jail was very different from Rosa's, and reflects Kelli's personality and her own brand of strength.

K: When I was first arrested I was carrying a lot of gear in a 'safe place'.

X: Didn't they search you?

K: Of course they searched me but they can't 'reach in' unless they're absolutely sure you're possessing. Even then a doctor has to do it. So in the two days I'm in a police cell, because I didn't have a needle, I had to snort it, but you need to use more to get the same effect. Then I get sent to Mulawa and the first thing I do is ask for a fit. So the fit comes but so do the vultures.

X: You don't ask for a needle unless you've got gear, and if you've got gear ...

K: (Nodding and winking) So I start heating some of the gear I still had in my 'safe place'.

X: How much had you gotten in?

K: I'd gone through a lot snorting while I was at the station. I still had a few grams, which is still a lot. I had prime stuff, but I wasn't about to tell them that. So I get all the stuff I need because everyone is so accommodating, because when you've got a fit you'll get a shot and whoever's friends with whoever has the fit may also get a shot. So I'd finished the mix, it's ready and I start to draw the needle and they take it away. I go straight to the leader, put her in a headlock and say, 'You'd better tell your flunkies to give me back my gear now or you're going to be dead.' And they gave in. They were just a bunch of wooses.

X: Your instincts were right. K: Survival skills! I have great instincts.

X: You're instantly in the role aren't you? You become Queen Bee! It didn't take you long to get to the top of the shit pile, did it?

K: They'd never seen this sort of feistiness from a newcomer before. They kept me three months in Mulawa and I'd be having four fights a day at the start. It was just a workout for me. And they all learnt very quickly. I went to court and Tom stood up for me and said he hadn't even known me at the time he did all his stuff. So I got out. They had nothing on me. I wasted three months of my life but I got a whole bunch of flunkies who loved me because normally a strong person treats them like shit but I always treated everyone like a human. But being locked up brought out the animal in me. All my natural instincts just came. I realise now how animals have their babies because it's just the natural call of the wild that they get. It's all there.

So I'm out. Tom got five years. I visit him every weekend—religiously. I was living normal. I'd had to go cold turkey in prison so I was off the gear. But I'm out and I'm still making a living dealing and I have to support Tom and his habit. We women are so much stauncher than men. We all look after our men's habits while they're in there. Whereas if it's to return the favour, no way! All they do is stuff us up.

X: So the kissy kissy stuff. I'm amazed that the prison authorities even let it happen.

K: They can't stop it and it keeps all the troublemakers sedated. As long as you do it like Houdini they let you get away with it, but if you make it obvious of course they're gonna bust you then.

X: So you're still dealing?

K: I was straight after I came out. But when Tom asked me to start bringing it in for him, I didn't want to do it ... but just to please my boyfriend ...

X: And you got tempted and hooked again.

K: I was dealing top quality stuff. The dealers usually do. It's the sellers that take it on the street that cut. They get greedy. Some are selling almost all sugar. I always cut too but my stuff was twice as strong. Not enough to get you an overdose but enough to get you a really good high. Enough to get wasted for a few hours at least.

X: So your stuff was in demand.

K: I took the market! I took the whole market. How the other dealers hated my guts! I was making a packet but all my profits were going up my veins and Tom's veins, and his mates and the entourage that started hanging around me.

X: Did that land you in prison again?

K: No it was for traffic offences. I ran though a road block. I was mad at my sister. We're very passionate people. Hot-blooded. I had an argument with her and I took it out on the accelerator. Soon I hear sirens but I dodged them. I'm an adrenaline junkie from my time when Tom was playing chases with the cops. We made it home. I hid the car at my uncle's. I put his car on the street. My sister insists on seeing her boyfriend. I can't leave her by herself so I decide to take her in my car.

X: You went in the same car! K: I know. I must have a screw loose.

X: Couldn't you have taken your uncle's car?

K: I didn't like his car. There was an unmarked police car searching for us and the chase was on again and I ran through a road block and got six months. That's just what my family's like! We do impulsive things. When you're in that frame of mind you're not thinking clearly anymore. And we'd been bonging like crazy. We were wasted. You won't believe it but Tom had been out of jail for a week when I was put back in. It was more of the same. I had to reinstate myself.

X: In your own inimitable way. But you got out again.

K: And I'm back on the streets, dealing. Tom is in and out of jail. I start dealing coke at this point. The real money's in the coke. The coke junkies buy more gear more often.

X: They're a richer crowd? K: Yes.

X: They're a classier crowd? K: They start off classier. Coke was my downfall.

X: Why?

K: Because we'd just be in a room taking shot after shot after shot.

X: Snort?

K: No shot.

X: You injected it?

K: It's the best. It pops brain cells. You can feel them popping. It's like the best climax that you've ever had in your life, times a hundred.

X: Is coke also dissolved in a heated spoon? K: With coke you don't have to heat it. Even with some heroin, the really good stuff you don't have to heat. When you snort coke, you get the nice high, you get all the numbness, but you don't get the extreme climax you get when you inject. It's like twenty seconds of an orgasm multiplied by a hundred.

X: No wonder people take it. But it's a fool's paradise because it doesn't last.

K: It doesn't last. So you have to score again and all my profits went up my arms. Heroin dealers and coke dealers are different types of people. Heroin dealers have this 'gangsta' mentality. They drive around in black Mercedes Benzs and black BMWs. They're so obvious. Coke dealers own antique stores.

X: It's a classier drug. K: With classier suppliers. The users start off classier but it only takes six months for them to see how they take a nosedive. Heroin users take a few years to fall. Coke's a faster drug, a more expensive drug, you use it more often.

X: So if you had to pick? Coke would win by a mile?

K: Oh yeah. The buzz is better. I stopped wanting to be a zombie. I wanted to be alive but it wasn't a real reality. Money came easy. Easy come, easy go. I spend the next three years like this until I go back in.

I was involved in a bungled bank robbery. I swear I didn't know it was going on. I met this man called George. He was gorgeous, although I thought he was called 'Dean' at the time because he had a new identity. George was the original Mr Asia. The guy that took the fall for him in Adelaide, he was just the front man. It all came out in the papers after he died. The chemistry we had—it was beyond Tom.

My best friend at the time, Chris, who was a transgender prostitute working the wall (boy by day, girl by night) had stolen some credit cards from his clients. We were trying to get them to work and getting nowhere. We're in George Street, Sydney and George comes around and we tell him we've got no money. He says, 'Hang on! I'll be back in a minute, just trust me, baby.' And he disappears. He was like that, so handsome.

There was a gift shop nearby and I thought he'd gone to get me something. Next thing I know there's sirens everywhere, cops. I got to the gift shop and as I pass I look in a bank and notice George on the floor surrounded by guards. I want to help, out of instinct, but I can't. Chris and I run to George's sports convertible. I just started the car and I get the feel of cold steel to my temple. The cop goes to the front of the car, points the gun at both of us and says, 'And put your bloody hands where I can fucking well see them!'

I go into reverse and then forward. The cop dives out of the way. I don't think straight sometimes.

He starts shooting. Instead of at our tyres he's shooting the boot. The bullets are coming straight through. It was already peak hour. I go to the wrong side of the road and start weaving in and out of oncoming cars. By now the TV networks are onto us. I get to a corner and I put on the indicator to warn people I'm coming through, because I don't want anyone to get hurt.

X: You must be the only getaway driver in the world that indicates.

K: That's what Chris was saying. We got on to Park Street. I got blocked by a ute at a traffic light. A cop on a bike intercepts me, opens the door, tries to grab my keys. I throw him out. The light turns green. There were two other cops who were not even originally involved in the beginning in the traffic lane next to me. They see me throw out the bike cop from my car. I don't know they're cops at the time, they're in plain clothes. One of these cops gets out of his car and he tries to get in to mine. I think, 'Who's this wanker trying to be a hero?' I was just in my lane, minding my own business. I pull out and the cop later claims compensation for damage, which is why my sentence was so stiff. I go up Clarence Street and this idiot goes through a red light and crashes into me. I can't turn the car. I run into a pole and into a car in front of me and that car crashes over the car in front of it. The judge later said that I was lucky I wasn't in for multiple manslaughter. I was convicted and spent eighteen months in jail before I was sentenced.

X: You spent most of your time in maximum. **K:** But boys' maximum was a holiday camp compared to maximum for women. Me and some other girls were sent to Parklea for a time while they built the segregation section at Mulawa, just for us. There was a wing there at Parklea for very naughty girls.

X: What was segro like?

K: I usually liked it. It gave me a chance to catch up on my letter-writing.

Kelli ultimately spent three years in jail. Tom later died of a heroin overdose. The experience of jail isn't the same everywhere. Here's the rest of Sophie's story, as told by her mother, Jean.

X: So in the years that followed, Sophie was just getting into drugs. It's easy. One shot leads to another. She steals to support her habit, but her dad keeps bailing her out, so she's not really dealing with the consequences of her actions. **Jean:** No. She was serving short sentences for burglary, maybe six months to a year. I'd say that there were times when she was dealing with the consequences of her actions, but it didn't stick. She just had this pathological desire to destroy herself.

X: So it's small stuff, and then something big happened. **J:** She was serving time in a penitentiary when the 'Three Strikes Law' came to effect on 7 March 1994. If you get three convictions you get twenty-five to life—it's Draconian. She was still on heroin in jail, apparently it's easier to get it in there than out. I don't know how. The security's so tight. Anyway, soon after it happens Hailey tells me that Sophie's in jail. Someone handed her five dollars worth of heroin as a payback for a favour. She'd already decided that she was going to be clean so she stuffs it in her bra to flush it down the toilet. The officers did a search, and that was her third strike.

Sophie's handwriting is large, rushed, curly, artistic even, and in a letter to her sister in 1996, one of scores she would write to her family, she tells about her addiction in her own words.

I'M AN ADDICT! I have made all the choices in my life. I choose to believe that I was conditioned to become an addict in childhood. Similar to how a dog salivates behind the smell of food. I would say that having to take a narcotic from 6 years old on inevitably did more damage than good. Do you realise that I never stopped using from the day I got off those pills? From coke to heroin. I know that I experimented with acid but I don't think I got crazy with any drug until later. I've spent 1/3 of my life in prison. I've gained nothing. I have a mother I hate, a father that has been my enabler for years and a sister who can't understand me. Not to mention the rest of my dysfunctional relatives. I've been in and out of the drug scene since I got here. Drugs are more than plentiful. You practically fall over them here. Last May I was caught with .05 gram (about $5.00 worth on the streets) in my bra. I'm mad at myself for not using them. They strip search me. I was thrown in the hole for 3 months. This is my third strike. 25 years to life in prison. I have to go to trial because they won't make a deal. I fight myself on a daily basis just to make it through a day without using, breaking down or even killing myself. I am a realist. I am facing the fact that I'm going to spend another 20 years here. It's my fault but damn I never thought my life would end up so worthless. I just don't see this as life. Existing yes. But not life. There is no love here. I never felt so scared, alone, unloved, unwanted, period, in all my life.

The Three Strikes Law in California is the direct result of a punitive social climate of zero tolerance for crime. Under this law if you're convicted of three serious offences sentencing is mandatory and with little chance of appeal. Three strikes and you're out. Or rather, you're in jail. Jean picks up Sophie's story:

Jean: She was the first woman in the history of the third strike law to be convicted while she was in jail. There was nothing I could do. And what could I do anyway, from here? **X:** You were twenty years over there in America, raising her, trying to do something, and it didn't work. Even if you had been over there once she was in jail, what could you have done?

J: Make myself crazy. That's why I turned off. A lot of people find it difficult to understand how a mother could do that, but it was like I was just saving myself. You get to the point where 'I'm sorry if I was a bad mother. I'm sorry about everything. But I have to move on. I cannot stay in this crap. I cannot listen to this shit. It's not good for my health, and it's not good for your health either. You need to move on too. If you don't like me or you don't like who I am, what am I supposed to get, a lobotomy? What am I supposed to do? Don't I ever get out of therapy? Can't I ever have any peace in this life?

X: But a lot of people with children in jail, cut them off.

J: And also with heroin addiction they cut them off because they come in and destroy everything, take everything and they finally have to get them out of their lives. She did that with my own family while I was away. **X:** She systematically alienated everyone. **J:** Including my husband, but he kept coming back to the party.

X: But was that a good thing?

J: Well you have to have somebody in your life, even if it's not good enough it's better than nobody. Because the desperation of somebody in prison, unless you see it for yourself...

X: So you started corresponding with her.

J: It had been many years. She was elated. We've been communicating ever since. Hailey visits her with her family and comes back devastated, she said that Sophie's body was more hyper than ever.

In a letter dated 2000 Sophie talks about a life she feels that she's wasted, and the injustice of the system:

I'm so old!? I should have been out of here five years ago. I hate myself for this place. The sad part of all this is that I do finally like myself and have realised a whole lot of my potential and I can't share it with my world because I don't have the real world only this makeshift world within the world it's awful and yeah, it's painful as hell?

What I went in for was worth $5.00 on the street but in here it would cost $100.00. It was given to me. I don't pay for it. It's not worth it. This is not to say that I don't use because I do Mom. Very seldom but sometimes I just need to escape. If it's free, I'll do it. Try to understand, I just need a vacation from the pain and the heartache and that's my addiction and the only way I know. I'm trying very hard these days because I have something to lose. Dad wants to come back and visit and I want my visits back? I love you Mom? I haven't liked you for many years but I've always loved you. You are one of my biggest hang-ups. It's taken me a long time to even talk to you with my psychologist but I can now. I just want to let it all go. But Mom, please don't hurt me anymore. If you can't handle being in my life, get out now. I can't deal with anymore heartache Mom. I want us to be friends. I want you in my life.

But according to Jean, it may not be all bad:

J: She has a job in jail. She's a gardener, so she's very fit and stuff.

In a letter dated shortly after 11 September 2001, her writing is less slanted, neater and more controlled. In spite of the fact that prisons are worlds unto themselves events on the outside do affect life on the inside.

As far as the Attorney goes, the laws aren't changing fast enough. I don't know. I need to get out of here. I'm tired of this life, Mom! I refuse to accept this. I don't deserve it at all. As far as what is happening in the world, I'm not afraid, Mom. Most women hear [sic] don't comprehend the whole thing. These are 80% idiots!: The majority here are just scumbags, trash! I mean people would really believe someone would waste Anthrax in prison. HEE HEE. Who would care if a bunch of high-priced baby-sitters and scum bags got sick?

During her time in jail, Sophie fights to have her case re-examined. In 2002 she wrote this letter to anyone who would listen.

Dear Sirs, I am a three-strike lifer, incarcerated in _. I have been in prison for 12 years. I started my sentence in 1990. I received 10 years for burglary. In 1995 I got caught with .05 grams of heroin while incarcerated. I was made an example of and became the first and only woman in _ to receive 25 to life in prison.

I had an attorney who did my appeal but never went further than the first level. It was denied in October of 1997, but I never heard a word until March 1998. The attorney to this day will not answer my letters and never spoke to me once during the appeal process. Since me many women in _ have been caught for possession, drug trafficking, or conspiracy to traffic, yet no one has received a Life sentence. Some have even fought 50 to Life, but many 25 to Life. They were all offered plea bargains. I was never offered a deal.

I have no violent crimes yet 80% of the women had large amounts of drugs and violent crimes, yet some were sentenced with _ time credit.

There must be something I can do. I desperately need help! I'm an addict who is finally clean, sober, old, and ready for society.

If there is someone who feels some compassion for my situation, and willing to help me fight the three-strikes, please contact me.

It may have become obvious by now that in Sophie's case we're dealing with substantial issues of inconsistency and injustice. Jean, like many parents of people in jail, knows what's going on but there's very little she can do. Jail can be enormously disempowering not only to the prisoner, but to their families too.

J: All this time she's in jail, and it's like, someone else's nightmare. She was recently in solitary confinement for a month because she talked back to one of the guards. I had to apply, from here, to visit her. When I got there, in 2003, it was a huge place— barbed-wire everywhere. It's very surreal. Prison is a huge industry.

And yet the relationships can survive. This letter from Jean to Sophie tells us that love will do whatever it can:

I don't hate you. I loved you so much. You'll never understand but somehow nothing ever worked for us as a team. What can I say honey? It's all so heavy and painful. I too had a hard life. My mother had a hard life. Her mother had a hard life. It's a hard life. I'm sorry to have to tell you Sophie, you are a genius and I cry privately whenever I think about the pain you're in, but what can I do? I keep myself together with a shoestring. Life's painful without drugs but it's too painful with drugs. You've got to show yourself that you can get out of it. Do it, Sophie!

When Jean finally got to see her daughter, it was a profound experience for both of them.

———

Jean: I hadn't seen her in twenty-six years. It was big. She told me all these stories of what had happened to her, her 'lousy, violent marriage', how she did her robberies, how someone kidnapped, raped her and almost killed her once. 'You don't understand, Mom,' she said. 'It's the drug. It's the drug. You'll do anything, anything to get the drug.' She was up before a parole board. Even though she wasn't eligible they go through the motions.

'What about your drug problem?' they asked. 'I'm not on drugs,' she says. 'Well, what are your plans?' they ask. 'Plans? What plans? I can't get out of here. I've had enough. I've been here for fourteen years for drugs. I was never violent, I never hurt anybody. I'm waiting for 2004 for the referendum for the law to change so I can get out.' 'What if it doesn't change and you don't get out?' they asked. 'Then I'm going back on drugs. Why wouldn't I?'

I don't blame her. Why wouldn't she? She has no future.

She can't even go to the bathroom without being searched and she's in a cell with eight women. Half of them are nuts and the food's horrible. But she's always been smart. She's learned how to cook in her cell. The last time I saw her she wanted one of my rings. I would have given her one but I couldn't. I would've had to get permission, fill out forms. We just hadn't prepared for it. I told her, 'You've got to understand. You have no freedom. Freedom is the most important thing in the world. If you have no freedom you have nothing. If you ever get out of here you have to remember that just being free is everything.'

I'd really like today's kids to understand the consequences of their actions. They tried to pass a law, just recently in California, to get rid of this Three Strikes Law. They held a referendum to get rid of it, but it didn't pass. She's still there.

X: They wanted it? The Californians want the Three Strikes Law?

J: The average person is sick of the crime. Enough is enough. Let's put them in jail. So now half the world is in jail.

Sophie's jail has 4000 inmates. There are twice as many female inmates in this one facility alone, than the total female prison population of Australia. Why? In a recent letter Sophie effectively sums up the agenda that keeps her in jail:

Legalising heroin will never happen in the States. Too much politics behind it. I mean, come on, dirty politicians are making a fortune covering up for the mafia and illegal drug transportation. Need I go on? California is a prison state and it has become one hell of an industry employing thousands of people and locking up twenty times as much, if not more. It's very sad. Many human beings are quite mentally ill, but they've closed down all but one state hospital so they are mingling with the rest of us. It's wild.

You're right about people not wanting to face the reality that there are prisons for bad people and for people with problems, but it seems to me that, eventually, I should be forgiven for the pain I have caused. Maybe then, I can forgive for the pain inflicted on me, in my life.

10   BEING A WOMAN—STAYING CONNECTED AND KEEPING IT ALL TOGETHER

Being in prison in Australia is a complex and confronting experience. It's different for everyone, though all terms of imprisonment have a lot in common. In this chapter I'll present a number of different points of view about a range of issues that come up to do with being in prison.

Even the term 'in prison' is an oversimplification, since men's and women's prisons are very different sorts of places and there is considerable variation between the various institutions—and even different sections of the larger complexes. Moreover, the prison system is dynamic and ever-changing. Rosa maintained that the Emu Plains she describes no longer exists. Due to the increase in the female prison population it is now more like Mulawa, and Dill-wynia is more like what Emu Plains used to be.

The entries below are in alphabetical order because I don't want to give you the impression that any one issue is more important than another, although some entries are longer than others simply because there was more information available about a particular subject at the time of writing. Read as a whole they should give a further idea of what prison is like experientially, and how the experience of being on the inside shapes prisoners, the people who work with them, and how the experiences relate to the world on the outside.

Prison also has its own language, and some definitions are explained below. The impression I get is that women's prisons are a strange sort of petty hell—more like a bureaucrat's idea of purgatory than an inferno. However you experience them, they're certainly not places where broken people seem to have a good chance at mending.

Americans:
Rosa: We pay for a lot of Americans. They come here, do their sentence and then get deported. What's unfair is that when they leave they're as free as a bird. They don't even have to sit out parole. ... Australia's a very lucky country for you if you want to import drugs. I read a book, *Twelve Years in a Bangkok Prison*. It's the only book I ever read and it was disgusting, some of the things that happened.

Appearances:
Rosa: There was a woman who came in one day. Big woman, covered in tatts. She looked scary. And all the other girls were shouting over her head, 'We don't want her in our room!' I was saying to myself, 'Please God, please don't let her in my room!' Anyway, she ends up in my room. But she ended up being a little girl in a big woman's body. She didn't have a clue. She was harmless.

Baab:

Derivation unknown, possibly short for Baba. A sort of affectionate term used when you're about to put someone down or ridicule them. Mulawa-speak in the nineties.

Being There:

Rosa: You know, [being there is] what the individual makes it. I could have made it hard for myself by getting involved with people who did drugs. Getting involved with another girl would have even made it harder for me. Just feeling sorry for myself and not accepting the situation would have made it hard for me. I did what I could to make the best of it. But it depends on who you are. Like, for Leona, Alfredo's wife, it was the most devastating thing that ever happened to her, but even she managed to get material to make curtains for her room and this was at Mulawa.

In jail I often felt as if I was walking in a bubble. I saw only what I wanted to see. I heard only what I wanted to hear. I just breathed in and out, in and out in my own little bubble. I think I was waiting for forgiveness, for all the sins I'd committed, or that I had to forgive myself for what I did to my family.

Bluey:

General all-purpose blue forms used for everything from reporting incidents to requesting services to making an application for anything in a system where everything has to be applied for.

Body Language:

I have heard that prisoners have real a talent for reading body language. Living in close proximity with people day in day out, where at any time someone could turn on you, and even kill you, puts a lot of pressure on you to develop this ability quickly. In the prison environment it pays to learn any way you can to avoid trouble.

Box Visit:

Visit in which the prisoner is subjected to a strip search prior to having to dress in a one-piece body suit. The prisoner's family must then talk to the prisoner through a glass or perspex barrier, as you see depicted in movies. No physical contact is allowed, a restriction which is terribly stressful and distressing in some cultures. Rosa in particular found box visits humiliating and did everything she could to avoid them.

Buy Up:

The prisoners' opportunity to spend money they've earned, or money their friends and family send them. There's a limited list of items and no single item can cost more than $100. Usually buy ups are for everyday items but once a month they get 'activity buy ups' where they can order things like cheap walkmans or shoes or CDs.

Rosa: I asked an inmate who'd been in a lot for recommendations about what I should get for buy up. She said toiletries, smokes and you could get extra food but if it went missing ... there's nothing you could do about it unless you wanted to break somebody's fingers with a door. They're big, steel doors. ... I've seen the injuries, but I never saw it happen. I did my first buy up. I got tweezers because my eyebrows were getting serious. I got nail clippers. Simple things, soap, soap holder, shampoo, razors, 'White Ox', the most disgusting tobacco of them all but everyone smokes them. Then I ended up liking it and I ended up getting hooked on it. A packet of tailor-mades—they're proper cigarettes, not rollies. They've not got many brands, but enough. I got my mother to bring some singlets, some more underwear, tracksuits with no labels or brand names. Once I got all that I was a bit more comfortable.

Children:

Women are allowed to look after only one child, up until the child is five years old. If you have more than one child, you have to choose. The other children either end up with a relative, friend or going through DoCS (Department of Community Services). The right to look after your child is not automatic. You have to apply for it. You have to be classified properly and installed at Jacaranda at Emu Plains, or Parramatta Transitional, the only institutions equipped to deal with children.

Christmas:

Kelli: It was Christmas at Lithgow. We were served pork. I saw something strange coming out of my friend's mouth. She spat out what she was eating and she had a mouthful of maggots. She starts screaming. She started spewing. All of them at the table start chundering. I thought it was hilarious because I was the only one who hadn't eaten yet. My friend said, 'This means war!' and organised everyone to barricade the dining room. We were furious. We demanded to see the Governor but he didn't have any time for us. We waited for hours. They brought in the Metropolitan Emergency Unit. They came through the roof. Forty of them against thirteen girls. They locked us up in our rooms. I covered my walls and ceiling in graffiti. That was my therapy.

Cliques and Ghettos:

Lee Rhiannon: At Goulbourn [a men's prison] the exercise yard is segregated, you have one section for Caucasians, other lots for the Lebanese, Asians, Aboriginals. The prison guards justify that by saying that that's the way to keep order. I've had a number of complaints from prisoners about this. Rosa: They actually encourage this because if you request to be put in with people who speak the same language as you they can't refuse you because that would be 'discrimination'. Farah: A lot of people choose to go into groups. But that's what stops them from advancing within the system.

Rosa: When I got a job as the education clerk I had to push away a lot of women who wanted things I couldn't give them. I never realised until I got out and one said to me, 'You used to be so stuck up.' What? I was just doing my job ... That's the problem if you mind your own business. If you keep to yourself who are you going to hear things from? How do you ever know what people are saying or thinking about you?

Clothes:

Geri: Family can send you clothes as long as it's green or white. You feel like a complete dag until you get some clothes of your own because prison issue is so ugly. It's really humiliating. They give you these volleys that have been bleached so many times by so many people that the white rubber's now all yellow. It's not a good look.

Communicating:

Joanne: You talk to other prisoners, or to the guards but that's it. You get visitors once or twice a week. Weekends. Letters get looked at. You get five-minute phone calls you have to pay for from what you earn. You have to apply. You only get allowed a certain number of numbers that you're allowed to call.

Daily Grind:

Eve: 5:00 am. A prison officer wakes you up by shining a torch in your face. I think everybody's like this. You're used to waking up to the sound of the keys jingling on the officer's uniform. Even after I left for a long time whenever I heard keys jingle I'd think it was the screws.

6:00 am. Muster. Then breakfast.

7:30 am. Work. Another muster.

12:00 pm. Lunch.

2:30 pm. Work ends.

5:00 pm. Locked in House. Dinner.

7:30 pm. Locked in cell.

Degradation:

Rosa: The most degrading, horrible thing was, right at the beginning having to share a room with someone while they went to the toilet. It was the smell more than anything. To make it worse I was sitting on the top bunk. The flavours rise. Leona, in her Bolivian way would say, 'My God, they should give us matches or something.' Later on in other cells we were in houses. Then, we could at least leave.

Dobbing:

Rosa: It might not always be wise to dob somebody in. It might not work to your benefit. You don't know where somebody is. You don't know when or if you're going to meet up with them again. You don't know what they're going to do to you if they find you. When I had my fight, the next day I've got this huge bruise which I try unsuccessfully to hide. They take me to the medical annex and they want me to fill in a bluey. They say, 'If you tell us what happened we can help you.' I tell them 'I've got four years nine months to do. I've only just started. The girl that did this to me is going to be in and out all her life. I don't want this burden hanging over me wondering what she's going to do. I don't want to live in fear.' So I just wrote on the form: 'accidentally hit chin'. The girl was in segro anyway. Dobbing her in wasn't going to put her in segro any longer. Once in segro you're supposed to go back to stage three, but when she got out she went straight back to stage one. There is no consistency in the prison system.

... When she got out of segro this girl ends up 'sending me a message' through another girl. This message was, 'If she looks at me again I'll smash her again.' All this did was make my remaining time at Mulawa really stressful. I didn't want to end up with a broken nose or a scar I'd be carrying with me the rest of my life. I started getting paranoid. A week went by and I was watching *Miracle on 34th Street* and started believing that maybe there really was a Santa Claus, so I figured I'd wish for something realistic. I wished I could get transferred to Emu Plains before Christmas, so I could have a normal visit and presents. I didn't want to spend a whole year before I could get presents again. I'm in the lounge the next day and through the window one of the guards points at me and draws a picture of an Emu on a piece of paper and puts it on the window for me to see. I got my transfer. It was Christmas Eve. I don't care what anyone says. I believe in Santa.

Drugs:

Linda: A girl came up to me once and said. 'Oh, I notice you're getting visits every weekend.'

'Yes.'

'No one would suspect you of bringing drugs in would they?'

'No.'

'Would you get a visit from my friend?' And I was so naïve I said 'What for?' The last thing I was thinking about was smuggling drugs into prison. And she says: 'You know. For a drop.' So I say, 'Look, I'm not going to tell my family not to come and see me.' [You're only allowed so many visitors]. 'If I let your friend visit me I'm going to have to tell them not to come. My family won't not come. They won't let me say 'no'. That's how I got out of that one. Putting it on my family. I wasn't the one who denied her. I used my family to get out of that one.

Eve: It's not that hard [to get drugs in prison] ... wrapped up in balloons, hidden in your mouth. You can pass it in a kiss. Or you can hold the balloon deeper in your throat and bring it up. You can practise with M&Ms .... But then it's up to me to get it in, undetected and then have the drug. I might need a syringe. ... Girls have them inside but they share them. They're really hard to get in. They have to be cut down and made smaller so that you can smuggle them in. But when you have one they're like gold. You're set for life. You'll get free drugs forever so that people can use your syringe. Needles usually get into maximum security because of transfers from minimum security when someone has done something wrong. They get really blunt and they do a lot of damage when you put them in, but at least it gets the stuff into your veins.

Rosa: I got my wires crossed once. I was at a compulsory education seminar about hygiene and drugs. This lady was telling me I had to bleach my spoons. I panicked because I hadn't been doing that and I thought I might have caught something. I didn't realise at the time she was talking about drug spoons. I thought she meant the spoons I'd been eating with ... I didn't know you needed spoons to do drugs! I was a coke head! What did I know about spoons?

Linda: There was a girl I shared with. I had tobacco but no paper. She got out a Bible to get papers from the pages. I said 'No way! You'd might as well shoot me now. I'm not smoking the Bible!' She said 'Why not? Everybody does it!' But I wasn't going to desecrate the Bible just so that I could have a rollie. So there were spare rolls of toilet paper in the room. You couldn't smoke the toilet paper but you could use the paper wrapping. You could make a bong out of a toilet roll. **Rosa:** Once the drug squad came in to Jacaranda to do a random search. It had been raining. They woke the kids up at two in the morning. There were dogs with muddy paws. The smell of wet dogs when they left was terrible. You just had to get the mess back together as best you could.

Education and Study:

Rosa: Once I had won my appeal and I knew that I only had eighteen months to go I really wanted to study. I put in a bluey but I had to wait for my case management meeting to come up so that they could say yes or no to my going for a business studies diploma. I did everything I could though to keep myself occupied. I did pottery, art, I learned to play the guitar. I did a drugs course. I did a course on Christianity. You're not really there to learn. You're there to get through the system. The system is there to teach prisoners who can't read or write how to read and write, or to get drug and alcohol counselling.

Food:

Emma: You've got to put up with cutting up raw vegetables with plastic knives. At some jails prisoners do their own cooking; at others, CSI, Corrective Services Industries, provides pre-packaged meals ... It's worse than airline food. Pre-packed sandwiches. You don't get to pick what's on them. You get whatever's given you ... Unless you're a diabetic, or a vegetarian or you've got an allergy you eat whatever's there. In some prisons a lot of what you got was pre-packaged stuff from CSI. Mulawa is right next to the Silverwater Men's Prison. There, male prisoners cook all these meals as part of their work. It's pretty disgusting ... I hardly ate any of it anyway. It was like really dry mashed potato and really dry fish. Frozen veggies, boiled. We called it 'food by the man next door'. I lost about five kilos from not eating.

Gate Gays:

Farah: You don't get conjugal visits in Australia, which is why a lot of women turn lesbian when they're inside. They're called Gate Gays because they're only gay 'inside the gate'. Gay women, or gate gays, were the only thing that gave me trouble while I was in jail. There'd be women who were attracted to me, then their girlfriends would get jealous. I made friends with a girl but her girlfriend thought I was going out with her. Anyway, this girl's girlfriend, she looked like a bloke. It was weird, at one point, it had been so long since I'd been with a man, I even looked at her and actually found her attractive! But it was just a thought that popped into my head. It's not like I dwelled on it or anything. But I remember thinking, 'Farah, what are you thinking. God, I must be desperate! Imagine what I'm going to be like when I finish my sentence!' I know that this blokey girl though would have liked to have had me, but she never got me. It would never have happened.

Getting Along:
Geri: All your relationships start with 'What are you in for? What did you do? Why are you here?' I usually said, 'Drugs'. Details could come later.

Getting Tipped:
Evie: If you were at Emu Plains and you were naughty you'd get sent back to Mulawa to that part called Dawn de Loas ... Standover tactics. You intimidate someone. So that's where all the worst women get sent. All the rubbish. That's why getting sent to Dawn de Loas is called 'getting tipped'. You have to get dobbed on, to be tipped.

Going Back, Recidivism:
Vera: Winter time you always will [get in trouble again if you're back on the streets]. In winter Juvenile Justice Centres are always packed because everyone comes off the streets to get three meals a day and a warm bed to sleep at night ... If you've been on the streets for a year, you get street smart. You know exactly what to do, how to do it and when to do it. I knew a lass once, the longest she ever lasted on the outside was three months. And she's doing exactly the same thing now in women's prisons.

Green:
Rosa: When you ask people in jail what's the colour they most hate, they say 'Green!' because they're just so sick of it. But once the circumstances change it's okay. I want a dark green lounge now. But you get flashbacks. The Blue Wiggle used to be green. To tell you the honest truth he looked as if he just came out of Long Bay. I think they changed him because they didn't want that association.

Home Brew:
Farah: You get white bread and you mix it with water, so it's like a sludge. You mix it with jelly crystals. So you've got yeast from the bread, and sugar from the jelly crystals ... You get very good at hiding stuff. They hid this batch in the laundry. They put it in a bucket that had had bulk laundry detergent in it. So they had this green sludge, like The Blob, I never saw it but I could imagine it ... And it's 90% alcohol. A group of women got drunk and there was a lock down. The officers said, 'We don't know who is going to do what under the influence. If we don't allow alcohol, it's to protect you.' That's when I finally realised, because I too tried to get some apple juice and make it nice by putting some Vegemite in it, but it didn't work ... Well, you know, in there, you'll try anything. I've even heard of people trying to inject Vegemite. I swear, they get that desperate for a fix. Eventually you could only get sugarless diet jelly because of the home brews, and for a while the whole jail was on Nutra-Sweet, and if you wanted to cook with sugar you had to ask the officers for sugar, just like you had to ask them for the knives.

Home Cooking:
Catalina: I used to do all the cooking. Maybe it has to do with my culture, but I couldn't sit there, having a meal and have everybody else watching. So I'd be cooking for all

of them, but I made a deal that I wouldn't be doing the washing as well. They were very appreciative because a lot of people in jails don't really have living skills. I'd been cooking since I was ten ... They were heavily into drugs, in and out and in and out of jail all the time. One girl was in and out four times in four years, doing six months here, nine months there? They didn't know how to do anything ... They were just very neglected kids ... At least they were getting a good meal. There was always a lot of food.

Oh, I could cook anything. Spaghetti bolognese was good, and stir fries were good because you only needed two pots. Shepherd's pie you only needed one. Whatever they ate a lot of, I just kept doing. I was even learning a lot of other dishes from some of the older Vietnamese women. [They were in for] drugs. Trafficking. Possession. One woman, a South American I met was in for twenty-five years for importing tonnes of the stuff. I liked cooking with her though. I was really doing it for myself, but I wasn't going to cook a little meal. That would've been pointless. At least I was getting my decent meal, once a day.

Hygiene:

Rosa: Anything for hygiene they give you heaps of. There's toilet paper, you see bleach everywhere, gallons of it. Soap, toothpaste, toothbrushes. They don't like to see people walking around dirty. But they won't supply you forever. Eventually you have to buy your own. They don't want to make things too easy else people take advantage. So the soap is one of those little soaps. You want a nice one? You buy it. You want flavoured toothpaste? You buy it.

Information:

Rosa: You just pick it up as you go along. You don't have a clue. They only gave me a booklet once with a whole bunch of addresses. 'This is Mulawa Correctional Centre, locked mailbag blah, blah, blah.'

Karma:

Rosa: I did headsets [the work that is repacking airline headsets] because a lot of Spanish-speaking women were in that section already. It was really funny because Leona was there too. The entire time I was on bail she was there. She looked all right ... It was strange meeting her again because I could have gotten them all into a lot of trouble but I didn't. I didn't tell the police anything that they didn't already know ... Leona knew this because there was nothing else put on her. Anyway I said hello and straightaway she started crying again. I said, 'Look. It's okay.' She said, 'What happened?' And I said, 'I'm guilty, that's what happened.' So she goes to her bag and gives me her stash of all her jams and coffees and sugars. And I thought, 'Is that all I get for keeping my mouth shut?' Later on she gave me a book. About being optimistic.

Locking Down:

If there's a major security problem in a prison the prisoners get locked in their cells and their houses for an indeterminate length of time.

Locking In:

Locking in is part of the normal routine in prisons. At five in the afternoon inmates are locked in their wings or houses. They can't get out but they are free to move within their houses. Inmates can also lock the doors of their rooms from the inside.

Maximum Security:

Linda: Everyone starts off in maximum security. It all depends on how you behave—how you progress through the system. Most girls aren't in Stage One, or Level Three for very long.

Meat Wagon:

Transport trucks that ferry prisoners between locations.

Linda: The walls are all steel. And the air-conditioning is freezing.

Medium Security:

Linda: Stage Two at Mulawa is a bit roomier than Stage One. You have more freedom. Your family can bring you stuff and you can go shopping. Stage Two is when you start to do courses. You also get metal cutlery, but it's blunt as. A butter knife is sharper.

MIN—Main Index Number:

All prisoners in New South Wales get a six-digit number and it's theirs for life. If you go back to jail, you're processed under the same MIN.

Misunderstandings:

Rosa: Then they put me in a room. Bed. Basin. Toilet. A window with chicken wire and bars looking out at bush. It's about nine o'clock at night by now. I'm told I'm only allowed out for one hour a day until they process me for the next section. But they only really allow me out the next day for breakfast, lunch and dinner. All I do is sleep all day. After being there for five days I wonder why I'm there. It's daylight. I don't know what time it is. There's a telephone so I ring the emergency number. Two officers come, so I say: 'Excuse me, but I've been lying on this bed for about five days. I haven't even been allowed out for a whole hour, to get exercise or something. My back is so sore I can't sleep.'

They started making a joke about it. 'Aaaah. You can't sleep. Maybe you'd like a Valium or some Rohypnol?' 'Actually I just wanted a Panadol, but, forget it.' So I turn around and they just leave.

The next day I ask someone else: 'Why am I here?' They say: 'Are you having suicidal thoughts?' 'No.' 'Are you threatening to kill yourself?' 'No.' 'Are you at the risk of harm?' 'No.' So they took me out and put me in Stage One. I was delayed a week ... I could've been there for ages. I don't know how long they would've forgotten about me. Later, I found out from one of the girls that that place was there if they thought you were going to kill yourself, or you were on drugs, or had a bad medical condition. Eventually I got an officer to talk to me and he told me that they'd received information that I was at risk of self-harm. I later found out that on the night I was transported to Mulawa I was sharing the meat wagon with six other girls. One of them was a Croatian who had tried to rob someone. She wasn't handling things well and kept threatening to kill herself. Her name was Mira. She looked a lot like me and they thought I was her ... The officers' job ... is to keep the peace and to let things go on, day by day. They don't worry about your health, or your work or whether or not you get an education. Their job is to make sure you don't get out the gates. That's it; and that's the end of it.

Minimum Security:

Rosa: When I was at Mulawa in Stage One there were four houses: A, B, C and D, and each house had fifteen rooms. Each house had a kitchen, with a refrigerator and freezer, a lounge room, a small dining room and an officer's room with a big perspex window so they can see you. It's dirty and it's got scratches but at least they can see. They give you all you need to cook: food, pots, pans.

Motherhood:

Rosa: At Emu Plains they have a special section for mothers. Seven houses with five rooms each at the time I was there. There were empty rooms when I was there so I got to stay with the mothers. It's called Jacaranda and if you're good you got to go to Jacaranda even if you didn't have a child. The people that didn't get to go there called it 'Suckaranda'. You can only have your baby with you until they're five. There was a German woman who was in for trafficking, she still had several years to go but her little girl was about to turn five and be deported. There was no one else who could take care of her in Germany so she made an application to be pardoned. She got it, she got her pardon. The women with children always got more privileges. They'd go on excursions during school holidays. They got an extra buy up for their children. They got more money. But it would have been hard for them. Kids are hard.

Moving:

Rosa: I moved about twenty times in the thirty months I was in jail. They never give you any notice. They just say, 'Pack up, you're going.' You have to put all you stuff into a blue garbage bag. You don't have any say. [Note: The DCS advises people visiting inmates to call the day before a visit to make sure their visitee is still at that prison.]

Mugs:

Linda: The mugs you got to use were plastic and they were all really disgusting. But some were porcelain. They were old but they were good. You couldn't just get them. You had to be given them by another prisoner, usually one that was leaving. Someone gave me one. I was so grateful! ... Some of them were Christmas presents. Some had been doing the rounds for years. They were the best way to have coffee. They were really valuable, mugs ... When I got out I found it really hard to deal with. I'd feel uncomfortable making coffee using my mother's mug. You couldn't touch some other prisoner's mug. It just wasn't allowed. You stole a mug. You were dead. They were very valuable things. Almost as valuable as needles. All you do there is smoke and drink coffee. So you at least want a good cup of coffee.

Muster:

Eve: Muster is like roll call. It's different in every jail. At Emu Plains all the houses have to show up in a cement quadrangle and be counted in a spot allocated for your house.

Offer Too Bad To Accept:

Kelli: At Mulawa I had a friend at the time who told me I had to see this new cell mate of hers. She said, 'Kell, you have to listen to this woman's story.' I went there and I met this woman called Mary. She's sitting on her bed, looking at the floor. She wouldn't even look me in the eye. 'So what's your story?' I ask. She bursts into tears and since she's already told my friend the story my friend tells me that in a couple of weeks there was this 'wicked' woman called Rosemary who was coming in. Rosemary, according to Mary, had been having an affair with Mary's husband. She'd already turned the whole jail against Rosemary.

My friend had told Mary that I was the best fighter in the jail and if she wanted anyone put in hospital she should talk to me. Mary then offers me $10 000 to put Rosemary into hospital.

She said that she had connections on the outside. Her 'connections' were Rosemary's husband and the cops that put her in there. Mary's story was all lies. It was Mary who had been having the affair with Rosemary's husband. They wanted Rosemary murdered before she came out because if she had any chance of getting out she was going to expose them all. I didn't know it at the time but I smelled something fishy about it. So Mary offers me ten grand to put Rosemary in hospital or fifteen grand to put her out altogether. I'm thinking, 'This is evil.' Fancy asking me that! I'm the protector. I'm watching this woman really closely. She never once looked at me in the eye. She gave me this really wimpy handshake.

I didn't say no; I didn't say yes. I said, 'I'll think about it.' Exactly two weeks after this proposition I met Rosemary. That morning we were going out for our first practice at softball. Someone pointed her out to me. I was expecting to see this really evil woman. I walked up to her and this wasn't the woman who'd been described to me. This woman looked angelic. At the time the universe was showing me she shone. The aura around her shone. It was all positive. This was the woman who was manipulative and had conspired to kill her own husband? That was crap. That very day I said, 'Hi, I'm Kelli.' She had soft hands but still gave me a firm handshake and I liked that. She wasn't a toughie. She wasn't showing any weakness either. I liked her vibe.

Everyone was hanging out of their windows or on balconies wondering what was going to happen. Gossip spreads like wildfire in jail. They were all expecting me to break this woman in half. Instead I said to everyone that anyone who lays a hand on her would have me to reckon with. From that day I stopped fighting. I still hold the record for the most charges in one day but after I met Rosemary the screws told me that I became 'boring'. They were a bunch of wankers. I had been giving them the excitement in their lives every day. Rosemary had been through hell. She'd had hot water poured all over her and God knows what else. I invited her to join the softball team.

Outings:
Rosa: After my punch up I got to go to x-ray. An officer took me and it was the first time I'd been outside in six months. It was so much fun! I heard the beep beep of the traffic lights. I missed that noise. When I heard that sound I just felt this great sense of loss.

Catalina: The whole system is set up so that you don't know whether to trust anybody. The officers don't know whether or not to trust the prisoners. But after a while I got so much trust I was trusted to go with an officer to go shopping for activity buy ups. It was like shopping therapy.

Pecking Order:
Vera: There's a pecking order in prisons. Murderers at the top, child molesters at the bottom. Women child molesters are very rare and they're in protection.

Pill Parade:
Rosa: The officers used to come, open the doors and shout 'Pill Parade' and shut the doors but then all of the girls would just bolt out the door, line up, go with an officer to the medical annex. Pill Parade was when everyone got their medication, whether they needed anti-depressants or Panadol or something. Pill Parade is one of the few opportunities you get to 'mingle' ... I used to go and get Panadol. They'd give you two at a time but I wouldn't always take them so I would stock up, so I wouldn't have to wait if I did get a headache.

Progressing:
Rosa: I was in max only for about five days before I was reclassified as a two—medium security. I think the officers in that first wing when you go to Mulawa [to make the assessment]. Stage Two had more room. And you had more freedom. [Note: Here and elsewhere you hear Rosa talk about Stage Three, Stage Two, Stage One. The Department of Corrective Services has a numerical system for classifying female prisoners. Women start at Stage Three, or Level Three: maximum and are progressively scaled down, depending mostly on how they behave. If they misbehave, they may get reclassified. Level Four is for those in Segregation or Protective custody.]

Protection:
Gerry: If you threaten to kill yourself, or if you think someone's going to hurt you, you get put in protective custody, where you're isolated. You can get put in a holding cell in a padded room with a camera watching you all the time. They only allow you out to eat, or for an hour of exercise, although you often don't even get that. [Note: This is what happened to Rosa as a result of a misunderstanding, although in her case the room had no camera, and no padding, she was just put in a room in the medical annex at Mulawa.]

Eve: Strict protection is like solitary confinement. They put you in a room underground and they only let you out at night so people who are in protection for a long time are so pale they look like ghosts.

Putting Up a Good Front:

Rosa: In our house we used to make picture frames out of cardboard and put our art up. One day we decided to polish the floor with cream cleanser. We 'borrowed' a polishing machine and discovered that the floor was white and blue tiles, not cream and green. Some days it would be over 40 degrees, so once we decided to wash the lounges. They dried in no time. We used to wash our curtains. We made stands from old lockers, sheets, plants that we grew in pots we had made and put pictures of our families on it. One of us became an aerobic instructor, one of us became a hairdresser. It's not easy. You take one step forward but if you make a mistake it's ten steps back ... It spread, our example ... But you have to keep doing it. We didn't have a clue but somebody had to do all these things. It was how we adapted to the situation. It was how we could wake up in the morning. It was our house that they used to show the commissioner whenever he came around.

Rights:

Australia is a signatory to the International Declaration of Human Rights. Unfortunately, in spite of all the press, such signings are little more than expensive public relations exercises because these international 'agreements' do not have the force of law. In the arrest process you are 'cautioned'. The police do not read you your rights because *in Australia you have no legally protected guaranteed right to free speech.* As a result you do not have the 'right' to remain silent. Whatever illusions about the rights that you believe that you may have, and whatever rights you may have, all seem to vanish after you are arrested. Ex-prisoners told me again and again that they had 'no rights' while in jail. Prisoners may not vote, but they still have the right to representation. They can, for example, write to or telephone a Member of Parliament.

Lee Rhiannon: But this is pretty unsatisfactory. Prison officers are listening in. You get this regular, distracting, 'beep' and you only get five minutes. It's hard to have a meaningful conversation in five minutes ... The figures show that the majority of people are in prisons for very short sentences, under six months. There's an increasing debate as to whether people should even go into jail for such short times ... I felt that being in prison was a life of deprivation, a very hard life. People have already been punished by losing their freedom, they don't need to be punished further by being housed under appalling conditions, being denied the right to have education, books.

Emma: You lose all rights when you go to prison. If you think you have a right, think again.

Rigmarole:

Vera: Everything in prisons is a rigmarole. When I want to initiate a program with a prisoner I have to go to the program manager to get a room allocated and document the details. Then the woman who wants to do the program has to fill in a bluey and write a paragraph repeating the information I've already given. The we have to wait to get it approved. Then when it's approved I get confirmation in writing. Everything you want in prisons is a rigmarole, but it's worth it ... You have to have a letter of approval, for everything you have in your bag. Every time you go in. That's why I don't take anything in except my diary, my lunch, and maybe a couple of biros. Depending on which prison I go to I have to have my car keys on a lanyard in my pocket or on a necklace around my neck ... I get screened every day when I walk into jail. It's all part and parcel of the day. I don't even think about it now. I have to get biscuits approved if I'm bringing in biscuits. These little things don't bug me ... It's part of the norm. It's part of life. You have to turn a blind eye and a deaf ear to it. If these things bug you, you're not going to do a day's work. You're just not going to cope.

Rosa: Everything has a form. Everything is structured. They don't want you creating trouble ... But where there's a will, there's a way.

Roomies:

Eve: The first time at Mulawa I was put in a room with two pregnant women. There was a bunk with a mattress on the floor.

Screws:

Rosa: I remember going to another section of the jail once and an officer says, 'Hello girls! Come to see the animals have you?' I mean they're dressed in green. We're in green. She's calling us animals too ... I think they've got personal issues in themselves. It has nothing to do with the jail system. They get paid good money and their job is very easy ... There were other officers that would be nice to you. They cared. Yet if you ask any officer they say that they prefer to work in a men's prison ... Why? Because women have big mouths. They talk back. They start arguing a point and they can argue for up to an hour. It won't work but they do it anyway.

Searches:

Joanne: Strip searches are really degrading. Cell searches, house searches. ... When you come off a visit you're strip searched, every time. They tell you to shake your hair. They look behind and inside your ears. Some women, if they are really overweight they have to lift up their boobs. You have to pull your underpants down to your knees then bend over. You even have to show them the soles of your feet.

Segregation (Segro):

Eve: Segro's a lot like protection but you're put in there if you've done something wrong, like gotten into a fight or you get caught with drugs. It's even harsher than protection because they only let you out to eat. Once you get out of segro you're reclassified as Level Three and you've got to make your way through the system all over again. You can't get anything into anybody when they're in segro.

Self Harm:

Rosa: A lot of people cut themselves in prison. I didn't but I had when I was twelve and

I understood why they did it ... You don't even know that there's pain in your body, but I got a piece of glass that I found in the park and I slashed myself and I used to love just watching my blood pour down. It was just so soothing, looking at it. I thought, 'Wow! What a relief!' ... It only hurts a week later when it starts healing. As you cut yourself and watch the blood pour out it's very soothing. There's this release. It's like you have this heavy, thick pain in your chest but once you cut yourself it's like 'Aaaaah. I can breathe again'. Then I just kept doing it.

Then I'd get artistic and do letters ... You watch the blood pour and it stops so you give yourself a little squeeze and it starts up again. How long it lasts, I don't know. I was very young at the time and I don't remember.

Smoking:

Rosa: You're not allowed to smoke in your room, but if you're in max they let you out for an hour of exercise. So you trudge out like zombies, walking around this tiny yard, walking in circles and smoking your cigarettes.

Stories:

Geri: You hear so many stories. One girl was in for manslaughter. She'd killed this guy who raped her daughter. Another girl was a manic-depressive; her grandmother was looking after her. Her grandmother was all she had in the world. One night the girl took some Rohypnol and she just stabbed her grandmother to death while she was sleeping. She did seven or eight years.

Liz: Girls don't walk into banks with guns. That's a guy thing. They'll hold you up with a syringe ... That's armed robbery.

Farah: There was this one girl. When she was fifteen or sixteen she was in a taxi-cab and the driver put his hand on her knee. She thought that he was going to rape her so she takes out a pocket-knife and stabs him in the side of the neck. The taxi driver turns his head and the knife cuts his jugular and he bleeds to death. The courts said that because she was carrying a knife that that just wasn't on. But this girl came from the country. There was a series of rapes in her home town when this happened. She was thinking, 'I'm a girl, on my own, in the country the police aren't going to be around if I get into trouble, I have to look after myself.' She gets this sleazebag cab driver. She panics. Wrong person, wrong place, wrong time. She got fifteen years.

Rosa: Not many people talk about where they come from. I believe that everybody in there has had problems. They're all broken people, with issues. They're all very delicate, I think. They won't really talk to you unless you've done a long time with them. You might talk to someone that's going to open up a whole can of worms for you and then tomorrow, they might be gone! So you can't confide in people.

... It's then like 'Why did I open up that can of worms, when it's so hard to let it out, for what?' When you do take that step you want to know that it's with someone that is going to be there to help, or who you know won't violate that trust.

Telephones:

Catalina: You're only allowed three numbers to call. And your calls can only be six minutes long. You can change the numbers but they have to check with the person taking the calls that they actually consent to you calling them. When you call someone they hear a recorded message 'You are about to receive a call from an inmate at Blah Blah Correctional Centre. If you do not wish to accept this call, please hang up now.'

Terms:

Geri: You've got long-termers and short-termers. Long-termers are fairly well respected because they know stuff.... Anyone who's been in there more than a year (is long-term). One year to do in Mulawa is a lifetime.

Urine:

Kelli: When I was in Mulawa they introduced random testing. All the 'leaders' of the Mulawa wings got together ... and we decided that we weren't going to have a bar of it. But when they start going around one by one they all caved in and submitted to the test. The head screw comes up to me with her entourage and says, 'Kelli, we have a situation here.' I said: 'Yes we have, Jonesy.'

'All we want is urine. Only your wing hasn't given urine.' I said, 'Jonesy, I'll do anything else you ask, because I like you, but no. This is a matter of principle.' She says, 'You realise this will mean losing all of your privileges, you'll have box visits and you'll lose buy ups. Is that you final word?' 'I'm afraid so, Jonesy.' So they left. ... It was all bluff. I lost my buy ups for two weeks but the girls all bought for me instead.

VIN:

Visitor Identification Number. Anyone visiting a prisoner in New South Wales gets allocated six-digit number and it's theirs for life. It doesn't matter who you're visiting or where you go when you're visiting a prisoner you'll need to take along some photo ID (or you'll be forced to undergo a Box Visit) and they'll look up your VIN, although getting through the red tape is a little easier if you remember your VIN in the first place.

Violence:

In adult jails the women seem to grow up a bit. They're more mature but then they have that nasty streak that will always try to get at someone when no one else is looking ... I haven't heard of rape. It could happen. Sooner or later you'd see someone acting out of the ordinary and something would have to happen. There are people cut up, but they're doing it to themselves. People get bashed up ... Just think of a bad cat fight.

Rosa: I didn't put myself in a position where someone would get aggro with me. But once there was this girl who got jealous because her girlfriend was spending a lot of time with me and this other girl. This girl was big, and she was a bully. Everybody hated her. She comes at me once when I'm in the kitchen and though I don't know it at the time, she's drunk from a home brew. I make eye contact with her, just by chance. She says: 'What the fuck are you looking at?'

'I'm not the fuck looking at nothing,' I say. That's how you've got to talk when you're in prison.

She says, 'Yeah, you were, you were looking at me and now I have to smash you.' So she climbs over the kitchen table and punches me in the mouth. I'm stunned. But then she just ran away and hid in her room. It was just so quick I'm, like, 'Where's my fight?' And I hear her, like, chanting, 'I smashed her! I smashed her!' And I see all of these faces peering at me from the little windows that they've all got in their rooms. I just went to my room and didn't talk to anybody. While I was in the room, that woman went around punching a whole lot of other people. A few hours later the authorities had a lock down on account of the home brew drunks. That was the only fight I got into while I was in prison.

Eve: Once, at Emu Plains there was a group of girls watching this big girl kicking this small girl around on the ground like a soccer ball. We broke it up and the girl doing the kicking, who was high on something, some pills, said it was because this girl left her mug in the sink. So this big girl smashed the small girl's mug. The girl's upset that her valuable mug is smashed and 'starts' the fight with the big girl, but the big girl smashes the small girl up. Thing is, the small mug girl is an Aboriginal, and trust me, you don't want the Aboriginals after you because a) there are a lot of them and b) they stick together and stick up for each other. It didn't take long for the Aboriginals to get their revenge. One of them pulled the big girl off a tractor and just started smashing the girl's face again and again. The officers broke it up but after that the big girl was on the black list. She was an outcast. They ended up dobbing her in for the drugs and she was tipped back to Mulawa.

Six months later she came back to Emu Plains and I didn't even recognise her because she lost so much weight because of the huge amount of drugs she'd been taking. Once I saw a girl in the toilets getting bashed— constant uppercuts to the face. She was just copping it all. When it was over she just washed her face, fixed her hair and straightened her clothes. A few weeks later I saw the damage, her face was all black and blue. I asked her, 'Are you all right?' She said, 'It's okay. It didn't really hurt me.' She was one of the girls that come in and out all the time. She was constantly getting treated like that. I don't know what her story was but for her being bashed was okay, in her world.

Visiting:

The conditions under which visitors are allowed to see prisoners are often difficult. Sometimes family and friends simply stop visiting because of the time and expense involved. In November 2004 the State Minister for Justice opened a new multi-million dollar visitors centre at Dillwynia.

Lee Rhiannon: At first glance that sounds great, but what that money has been poured into is all this new search equipment. So before people even get in there, it's very intimidating. Visitors are searched by dogs. There's a whole rigmarole, even fingerprints. It adds up to an atmosphere that is very disturbing.

Children in particular, visiting their parents, often spend a lot of energy putting on a good front and trying not to cry.

Visits can get complicated. Some people spend days travelling to visit someone and have to call long distance every one of those days to verify that the person hasn't been moved. It's not easy for the prisoners either. In maximum security or other instances prisoners are required to strip completely, get into a large set of white, baggy overalls that are tied tightly round the neck to minimise hiding anything. The clothes go into a locker and the key goes in a bag that hangs from a bag tied to the back of your neck. You're family and friends see you looking like a demented, over-sized toddler.

Rosa: One woman—she was like a one-woman distribution centre for Drugs—invited me into her room. She had an apple that she'd converted into a bong. It had a cone inside it. I tried to 'politely refuse'. I didn't want to get caught in a urine test because my visits were too important to me and if I'd been caught I would have had to do twenty-one days of box visits. One week my brother forgot his ID so we had to do one of those. You're in a room with this wall between you. It's awful if you come from a culture where you hug and kiss. I didn't want to put them through that. I told this woman that I didn't want anyone hassling me about it so she was cool with that. At Mulawa we were allowed three hour visits, Fridays, Saturdays and Sundays. At Emu Plains the visits were Saturdays and Sundays from nine to five. You could have as many visits as you wanted, but only four people at a time. You could wear your own clothes and the strip searches were random.

Volleys:
White rubber-soled shoes made by Dunlop. Prison issue footwear.

Waiting:
Eve: Everything you do has to be approved. You have to wait for approval. You can't go anywhere on your own. You have to wait for an officer to escort you. They say to you, 'Pack your room, because you're moving.' You could be packed and ready four, five hours until you go. You want your drugs from the Pill Parade? You wait. You want to see the dentist, the doctor, the nurse—you've got to wait. You're at a gate, you've got to wait for some officer to unlock it, and they do it in their own time. You could never get anything up front, as soon as you wanted it. They call it the Waiting Game.

Withdrawal:
Kelli: What's withdrawal like? Imagine the worst 'flu you've ever had in you life, times a thousand. Everything hurts, everything aches—your head, your muscles. Withdrawal is awful. It's withdrawal that keeps a lot of people hooked, because you don't want to go through that. It's a real barrier to healing.

142

Work and the Prison Economy:

Farah: At Emu Plains you could work in the nursery. You had clerks. I got a job as the education clerk. I got $30 a week for being there from nine to three. They had cows that provided milk for the whole prison system. The girls working the dairy got up at three in the morning and at six in the afternoon to milk the cows. They got $50 a week. The industries clerk who looked after all the girls' pay got the top job at $60 per week. You got more buy ups at Emu Plains than at Mulawa. You could buy a television set for $300, but you had to buy it through the prison system. There was only one model. You can't have everyone getting different things in prison. It causes problems.

Geri: The sweeper is the girl who's in charge of cleaning the wing. You get about $20 a week for that. It's a job with trust because you also get to clean the officers' office. ... You ask the officers (to get that job) ... They decide. These are the things you could do at Mulawa—you could do a course and get some education. You could go to headsets. This is when all the headsets from the plane companies come in bags. We untangle them and change the muffs and seal them up again. And for every fifty headsets you get—wait for it—twenty-five cents! ... We called it rolling the headsets, because you had to roll the cords up to put them in their bags. We were machines. We'd do fifteen bags of fifty at a shift. It was the only way you made any money. On a good week you'd get $30.

Only two people were allowed to take in the headsets and sort through them because sometimes you'd get little bottles of alcohol ... There'd be cameras watching you all the time anyway. There were four women at each table, and twelve tables to a room, and there were four rooms ... But if there weren't enough headsets, there was no money. You could work in the nursery, potting seedlings ... The nursery just paid you $30 a week for doing what you have to do. But if you had to leave work even for a minute, you'd be docked. It didn't matter if you had to go to the doctor or anything.

Jenny: When I was at Mulawa there was a paper making class. They set up a business selling cards, made from recycled paper, to all the other prisoners. The painting I did ended up as a print on their most popular card. They wanted to give me a percentage but I told them that I wanted them to keep the money to help them get materials.

Working the System:

Eve: I was sharing a room with this girl at Mulawa. She was transferred to Emu Plains while I was at work, so while I was at work she stole everything I had: from the soap to my underwear. I came back to my room. It was stripped bare. I asked the officers where this girl was and they told me ... Anyway this girl was afraid that I would do something to her so she put a hold on me and stopped me from getting transferred to Emu Plains until she had left.

Writing:

Vera: Anyone from the general public can ring up Sentence Administration and say, 'Can you give me the MIN number of Jane Doe? Her birthday is 'blah, blah' and then write to them care of the correctional centre they're in. They have to do that. It's public knowledge. If you don't have a birth date you can generally get by with just a name, unless it's Jane Doe. Or you can write to the Prison Fellowship (see address in Appendix at the back of this book).

No one is an island, but prisons come pretty close to being isolated worlds that are nothing like the rest of the society that supports them. Prisons are intense environments that demand rigorous standards of behaviour that have little or no value in the outside world. This is deeply ironic, in that prisons aspire to achieve 'corrections' but the endless rules and regulations you need to follow, and the games you need to play to survive in prison, actually train you to be maladjusted for the outside world. How then are prisoners helped to readjust to our reality on the outside?

X: My understanding is that there's very little support for prisoners returning to normal life.

Vera: It's there, but you've got to dig deep to find it.

And even when you do find help it can be very limited and limiting.

Eve: I'm in a refuge at the moment and it reminds me so much of prison every day is a struggle. Even the windows have bars.

X: But there is hope that you'll get housing.

E: In the meantime I just have to bide my time.

———

After over two years in prison Rosa had to spend a year in a halfway house, the Parramatta Transitional Centre. It was the outside, but her life was as controlled as it had been during her bail. Even her last day inside Emu Plains had been problematic.

Rosa: The day I left a woman's mother died. She was a wreck, hysterical. I wanted to stay and help but I couldn't stay because I had to go. I felt terrible because I wasn't able to help.

When I first got out I noticed how stinky the road is and how everyone was wearing different clothes. At one point I was crossing the road and thought I was going to get run over. I'd lost the ability to judge distances. All the distances in prison are short. I'd lost the skill of crossing the street. I was put in a room where I couldn't sleep for days because of the traffic noise. I hadn't heard traffic for years. Prisons are quiet places. In that way they're good. You can get your thoughts back into place. Walking was amazing. You never go for long walks in jail because you just walk around and around in circles, but it's hard to walk in your shoes because you've been wearing Volleys all the time and you've been wearing tracksuits for so long that when you wear real clothes it doesn't feel right.

X: Do friendships last, outside of prison?

R: No. Everyone comes from a different world. Everyone in jail has problems. Big problems. And when you get two broken people together you just start brewing up problems.

X: What you're saying is that broken people can't mend broken people.

R: They need whole people. They don't need to be living in the same way that got them to where they are. Like, when you're in a refuge you're full of other broken people and you get depressed. Your body feels like lead. You don't want to get up.

My relationship with a lot of my family changed too. They said to me 'You know, Rosa, a lot of our lives have changed because of what's happened to you.' One of my cousins didn't value anything, but when he saw what had happened to me he said, 'Hey, that could be any of us'. I told them about a lady who had had a drink in a club, got into a car, it was raining and a drunk guy just ran in front of her and was killed. She was in for manslaughter. It was just an accident. Just a mistake. She wasn't over the limit. She wasn't even drunk but because she had alcohol in her she did eighteen months because the drunk's family wanted 'justice'.

A lot of my family came to me and started admitting some of the things that they'd done.

X: You became a 'Mother Confessor' for the whole family?

R: They were saying, 'Don't feel rejected by what happened. We've also done wrong; we just didn't get caught.' Someone told me that they found some credit cards once and just went shopping with them. They never got caught. But I still felt bad about what I'd put my family through. You know my mother and my younger brother? I don't think they ever missed a weekend to visit me. They used to give me money and I hated it. I felt that I didn't deserve it. So I was lucky that when I was in the halfway house I had finished my first year of TAFE and I got on a work release program and got a job. You know, when I was finally released I couldn't even get a Centrelink 'get out of jail' payment of around 200 bucks because I had saved up $1000 from working for almost a year.

X: So you were 'punished' for being effective.

R: I couldn't even get housing because the government said, 'You're working, you're studying.' My work was giving me, what, $200 a week and I was paying rent to the halfway house.

X: So you were penalised for doing what everybody wants ex-prisoners to be doing.

R: They even gave me a budget. I'd get my money but would get told how much I could spend on cigarettes. I wanted to buy a $50 handbag and they wouldn't let me. They wanted me to buy a crappy $15 one. I had to justify my expenses to my caseworker. But she'd named her son 'Che Guevara'. What does that tell you? I argued that the $50 one would last a lot longer and look better. She told me I was being 'passive aggressive'. They wouldn't let me spend my money. Another thing I hated was that on weekends we'd have to do gardening but it was on weekends that men would be doing periodic detention at the nearby jail. They'd call out and wolf whistle. It was awful.

At the end of my year, because of my parole conditions I had to reside with my mother. But I never felt right there because my stepfather had turned my brother's room into a computer room, my brother moved into my old room and I ended up having to share my room with him. By the end of my sentence I had my own room, my own space and suddenly, wham! I started to wake up in the morning, furious. I was paying rent at home, cleaning the bathroom and I was never consulted about any changes, like when my stepfather changed the shower head to this dinky little sprinkler. It drove me crazy. All these little things piled up. I started getting panic attacks. I had a nervous breakdown after six months. I'm still on medication.

X: Were you afraid of being released?

R: I wanted to be released because I wanted my freedom, but because I hadn't had my freedom it was a scary feeling. I couldn't remember my freedom. Even before I went to prison I couldn't see past my hand. So even then I didn't have the freedom that I was longing for. When I was finally leaving the Centre I was so scared my legs started shaking. I kept asking myself, 'What am I going to do? I'm going to be on my own. I'm going to have to make it by myself.' X: You'd learned to be dependant, because everything was regulated. R: 'Institutionalised' is probably the term.

X: How long do you think it takes before you get institutionalised. R: It all depends on the person. If you accept everything you become institutionalised very quickly.

X: And you're a very accepting person. But when you were on the outside how did you accept freedom? You don't sound as if you found freedom all that easy to accept. R: Not as I was walking out. You don't know if you're going to be all right, you think that something tragic's going to happen.

The Community Restorative Centre in Broadway in Sydney specialises in helping ex-prisoners adjust to life on the outside. Their services are free to anyone with a MIN number.

V: We do whatever we can. We can help them access resources, we can help them fill forms. We really assist them with the daily grind. That's how they feel. I visit the girls at home, see how they are, see how they're doing. The temptation is to go 'I see what you need, blah, blah, blah' but some women aren't even up to that first step.

X: Where are they up to then? V: It really depends on whether or not there's someone waiting for them when they get outside. Most of them don't have anyone. Initially they're excited when they get out because they're out, but then it hits them that they have nothing except the clothes on their back and their release certificate and maybe half a Centrelink payment. The jails are supposed to look after them but they're under-staffed. At a jail there may be hundreds of women and only two welfare staff. It's very under-resourced. The woman may have a phone number of an old crony but that old crony may be the reason that they got into jail in the first place. They may know that they shouldn't be hanging around with them but they're the only friends they've got.

They've got nothing, but they won't always appear that way because they want to be tough and strong.

X: Like they've learned to be in prison.

V: A lot of them get through by teaming up. They'll wait for their gal pals to get out of prison but, temporarily, they've lost that support. Nevertheless, we have to step back and let them tell us what their needs are.

X: Why do you have to step back? Why can't you just say, 'I know what's best for you because I've not only seen you I've seen hundreds of other people'? Why wouldn't that approach work?

V: A lot of the women have never learned to look after themselves. They've never learned how to love themselves or anybody else so it's like telling someone that they've got to learn Japanese, because I know that Japanese will get you further. They just won't get it.

X: It's out of their frame of reference.

V: They've never learned how to 'make it'. Nobody's ever shown them. It takes me a long time to get the women to care.

X: So what are the techniques that you use to get women who have never learned to care enough about themselves, to love themselves, to care enough to make it?

V: I'm often not sure after one year, two years, whatever, that anything I've done is working, because the very first thing that I'm very conscious of is that they don't trust you. I mean, if my girls do a crime while I'm helping them, I don't tell. We're not policing people here. We're here to assist them. I encourage them not to commit crimes, but they have to trust first, and that is huge.

X: Trust is the big issue—more than anything. You trust and then doors begin to open. Light trickles in?

V: And they start to listen. They've lost trust and, as you know, once you lose trust it's very difficult to get it back again. So I'm there for them.

X: And that's important too—that continuity—because they've been shoved from one relationship to another, one institution to another, one helpful agency to another.

V: And some of those people are not very helpful. All talk, no action. We're a unique group of people. We deliver. It's like people out there in the world, they don't connect to the caring thing. They'll hear about all the bad things that have happened to these women and they say, 'Oh, that's terrible' but they don't think about it after, because 'they're bad and I'm good and that's why they're in jail and I'm not' and they don't want to associate with people who have been in jail because they're not 'my sort of person' and they're 'all terrible and dangerous people'.

X: So you provide trust and continuity.

V: I spend time with them and they can't believe I mean what I say. I help them with grief counselling because a lot of them have family that die while they're in jail. I help them stay on methadone because a lot of them don't want to be on methadone because your saliva dries up and your teeth fall out and it makes you feel crappy so I get them dental appointments, drug and alcohol counselling, housing.

X: So the fact that you can get them concrete help is enormous.

V: They're so used to people saying they'll do something and then nothing happens.

X: So the default assumption is that you are just another bag of hot air.

V: But they also sometimes don't turn up to appointments.

X: They don't take responsibility.

V: Their lives appear to be a day-by-day thing. In prison you know exactly what's going to happen. The day is planned for you.

X: Every Tuesday is just like every other Tuesday.

V: Which is totally unlike the real world.

X: So you could argue that the prison system conditions you to behave in a way that is totally maladaptive to the real world.

V: Oh, yes. Absolutely. And prison will affect you differently if you're forty-five and this is your first time, or if you've been in and out all your life.

X: What's the difference?

V: I've got girls that really push to move on. They're trying to get work or to go to college, but there's like this invisible rope around your neck. They're still carrying the ball and chain. Somehow, being in prison has done something.

X: A lot of them seem to imagine that there's an aura around them, that somehow people will be able to spot them. And they may be right, but I think it's a body language thing and others pick up a subconscious cue.

V: I don't think that the general public would spot them, unless it's really obvious and they're covered in tattoos.

X: But that's part of the ball-and-chain isn't it? Self-inflicted.

V: But the girls that are trying to get on with their lives aren't covered in tattoos.

X: Then what is it?

V: In jail you get told what to do and apart from putting your own clothes on, everything is done for you. So everything that you and I do, the stuff that we just get on with, is all too hard. They've got to go to too many places, talk to too many people and put on the nice face.

X: All those facades we put on subconsciously, but they've lost that.

V: They've never had that. They've never learned that.

X: Who is this 'they', the classic criminalised, institutionalised woman?

V: About 90% of the female prison population. And it's been done to them. They had no responsibility over their criminalisation or their institutionalisation.

X: Aside from the responsibility for the crime that got them there in the first place.

V: And even there, about half do and half don't take responsibility, anecdotally. Some say, 'I know why I did it. I was broke. I was desperate. I was hanging out for my shot.' The other half don't last because they're angry. Angry about poverty. Angry about domestic violence. They're unable to get up or do any creative thinking that could make them see a silver lining in the midst of all that bleakness. Somehow they have to find their way. And a lot of my girls in moments of exasperation say, 'Fuck it. I'm going to go back.' Especially when they have no one. A lot of men have women waiting for them, but a lot of women don't have men.

X: That's just what happens in society though. It's been my observation that prison is just like the outside world, but with the volume turned up. If there's an unresolved thing in society in general, it will show up in prison. The sort of petty abuses and power plays that happen in prison happen in the outside world all the time, but in prison there's nowhere to hide, nowhere to run away.

V: It's a great wake-up call to society, but nobody wants to hear what prisons are telling us. Prison does absolutely reflect what's going on in society, what happens in jail and what happens to women and men. If you talk to the staff member who works with men, she'll tell you that it's so much easier dealing with them. It's not that men have fewer issues, it's that, being men, they don't talk about it. Men will say, 'I'm okay. I just need somewhere to live, and I'll be right.' Women will tell you everything on every level that they need and there are many, many levels. I talked to someone that had worked in men's and women's jails and he said, 'The women are driving me mad. They're just so needy!' **X:** Men are equally needy but they tend to anaesthetise themselves with drugs and alcohol and give themselves cirrhosis because they repress everything. **V:** Women do the drugs and alcohol too but they talk more. In normal society women operate on a lot more levels because we are a lot more people. We're a transitional worker; we're a mother; we're a lover, a sister. Whereas men don't reflect as much.

X: I'm trying not to feel insulted about having a penis. But who cares? I'll deal with it, because I'm a male and I'll repress it and die of prostate or testicular cancer on average ten years before the average women. She'll be right, mate.

V: Women also tend to miss their support systems more. I've known instances of families that have lost face, and they don't want any more to do with them. Or they just expect their children to just get on with it. No rehab, no counselling. Nothing. Some cultural expectations are: 'Okay. It's in the past. I don't want to hear any more about it.'

X: The last two years didn't exist, you were away 'on holiday'.

I wondered what might be the hardest part about being outside. I had a clear idea of where Vera stood on the matter so I asked Rosa.

Rosa: The hardest part was the temptation: to take drugs, to do the wrong thing. I saw so many people taking drugs in jail but I turned away from it but it was something that I wanted—maybe to shut out all the pain.

X: It sounds strange. It's as if you were stronger in jail than when you got out.

R: It's because in jail I had a purpose.

X: What was the purpose in jail?

R: I didn't want to get a box visit. I saw the effort my mother and brother went to every week to visit me. If I'd taken drugs I would've risked getting a box visit. That would've been the worse thing I could do to them. But outside, what was my purpose? It didn't matter where I stood, on what ground anywhere, I felt I didn't belong. Don't you ever feel like that?

X: All the time. I feel as if I come from somewhere else and I know what life is like without all this craziness I see around me and the only reason I'm here is to remind myself just how bad it can get. One of the reasons I'm interested in writing this book is because I'm trying to find an answer to the question 'Why do people behave so atrociously to each other?'

R: I believe it's because they don't know any better. It's their normality and they believe it's okay. It's when men abuse women. They think it's normal. One thing I want to let people know is that people in prison are people with problems. In childhood they have been demoralised, abused—even men, even rich kids because some of them, they're the most neglected. If you're brought up by nannies, who's your role model? Even if you aren't, who's your role model?

X: So people in prisons have had crappy childhoods?

R: And they don't know any better. They don't feel worthy of anything better. You end up in jail because you feel so unworthy that you're supposed to be there. After I got caught I felt the same way. I know what damage drugs can do to people. I had an uncle that died of an overdose, a cousin who, well, he was depressed but maybe it was all the dope that he smoked and all the coke he took that made it easier for him to pull the trigger. I worked to support my habit but some people have to get so much, they're so out of control that they have no choice but to become prostitutes and sell themselves to support their habit. And it becomes a vicious circle because they need more drugs to get them through being a prostitute.

X: I'm depressed. I'm alone. I'm looking after number one all the time. I'm a prostitute. I don't really like it very much but I'm making all this money. I spend all the money on drugs because it makes me feel better. But the more I take the less it works so I need more money for more drugs so I do more tricks so I get more depressed and at the end of the day ...

R: You end up in jail because you start stealing or dealing to support your habit. It's the same with a gambling problem. You'll spend all your money, but you got your high. If you mix gambling and drugs your health suffers.

X: Your brain doesn't work properly because it's polluted by all this chemistry.

R: You end up in jail. Sooner or later.

X: So now that you're out has it gotten better? Has it gotten worse?

R: You know what makes me sad. There's no common courtesy anymore. People don't even stand up for pregnant women on buses or trains. Even school children don't bother. But still, I don't even know where I'm going.

X: Do you think that's true of a lot of ex-prisoners, that they don't know where they are going?

R: Where are you supposed to go? What are you supposed to do? Even when you behave decently you get screwed. Don't get me wrong. I haven't lost hope, but with ex-prisoners it's, like, you could be working, but what are you working for? Not many people who end up in jail had hopes and dreams to begin with because, obviously, if you had hopes and dreams you wouldn't have ended up where you were.

X: Because you would have been too busy pursuing those dreams. But it's been my experience that lots of people don't have hopes and dreams.

R: They'll be in jail soon.

X: If they aren't in some sort of prison already.

R: You need something.

12   CHANGING THE SYSTEM

There are a lot of people out there who do not believe that prisons are 'good things' and that there is a rather large gap between what prisons aspire to do, that is, to 'correct', and what they actually accomplish. After having listened to so many women talk about their experiences I had to ask Liz the obvious question.

X: It's called 'Corrective Services'. Where's the correction?
L: It's there.
X: What does the correction look like?
L: A good officer is a correction.
X: What else?
L: Good programs. But you see it's hard to get through all the rules and regulations.

———

I think many people perceive 'the system' to be the 'baddy' in all this. Few people appreciate though that the system is made up of many people trying to do their jobs. The system is also capable of being victimised and abused. It should be pretty obvious by now that when you abuse people, they become abusers.

What's less obvious is that when you abuse systems the systems also become abusive.

A system is like a machine: if you don't maintain it properly, or if you damage it with exploitation or misuse, you will get hurt. You too will become a victim of an abused system.

This is true regardless of why or how people designed the system in the first place, or what the rationale is now to maintain it as it becomes increasingly dysfunctional, as all systems must, over time, if they fail to adapt.

What justification is there then in people's minds for maintaining prisons. I asked Terry, 'What crimes fit the punishment?'

T: There'll always be fraud.
X: Is jail the best answer for fraud? Why not community service?
T: Fraud's pretty bad. The money's got to come from somewhere. People seem to think that it's okay to defraud Centrelink, but it's the honest person who's desperate and can't get a payment because they've got no ID. Centrelink makes the rules to stop fraud but then honest people get turned back because they can't get around the rules.

X: This then gets us into the broader issue of 'law and order'. We make rules to protect ourselves but the rules then get in the way of reasonableness and justice. **T:** People exploit systems of social welfare so the social welfare services have to create barriers and assessments to make sure you're legit.

X: And setting up those barriers and assessments takes time and resources better spent on actually helping people.

So some of this whole issue is about theft and abusing the system. Whatever the system is. People abuse society's rules and go to jail. The courts abuse the Corrective Services system by putting people in jail who really don't belong there. Offenders abuse the Corrective Services system by committing crimes so that they can treat jail like a winter hotel. Citizens abuse democracy by caring more about some American actress' love affair than what's happening to their neighbour to screw her up so much that she ends up going to jail.

We all have to face the reality that we are, all of us, dealing with each other in a society and in a system of criminalisation bound by history and historical inertia and that it is our indifference that gives that inertia its power.

In the criminal justice system things tend to stay the same and change slowly. Why? I asked Green MP, Lee Rhiannon, in order to get a political point of view.

X: What can you do, as an MP to initiate change? What can you do to help a prisoner?

Lee: Individual MPs are limited. As an individual MP there are opportunities to ask questions of Ministers, make representation and to try to get accurate information, but I'd have to say it's limited. History shows that change comes about by people working together, by people struggling together, by being outspoken and taking a radical stance. That's certainly needed when it comes to prison reform. Prison reform is lagging behind other improvements we've made as a society. Sydney was a penal colony and while things aren't quite as ruthless as they used to be it's still pretty bad.

X: Who has the power to change things? Who ultimately has the power to say, 'This has to stop, and I'm telling you to stop it, and you will do this now.' How does that work in a democratic society?

L: Power is held by the state. On one level you'd say that power lies in the government and its agents. But history demonstrates that social change comes through people's movements. Our public education system wasn't the good idea of a politician, it was people in society campaigning for that, pressing for that, talking about the need for that. Then politicians are willing to change the laws. It's the same with environmental laws and occupational health laws. That isn't happening at the moment with prison reform.

X: But what you're saying is that even with the movement, politicians may change the laws but they can't change the attitudes of the people at the coal face.

L: We can pass laws and assign money but that power that politicians have not only comes from the ballot box but the movements that make up our society. To this date the social movement for prison reform has not had a strong voice.

X: If I am a person in a position of power there are so many things to do just to get through the day, the only way that I will listen is if the wheel squeaks really loudly. But if, as a citizen in a democracy, I wanted to change one thing in a prison, how would I go about it? Who do I talk to? Who can ultimately say, 'This is ridiculous. This has got to stop!'?

L: It would be an interesting question to put to the Minister because one thing that I am noticing more frequently with ministers, particularly when it comes to issues of prisons and police is that, you ask them a question and they say, 'That is an operational matter, it has nothing to do with me. I just set the policy.' So you talk to the operations people, like the Commissioner of Corrective Services, and you try to speak to those.

X: They say it's up to the Minister to set policy.

L: That's why you've got to get out on the streets and rattle the chains. It's not a linear process.

X: It's also a discontinuous one. You have one status quo, where everything tends to be the way it's 'always' been, and then a revolution where you get 'chaos' and then a new, stable, hopefully better state. It remains a fundamental question though. Ultimately somebody's got to say 'yes' or 'no' to something. Who is that person and why aren't they saying it?

L: Take the Roseanne Catt case. She fought.

X: How?

L: In a variety of ways. She had a very strong support group outside. They set up a website. I met her when I visited Mulawa as part of our enquiry. Our committee met with a group of prisoners and a point came when the prisoners asked the male committee members to leave, because the prisoners wanted to speak to the female MPs on their own. It was an unusual situation and it annoyed some of the prison officials. We were alone with those prisoners about an hour. Among others, Roseanne talked to us in detail about her case. Eventually the authorities decided to release her early. Her case demonstrates what I was talking about earlier. If Roseanne had been on her own, without the support base, she would have probably served her full sentence.

X: So it's almost impossible to change things if you're acting alone unless you are extraordinarily powerful. L: Or have money.

X: Another form of power. But connections imply a support base, but if you don't have them, you have nothing.

L: We hear of some horrendous cases. There's a whistleblower in Goulburn who fell foul of the authorities and his life is just a total mess. You would have to assume that there are some people inside who are innocent. Who knows?

X: Well that's the question. Who does know? Is there anything in the system that looks at this.

L: There was something that the government called the 'Innocence Panel' but that fell by the wayside. Sometimes you don't get much government cooperation. I remember certain people involved in our enquiry making inappropriate and derogatory remarks about the Catt case. I was left with the impression that they were using their position inappropriately to attempt to discredit her. Why? I don't care to speculate.

X: It's hard to get honest answers?

L: You don't hear much about prisons in the paper at the moment. The government has been very good at that. Prisoners tell me all sorts of things. The number of times they get locked down is simply unacceptable. Like at Goulburn, they have a lock down once a week. On those days they're confined to their cells for about twenty-four hours. This is unacceptable. Partly it's because there are insufficient officers, but partly it's because it suits them. When the prisoners are locked down the officers have a relatively easy day. That's what the prisoners tell me. I'll put the question to the Minister about the number of lock downs.

X: How does that work?

L: I put the questions in on notice, because the Minister will not have the figures on hand, and I know he wouldn't answer me in the House, that means that on notice, he'll have thirty-five days to answer.

———

In a political system where it takes *over a month just to ask a question*, you can't hold your breath on a purely political mechanism of prison reform.

Notwithstanding the efforts of compassionate and enlightened MPs, in the absence of a cohesive or even coherent policy/operation strategy from the people that we're paying to come up with one and to actually implement, what can be done at the 'lower levels' of power? Inevitably I had to talk to the people who actually have to deal with all this political and administrative schizophrenia at a day-to-day level.

X: What about change at the coal face? What would you do?

Vera: Dillwynia is supposed to be the new model of what a women's prison is supposed to be like. The women who go to Dillwynia have come from all the other prisons throughout New South Wales. In these other jails the culture is that the prisoners don't think for themselves, but when they come to Dillwynia they've got to drop that, because the culture of Dillwynia is that the prison officers have to respect the prisoners, they're not allowed to speak rudely to them. Inmates are locked out of their houses at eight thirty in the morning. They have to work. They're locked in again for lunch, in their houses, not in their cells because there are no cells at Dillwynia, so they're still free to move around. The officers all have lunch together so they have a chance to talk about anything that's happened in the morning. They can air their stuff or offload anything they need to get rid of. That doesn't happen anywhere else. That means fewer officers quit.

X: We're talking about changing people here now, aren't we? Or, at least the way people relate. We're not talking about institutional reform so much as allowing the institution to allow people to change.

V: If I could wave a magic wand I'd wave it over the women and say, 'Start being responsible for your behaviour. If your keep behaving in this way you'll be put in the behavioural wing for up to a week and that won't be very nice.'

X: We're talking solitary confinement here?

V: Yes. It's shape up or ship out. Their behaviour leaves a lot to be desired at times. They'll say, 'Oh well, who cares?' Well, we all care. Dillwynia is trying to tell women 'If you want respect, you show it'.

X: The idea is that if you treat people like responsible adults then they'll live up to that.

V: Exactly!

X: Whereas places like Mulawa are still treating people ...

V: Like dogs.

X: When we're talking about 'they' we're talking about the institution and the people who make the rules?

V: And they're starting to respond to the way that the head of Dillwynia wants things done.

Collette confirmed this.

C: If we hear an officer talking to an inmate in a way that we consider inappropriate we have to report it. If Dillwynia is to continue to be what we want it to be this has to happen. Even the Governor isn't the Governor, at Dillwynia her title is 'General Manager'.

X: So even the paradigm is different.

C: They're trying this whole, new thing. Horror stories are dwindling.

I don't know whether the threat of solitary works any better than anything else at teaching people to be responsible. I also wonder how much credibility the 'powers that be' have when they themselves don't seem to be taking full responsibility. The reason I say this is that in order to be responsible you have to be informed. You can't make a responsible decision unless it is an informed decision. If you look at the total number of authority figures that a criminal woman comes in contact with you get the overwhelming impression that *the authorities don't talk to each other.*

The police confine themselves to the arrest process and the gathering of evidence.

The courts confine themselves to looking at each case in isolation.

Corrective services deal with whatever the courts decide, without consultation from the courts, or even from the public, for that matter.

The chaplains don't get the chance to talk much to the prison psychologists or the guards, and, except at Dillwynia, the guards don't even talk to each other except informally.

Overworked parole officers don't get much of a chance to talk to the few support services that are out there and Centrelink, which provides what limited financial support it can, is a world of its own.

Covering all of this is a culture of 'duty of care', which is supposed to protect people but which frequently provides a cloak to cover up embarrassing realities and which prohibits people talking openly about these issues in a society where freedom of speech is not protected by law and you can be sued just for giving an opinion.

Confidentiality clauses also cover a multitude of sins, which necessitate writers (like me) having to protect the identities of sources who could be sued for daring to tell you what things are really like.

When you punish people for being honest, there's no incentive to give you the truth.

The end result is that you have abused, dysfunctional women (and I dare say, men) being tossed about from one authority to another, one agency to another, one professional to another, while mainstream culture looks away because it's all too hard. People are 'too busy' to talk to each other; or when they do there are a lot of 'just quietly' conversations that protect the guilty and cover arses. And, because so many people aren't being open about anything, 'Chinese whispers' ensure that the message that starts at one end is unlikely to be the message that is received at the other. The criminal justice system is like a sinking ship. We're too busy bailing water to plug holes—and meanwhile, people are drowning. And too often, if someone says, 'Hold on, this stinks!', the messenger gets shot.

On top of everything else offenders, male and female, are often their own worse enemies and let their anger and mistrust get in the way of forming relations with people and formulating strategies that would stand a chance of actually solving their problems. The result is that the comparatively few people who actually want to help them find themselves the brunt of so much bullshit that they are often tempted to tell the offenders, 'For God's sake, I'm not the enemy!

I know you've had a rough deal, but stop being a victim and stop victimising the people who care enough to be bothered with you.'

There is no integrated strategy here. Files get filled, reports written, inquiries held but even the politicians (who supposedly 'set policy', whatever that means) don't talk to each other—and it can take a month to get an answer to a question, and if you've ever heard parliamentary sessions then, well, you get the picture.

Is the situation going to get better? Will there be fewer people committing crimes and fewer jails built because there will be fewer people going there?

One hundred years from now it's almost certain that every criminal alive today, every inmate in every jail, anywhere, every politician, officer or professional working in the criminal justice system will be dead. People who haven't even been born yet will replace them. That's the way of it. If we don't replace today's criminals with new ones there will be no justification for perpetuating a large proportion of the criminal justice system. If we stop creating criminals there will be no need to build and maintain courthouses, jails and all the other agencies and institutions that arise from criminality. There will be no cause to employ people to 'process' criminals or to protect 'us' from 'them'. And the billions of dollars and tens of thousands of lives wasted in this ugly dance of damage, anger and pain can be invested in something better.

I think things can improve, but we will have to put a spanner in the works of the factory that produces criminals. We have to interrupt the virus that infects the minds of children that turns them into criminals. We have to wake up from the corrupt dreaming and stop creating criminals in the first place.

13   HOW TO CREATE A CRIMINAL

Long before a woman ever steals anything, long before she ever takes anything from anyone, long before she robs, she is robbed. The one common element in all the stories that I heard was this: In some way or another all these women were, sooner or later, cheated. Cheated—of their right to be safe, secure, protected, cared for, looked after. Cheated of the right to respect—from their families, their peers and their teachers. Although many, by their own admission made it difficult (and keep making it difficult) for people to help them, and though many have often become their own worst enemies, they are all cheated people.

Fundamentally and basically, these women were betrayed. Someone who they trusted betrayed them, or fed them to the wolves, which amounts to the same thing. Nothing hurts more than betrayal, and the pain from that is something that some women have carried all their lives. They will continue to carry the burden of that betrayal—and all the betrayals that followed—until somehow, some way, they deal with it. The pain of that betrayal made certain choices, certain lousy choices, easier. These women aren't saints, but you should remember that they were once little girls. They could have been your daughters, or your sisters. They could still be.

A woman is in prison long before anyone ever puts her in jail.

———

The connection between the majority of female criminals and some form of abuse is, in my opinion, undeniable. It's beyond my humble abilities to give you an accurate figure of the proportion of the general adult population who were abused as children. From skim-reading a whole bunch of reports from around the developed, English-speaking world I get the impression that virtually everyone has an abuse story. How many people have lived in an environment of sustained abuse as a child? How many people were sexually abused as children? I don't know. No one does. But it doesn't matter. Even one abused child is too many.

Nevertheless there is one question I haven't addressed. Given that so many women have been sexually abused, why do only a small fraction of them take drugs, commit crimes and end up in jail? I asked my psychotherapist friend Virginia for her take on this. It took me a little time to get my head around it, but I hope her explanation is clear to you. If you find it hard to understand all this as an adult, imagine how confusing it is to deal with molestation as a child.

Virginia: The world of psychology acknowledges that it's likely that if you've got a group of five women in a room, then three of them have been tampered with, sexually. We're talking 60% of all women have been molested. Now it's important to define what sexual molestation is. Sexual molestation is not rape. Rape happens when someone has violated your boundaries. Child sexual abuse happens before those boundaries are ever formed in the first place, and that's why it affects you so profoundly.

X: There are 'windows of developmental opportunity', aren't there? If you don't learn a language, any language, by the time you're twelve, it's almost impossible to learn, because by then the parts of the brain and the muscles of the mouth that deal with language are no longer flexible enough to take in new stuff easily. That's also why people learning foreign languages as adults speak with accents, unless they under-take considerable training, because even if you do learn a language or two the 'jelly is set'.

V: And just like language the sense of self and identity happens within a window of opportunity. The sense of self, the rules of where you end and everything else begins takes about seven to ten years. By then your personality is 'set', although you can change personality after that if you're willing to put in a lot of effort. That's why there's the saying: 'Give me the boy until he is seven, and I will give you the man'. It's also why you 'can't teach an old dog new tricks' and why adults and children learn differently. They are different people. **X:** So how does this explain why some women who are molested end up with such crappy lives, and others don't?

V: Things don't happen to children if they're watched all the time, but who is? Parents leave children alone for all sorts of reasons and, in fact, it's healthy to do so in a safe world because we all have to become independent at some point. But in a not-so-safe world all sorts of negative things happen. Okay. Put yourself in the position of a four-year-old girl, let's call her, Ella. She's bouncing on Grand-dad's knee (it's classi-cally a 'trusted' male that does this). Ella's happy, she loves her Poppy and everything feels good which is really nice because love is supposed to feel good. Now Grand-dad gets a boner and starts rubbing it against Ella. Ella now doesn't like this at all because instinctively she knows this is wrong.

X: She feels bad and as we all know sex brings on strong feelings because it's supposed to. Sex is the bribe that keeps the race going, it has to be compelling for us to want to do it. So it literally arouses strong emotions, no matter the context.

V: And that instinct is now sabotaged. There's this charged sexual atmosphere and maybe Ella can even smell it on Poppy. Now Ella's soul feels violated, she wants to get away, but Poppy keeps going, because he has major issues, and Poppy's much bigger than Ella. Ella is in no position to fight. Now in Ella's soul this is horrible and she feels dirty. Ella's still young, and her boundaries aren't set yet, so she can't distin-guish between feeling bad and being bad. So if this is happening to her it must be because she is a bad girl and she deserves this. When you're a child there's no boundary between feeling bad and identifying with the badness.

None of this is logical, but children aren't logical. They learn by association and some of the connections they make are creative, but wrong. In her undeveloped mind Ella is bad and she has also learned that even if it feels bad, it must be love. But in her soul she remembers being close and feeling good and that once love felt unconditionally good. Someone Ella trusted betrayed her expectation that love feels good. At this point, when Ella is in a highly disturbed state, Poppy says to her, 'Now don't tell anyone, it's our little secret'. Ella doesn't want to say anything. Even if Poppy hadn't said anything she feels so bad it would take enormous courage to tell anyone what happened. Somebody may punish Poppy and maybe Poppy didn't mean it, after all people punish Ella when she does things she doesn't mean. Any number of thoughts and feelings could be going through her mind.

X: Several things can now happen to Ella.

V: It all depends on what Ella decides is safe to do. Is it safe to go to mummy and daddy and tell them what happened? Her mother may be an alcoholic who doesn't care. She may be in the habit of not believing Ella anyway because she is in denial. Both parents may be too busy at work. Her father or mother may even be absent for long periods. Then there is the question of whether there is any back-up for her at all. In the majority of these cases Ella is on her own. The number of reported cases of sexual abuse is just the tip of the iceberg. Therapists deal with the consequences of it years later, but only if the children eventually end up in therapy. Most don't.

So sexual abuse isn't necessarily penetration, it's any tampering in a sexual manner that alters the perception of self. Ella has now become a bad girl in her own mind and this inappropriate behaviour becomes the benchmark of what love is. Love has been violated. It is now confused with bad sexual feeling. Ella hates herself because there must be something wrong with her.

These acts may happen only once or they may happen hundreds of times, but what's important is that Ella has started making these connections. Unfortunately these events usually happen a lot more than once. Each time the connections get stronger and they become more familiar. Corrupted love is now the norm for her and because no one protected her from this, or she didn't feel it was safe to say anything, Ella now can't distinguish between who is safe and who isn't. She grows up and begins to be attracted to bastards because her role models are bastards. Corrupted love is familiar, despite being painful. Decent men don't interest them, because they can't relate to kindness. That's not to say that being abused is the only reason that women seek out such men.

X: Some women like the excitement of 'bad boys'. Bad boys make them feel something.

V: But women who stay in abusive relationships do so because that's what they learned. And these damaged men are very good at finding women who will let them abuse them.

X: It doesn't matter though, if the abuse is sexual. Sexual abuse is extremely damaging but even physical abuse or emotional abuse can have similar effects. **V:** Children associate love with attention too. Some work out that the only attention they'll get is if they're hit. They adapt to loveless inattention by rebelling against their pain. Rebellion may well look like delinquency and in some repressive authoritarian households any independence is a beatable offence. But in some cases they can't win because neglect is so damaging too. So getting beaten up is at least some form of attention, some form of love.

X: Children need love because they know in their soul it's the only reason to be alive. Even abusive love is better than none, in their minds.

V: And the opposite-sexed parent is the role model of how the opposite sex should behave. If the men in your early developmental life are abusive, well that's normal. If your early experiences of love are abusive, that's normal too. And if you never revise your opinion of what's normal, you carry around this baggage and go from one abusive relationship to another, trying desperately to make it work each time and feeling like a failure every time it doesn't.

X: Or feeling that you deserve it because you've never examined the conclusion you made when you were four, or eight, or ten or whatever that you are a bad girl that deserves this.

V: Unhealthy love still feels like love. All love feels wrong because you've forgotten what real love feels like.

X: So that explains why abused women seek bastards that make their lives hell. And this leads to the classic precursors of women being in jail because of domestic violence, or poverty, like they almost did for Angie. Angie's stepmother was the 'Wicked Witch of the West' and crushed her self-esteem. Her father didn't hit her or abuse her, but he neglected her and left her prey to bastards.

V: By her own admission she didn't know any better, she was totally naïve. Her version of reality was that she could make it better somehow because she wanted to please the daddy in her head. **X:** She didn't want to make trouble.

V: And she couldn't go home because of the 'Wicked Witch'. There was no lifeboat for her. Remember what I said about rebellion? The other way a child chooses to adapt to these horrible abuse situations is through compliance. The child will do whatever it thinks is safe to do. If rebellion is safe, she'll pick rebellion because rebelling against a bad situation is the most functional way to adapt.

X: If your hand is in the fire you rebel by pulling your hand away from the flame, or you put out the fire.

V: Putting out the abusers. But the less healthy way is to comply.

X: Keeping your hand in the fire and 'grinning and bearing it'. Or taking painkillers while keeping your hand in.

V: Smiling while drowning in shit. Self-blame leading to self-medication to shut up the inner voice that's screaming 'this sucks!', like Rosa. People only comply because they're either so browbeaten they're exhausted, like Angie, or like Kelli, there was no space for expressing their pain without paying huge, unacceptable consequences.

X: So Kelli grinned and bore it. Even taking satisfaction in being able to take it, at least until her father, her rock, died and she couldn't take the pain. Why did Kelli pick bastards?

V: By her own admission she was a child when she left home. Children on the streets get into trouble because they're so vulnerable. And taking drugs to kill the pain is a child's way of dealing with hurt.

X: Kelli told me later that when she got out of jail her younger sister died and that was a turning point for her. She'd just been told that her sister committed suicide by putting a gun to her head. As she was driving to the house where it happened she blanked out. She didn't know where she was or what she was doing. She stayed like that for twenty minutes. When she came to her senses she actually had to call the house again to find out what had happened. But she felt as if she'd finally woken up after the eleven and a half years since her daddy died. She said it was as if she'd woken up from a completely unreal life. She'd been through so much, but she was strong.

V: Not all women have that strength. Some people just end up killing themselves, to the surprise of the people who are 'closest' to them. They're the ones who held it all inside until they couldn't take it anymore.

X: But much more common is the slow suicide. People who kill themselves through too many chemicals, or overeating, or overworking. We still haven't explained why of the 60% of all women who are abused only some women end up in jail.

V: You've been looking at the extreme underdogs of life. To a certain extent it's a class thing. If you're working class you have no resources to fall back on.

X: And you're at the mercy of a system that originated hundreds of years ago to protect the rich and powerful, and it is still doing so, as long as the rich and powerful play by the rules.

V: But if you're rich, and come from a background with a lot of money you can hide a multitude of sins. You can keep bailing your drug addict kids out. You can buy expensive lawyers that know the ropes. Or you can ignore the pain and buy Ella a nice car or marry her off to another rich bastard who'll end up treating her badly and have affairs under her nose because that's exactly how daddy was with mummy.

X: But at least she can suffer in style. And the great middle classes?

V: They usually get by on a lot of denial and prescription medicines. It keeps them out of jail, for the most part.

14   HOW TO CREATE A MONSTER

As great as the recipe for creating an ordinary, garden-variety criminal might be, if you're really serious about what you're doing you'll want to create a monster. Female monsters are exceptionally rare. Far more often it's boys who get the hard-core, industrial-strength abuse that turns them into criminal psychopaths. However, history has shown that given the same treatment little girls can be made into demons. Their methods of operation will differ, but they can be just as deadly and destructive as men. So how do you create a monster? Here's how.

Do everything you do to create an ordinary criminal (the abuse, the programming) but turn the volume way up. Do everything you can to violate a human being short of killing her (or him). Oh, and try not to cause too much permanent physical damage. There aren't too many sadistic mass murderers out there in wheelchairs.

Do this to any young girl and I guarantee you that the ones you don't kill will end up becoming the sort of people who justify having prisons around.

If you're going to create a criminal out of a potentially sane, healthy and loving little girl start with abuse, lots of it, and inflict it regularly. Sooner or later she'll crack under the strain. Start early to make the deepest impression, then isolate her, and set her up in a game she's not likely to win because the answers she sees in front of her face all lead to breaking the rules. When she breaks the rules, put her in a big cage with a lot of other damaged young women, and watch as they spread their viruses of the psyche to each other.

You can define a lot of socio-criminalisation as 'writing the rules of the game to set people up for a fall'. You can define psycho-criminalisation as 'screwing with somebody's head until they're so screwed up that they're going to make lousy choices.'

Separately they do not explain all crime. And while I did not start out to discover a fully comprehensive theory of crime, a fully comprehensive theory of crime is simple: crime is an expression of crappy values.

Our society's definition of crime is an expression of our collective values and priorities.

Individuals' choices to commit crimes are expressions of individual values. Sometimes, no matter what the programming, some people just ignore it. They distance themselves.

Stanton Samenow, a clinical psychologist in Alexandria, Virginia, related the following fascinating story on the program PBS *Think Tank—Rethinking Violent Crime*, which aired 31 July 2003:

> I interviewed a woman who had been a Red Cross worker for twenty years, a responsible person. She had a father who was in prison, a brother who was in jail, another brother who was in prison, lived in a very, very difficult run-down part of Washington, DC. I asked her, 'Why is it, with such terrible role models, even within your own family, temptation at your doorstep, why is it that you didn't follow in their path?' She responded in three words: 'I wasn't interested.' Now, if this woman had become a junkie, a thief, and a drug pusher, people in my field, psychology, after the fact would have said, 'Oh, of course. Look at the role models.' But that isn't what happened. She made choices to go against the negative role models.

Some people approach crime and embrace the values to the point that the values become their identity. As Stanton Samenow continued:

> One man said to me, 'If you take my crime away, you take my world away.' Another said, 'Crime is like ice-cream. It's delicious.' In both of these cases these individuals, as far back as they or anyone else could remember, they rejected whatever forces were in their environment for obeying the law or living a responsible life. For them life had to be a series of searches for control, power, high-voltage excitement. They rejected the world of the responsible person. And this goes as far back as they or anybody else can remember. You ask me why? I'll say I don't know and you can get ten experts on your program and you're going to get maybe ten opinions.

I can tell you why. It's because their experiences turned them on. Maybe someone should have introduced them early in their lives to computer games and pro-wrestling—or castration.

Some experts confirmed for me that some forms of programming for crappy values are more effective than others. As criminologist Lonnie Athens, Professor of Criminal Justice at Seton Hall University, said on the same program:

> Although crime is in the mind, it is not solely in the mind. And I think that violent criminals are made through a brutalisation process during which they make choices but at certain points they have greater leeway to make choices than other parts. And it starts with the process of being brutalised. And they don't make the choice to be brutalised. Their brutalisers make the choices for them. They're the subject of violent subjugation. They're subject to personal horrification, where mentors violently coach them. Then in the second stage, if they get there, they

get in a defiant stage, they become belligerent. And as a result of reliving their brutalisation they have an epiphany that the only way they can stop their brutalisation is to become violent themselves. And then they enter into a violent performance stage where they test their resolve. People become fearful in your presence and then you can come to embrace that, having experience of malevolency, deciding that you enjoy your violent notoriety. You delight in social trepidation—notwithstanding the punishment that may ensue. And then you decide at this point that for the slightest dominative provocation you will attack people with the serious intention of killing them or gravely injuring them.[13]

Crappy values.

It only takes crappy values to create crime—that and the power equation inherent in any particular situation. This is true of even mass crimes or even war crimes. Crime is crappy values—expressed. Psychologist Stanley Milgram conducted what were later to become famous experiments at Yale University in 1961–62. The experiments focused on the conflict between individual conscience and obedience to authority.

Milgram recruited 'teachers' who experimenters persuaded to 'electrocute' 'learners' as part of a series of 'lessons'.

In reality the 'learners' were actors, the electric shocks were phoney and the 'teachers' were the real subjects of the experiment. Milgram's question was: 'can people be persuaded to do things contrary to their conscience if an 'authority' tells them it's okay. The answer was overwhelmingly 'yes'. The experimenters relatively easily persuaded the 'teachers' to give ever more powerful 'shocks' to the 'students' even when the 'voltage' was over 300 and the 'students' were screaming with 'pain'. It was all 'okay' as long as the experimenters accepted 'responsibility' for what the 'teachers' were doing.

These experiments were triumphs of the expression of the value that obedience was a more important value than taking personal responsibility for inflicting pain on another human being, and that expressing conformity was more important than rebellion.

In a similar way warfare and its crimes express the value that it's okay to kill people as long as 'the state' sanctions it, while we conveniently forget that the state will kill you if you don't fight. Even if it doesn't, it can brainwash your fellow citizens into believing that you're a traitor or a coward for refusing to play the game, and they'll volunteer as unpaid enforcers of the state's version of reality.

Terrorism expresses the value that it's okay to kill 'heathens' because they're not real people. Infanticide expresses the value that babies, particularly baby girls, are worthless. Even 'victimless crimes' express the value that the law has greater authority than individuals to decide what the individuals do with their lives—even when the individuals are not harming anyone else.

The most chilling thing is that you can create criminals just by setting up a system, a bureaucracy, a machine, in which no one person does anything horrible, but the cumulative effects are horrible. You can set up Auschwitz, where someone is innocently turning a lever, but the effect is that thousands die in gas showers. You can also set up a system where the police are doing the right thing, the courts are doing the right thing, the jails are doing the right thing and the community services are doing the right thing—they are all doing their best, but the cumulative effect is that people's lives are being destroyed.

That doesn't let us off the hook. We are the ones that allow the system to grow into something it was never supposed to be, whether it is our system of criminal justice, or our wider social system—'arsesiety', the society that thinks through its arse. We allow these injustices to happen through our neglect, in spite of, or perhaps even because, everyone is looking after their own patch of ground, and failing to look at the whole field.

If we're really serious about crime all we really have to do is stop doing the things that turn people into criminals. It won't be universal— some people will be determined to be sociopathic whatever you do—but we can start, by stopping.

While we're busy creating a world without abuse we still have to deal with the sins of our fathers and mothers. Society manufactures people according to the values we collectively hold. Society breaks people, but can we mend them?

15   CAN YOU UNCOOK THE EGG?

Theoretically all chemical reactions are reversible. If I light a match to a hydrogen balloon in the presence of oxygen I can get a lot of water, as the *Hindenburg* famously demonstrated on 6 May 1937 at Lakehurst in New Jersey. I can also run a current of electricity through water and separate it into hydrogen and oxygen again. Cooking an egg is also a chemical reaction (in fact a vast number of them).

Now assuming that the criminalised mind is stored in a physical brain that records programming engraved in a bunch of chemicals, I ask myself a few deceptively simple questions. What can be done to 'erase the programming'?

What can be done to shake up the chemicals and settle them into a new, more life-affirming pattern? In short, can you unset the jelly? Can you uncook the egg? Does prison, sorry, does a 'correctional institution' correct the egg— the mind, the brain, the seat of the human soul? Even people like Vera who have worked a long time within the system, at the coal face, admit to being confused.

X: What's the point of jail? What's the functional benefit of jail to society?

V: Hopefully to rehabilitate.

X: Do you see any value in punishment?

V: To a certain degree.

X: Do you know the origin of the word punish? It comes from the Latin verb 'punire' which means 'to punish' but also 'to avenge'.

V: Being in prison is enough punishment, enough vengeance for anyone.

X: Imprisonment is bad enough for the human spirit?

V: Without everything else.

X: Everything else is like icing on the cake. In what cases is punishment appropriate?

V: Hardly an adult alive doesn't know what drugs are and what they can do to people. For someone to traffic in drugs, knowing that those drugs will either end up in children, or that children will be the victims of what the drugs do to adults, someone like that deserves punishment.

X: 'Deserving' meaning that it's appropriate to put people into prison in order to accomplish what?

V: Change their attitude, although I doubt that prisons do that.

X: But you think that for the time being society is better off with these people locked up?

V: For the moment, yes. What I'm saying is that if there are fewer dealers out there it will be harder for the kids to get stuff, and you're going to have a better chance of keeping the kids away from it. I know in reality that's not going to happen but in my mind it's going to happen. I just hate what the drugs are doing to the kids. And I hope that when there is a drug bust that we have honest and truthful police that don't just steal the drugs they confiscate and sell it on the streets.

If the issue is punishment, prisons are great. I can't imagine a more civilised way of torturing people who have committed crimes. After a lifetime of observations of and dealings with criminal cases, US Judge, His Honour Judge Dennis Challeen, had this to say about what we expect from, and what we do to people who commit crimes:

> We want them to have self-worth so we destroy their self-worth. We want them to be responsible so we take away all responsibilities. We want them to be part of our community so we isolate them from our community. We want them to be positive and constructive so we degrade them and make them useless. We want them to be non-violent so we put them where there is violence all around them. We want them to be kind and loving people so we subject them to hatred and cruelty. We want them to quit being the tough guy so we put them where the tough guy is respected. We want them to quit hanging around with losers, so we put all the losers under one roof. We want them to quit exploiting us so we put them where they exploit each other. We want them to take control of their own lives, own their own problems and quit being parasites so we make them totally dependent on us. [14]

A lot of Australians I spoke to while writing this book weren't too happy about jails either.

> Women don't belong in cages. 80% of imprisoned women are inside for poverty related offenses. 85% of women in prison are survivors of incest and sexual assault. The women's prison population has increased 300% in the last ten years. Prisons are the real crime. [15]

Hundreds of people are working on the issue of prison reform. I think they're hitting their heads against a brick wall and getting a lot of headaches for their trouble. The whole criminal justice system is showing signs of dysfunction, because it's operating in an archaic culture, a programming way past its use-by date. We could devote more time to creating a more enlightened society, one that doesn't think with its arse. But I guess that no matter how rich we are the poor will always be with us.

No matter how enlightened our society might become, or how sane or functional we might become as individuals, criminals will always be with us too. But I live in the hope that if we invest in intervening in the criminalisation process—especially in the psycho-criminalisation process—the supply of criminals will be ever-dwindling. What sort of investment in prevention and cure do we have to make?

Angie, Kelli and Rosa all survived their abusive backgrounds. Kelli and Rosa survived their jail terms. All three are now living their lives, doing the best they can, day by day.

One reason they all survived, I think, is that they all learned responsibility from a very young age. Angie had to look after her sick brother and later had to protect her children from a violent, indifferent husband. Kelli and Rosa looked after their brothers and sisters when their parents couldn't. Kelli in particular, for a time, protected her younger siblings from repeated rapes by their older brother. Rosa did what all 'good' South American girls do. She kept house.

Perhaps the salvation of women, and men, is to give them something to be responsible for—something beyond themselves. Maybe becoming responsible for someone else is a step towards becoming responsible for yourself. The one thing I found in common with all delinquent children, and delinquent adults, is that they weren't answerable for the care of anyone, not even themselves. They don't care about anyone, because there's no one they have to care about. Perhaps taking responsibility not only protects you from damage in the first place, but also helps you heal. In healing others there may be the path to healing the self.

Mending psychological damage is not easy. It is a path fraught with difficulty. We're really dealing with poverty here, not just the financial poverty that drove Angie to make her choices, but the poverty that arises from neglect and abuse, and all the other poverties that follow: the poverty that begins with ordinary evil, the poverty that comes from the absence of empathy, the absence of feeling that makes you think that giving people a decent childhood doesn't matter.

———

Liz worked for many years in the prison system and spoke to hundreds of women about their lives in that time. She talked to me about ordinary evil.

X: Do you believe in evil?
L: Yes. I can answer that without hesitation.
X: Where does evil come from? What feeds it? What stops it? And what exactly is evil, in your understanding?
L: Evil is anything I don't class as good. It can be fed by anything and the only thing that stops it is a determination to turn themselves around completely.

X: I get the impression that for some people evil is the easy option.

L: Sometimes evil is the only way they know. Some women have had horrendous things happen to them. I know a lot of women who don't know what TLC is. And when you start to show it to them they say, 'Whoa! I don't know about this! I don't know how to handle this!' And because we start being nice to them they start thinking that there is a condition to it. That's how they've come through life. They've never experienced someone being nice to them without a condition.

X: If someone's being nice they're after something. I imagine that it's difficult for Mr and Ms Middle Class to imagine a life like that.

L: It's more common than you think. It's a life without hope. A life that hasn't got nice things in it, that's only got abuse. You take someone who's been abused all their life. Maybe their father has abused them, sexually, and abused them every other way from the age of say, ten. Then somewhere along the line it stopped and now their younger brother or sister cops it. She leaves home at an early age to escape it, but also often just to get enough money to eat. Then their husband or boyfriend starts doing the same thing as what the father used to do.

X: That's interesting in itself, abused people have a talent for finding more abuse.

L: I don't think they're looking for it.

X: Not consciously, anyway.

L: It's because of their state of mind. The majority of these people have never had counselling so they're carrying all their junk with them and they can't assess reality clearly enough to determine what is in their best interests. It's clouded.

X: If your reality is screwy you'll make screwy decisions.

L: If you offload your junk you see more clearly and you feel a lot stronger. Some people aren't in tune with themselves. They go from one abusive situation to another. So you ask:

'Have you had counselling?'

'No.' 'Do you know how to get it?'

'No.'

'Would you like to get some?'

'Ohhh, I don't know about that. It would mean talking about everything? No, can't do that.'

They have no idea that when someone's asking them these questions what they're saying is, 'If you can come through this, just a little bit longer with someone to help you and guide you through the way; you'd be free of it. You'd have a better life.' But with some people it's so huge and so sore and so painful that they can't.

X: So the cure is worse than the disease? If the disease is having a horrible life with less-than-wonderful outcomes, the cure would involve actually confronting that junk, looking at it, taking responsibility for how you've reacted to your life, growing through it and experiencing all the pain?

L: Sometimes to come through all that and into an area they're not familiar with is too much. It's too huge a step. Sometimes, because all that muck is familiar, it's hard for them to picture a world without that. They say, 'You're telling me that if I talk to you or I talk to a counsellor that there's a better life for me? I want it, but I don't know if I can.' They can't make a decision. It can take years for someone to come around and finally say 'yes'. Regardless of how we see it they don't see it like that. They see the work that they've got to do. We might be saying that their lives will be free of pain. They can't see that.

X: They don't know what it looks like?

L: No. Because this abuse is all they've known all their life. What happens, do you think, when mum and dad have been fighting like cats and dogs and you've got a six-year-old and an eight-year-old looking at this and it's been like this ever since they were little babies. Do they know anything else? No. For them it's normal. You take those two children away from mum and dad because they've been accused of abusing their children. You put them in with a loving, caring foster family who are going to care for those two together. They've got a room each. They've never slept alone! They've probably only slept in one single bed. They've probably only had one blanket, if that. They've probably never gone to bed with a full tummy. The new parents say, 'Eat what's on your plate.' The children say, 'We have eaten. What? We have to eat all that?' They've never had that much to eat. 'You mean I can have a drink of milk? I can't have milk! Mum said there had to be enough milk for breakfast in the morning.'

X: It comes down to something as simple as that.

L: And some of the women are just mere children inside, screaming to get out. They've never been allowed to be children, from the age of maybe eight up.

X: Because someone had to be the grown-up.

L: I'm not saying they're all like that, but there are a fair few.

For many women in jail, the continuity issue is an important one. Even if you want to heal, how can you trust the healer?

Rosa: I remember being at Mulawa going through this stuff with this psychologist and thinking, 'Why am I going through all this stuff with this woman when I'm going to get sentenced then transferred?'

X: You can't build up a rapport.

R: Or something. Maybe a lot of women in prisons feel like this. Maybe it's just like what their lives were like outside of jail. Like, were their parents consistent? Were they there for them? Were the parents alcoholics or drug-addicted and in and out of the house or whatever. Even now, out of jail I see this counsellor and I'm thinking, 'What is she going to be able to change in my life that's going to stop me from taking drugs?' I mean, I don't do it every day, but I still do it. What is she going to do with my issues that's going to make me stop wanting to block out this pain.

X: Have you asked her?

R: No.

X: Maybe you should. Maybe you'll get an answer. She can't take away the fact that when you were ten years old you were molested. She can't undo that.

R: That's why I wonder 'What's the point?' When I was at Emu Plains I saw a psychologist for over a year. I understand more about the perpetrator of child molestation, and how what happened had nothing to do with me, because you do blame yourself for basically everything that happens. But I keep wondering 'What more do I have to do?' I mean, I've dealt with it.

X: But you're still taking drugs. Is that to block out the pain?

R: I guess.

X: But if you've still got the pain maybe you haven't dealt with it.

R: Okay. But then I just want to know, what more do I have to do to deal with it? I've dealt with them in my head, but in my heart, I'm still aching.

X: It's interesting that you say 'them'. The significant people in our lives continue to live inside us, influencing what we do. Somewhere inside you, you still have the pain. If you can get rid of the pain you wouldn't have to do drugs anymore. And if you don't do drugs anymore none of the other crap happens because drugs screw you up.

R: It's not like I even like it. I don't even know why I'm doing it half the time.

So a woman can run away and be on the streets and be cheated of her childhood. Or she can stay home and be cheated of her childhood. Either way, she can spend the rest of her life catching up while the little girl inside her keeps on screaming for some real caring, some real nurturing, some real love. Either way unless something happens she won't be able to see, hear or feel her way past her junk, her unresolved issues, her pain. The junk hurts, so she'll take more junk, chemical junk, to dull the pain. The junk she takes to dull the pain screws her up even more so that her brain doesn't work so she makes bad choices. She can't see past the junk, so she takes bad turns. She does things that land her in jail, where she collects more junk, until the junk becomes so familiar she'd be lost without it and leaving the junk behind frightens her so much she'd rather stew in it for the rest of her life—unless something happens.

Unfortunately, if there's one value our society seldom examines, it's the assumption that most families are happy families, and that you shouldn't intervene in the bringing up of other people's children, because it's 'none of your business'. You can see this in supermarkets, when a woman starts screaming at her child, belting it, and you watch the number of people who are within spitting distance and notice how they all look away, pretending that nothing is going on. I know I have. There's that, and then there's the sort of abuse that may eventually turn a woman to crime, and that nearly always happens behind closed doors. And when things happen behind closed doors we certainly don't want to 'get involved'. An ex-friend of mine could hear the wailing of a child next door to her house. The child was begging to be fed, because this child's new-age, air-head parents thought it would be a good idea if a three-year-old went on a 'cleansing fast' for a week. My ex-friend didn't 'get involved' either.

I have often wondered why 'they' don't hand out parenting licences, but then who would be qualified to issue them? DoCS? I don't think so.

———

Even when an abused woman is finally strong enough to face her demons, her junk, she's still up against a lot of work. I asked Angie what she thought of Virginia's analysis of why she had the life she had.

X: I understand that with everything that happened if you were a lesser person you would not have survived.

Angie: For sure.

X: But I could also argue that the abuse you suffered as a child left you vulnerable to having the experiences you had later.

A: Possibly.

X: So the abuse leaves you fucked up and vulnerable to more abuse. In that sense, abuse is something that really doesn't help you because without the abuse you might never have been vulnerable enough to be a victim.

A: I don't know about that, because the piranhas are there anyway.

X: But some of us never meet them.

A: But how come? I'm such a normal person and I meet all these dysfunctional, fucked-up weirdos. How does that happen?

X: Well, if you haven't been abused and your elders do the right job (and you're mature enough to understand the lessons) you grow up knowing what the rules are, where the boundaries are and what love is and what it isn't. Your elders also give you a value system that says it's not okay to be treated like crap, and what the appropriate responses to being treated like crap are. Your elders can't protect you from all the piranhas, but they teach you how to spot them before they ever get near you. Even if they're in disguise the piranhas will sense that they won't be able to get away with anything with you so most of them will leave you alone. Also, you won't seek them out, because they won't interest you; you'll be interested in other things besides playing junkie or cops and robbers. You won't have as much reason to play junkie or cops and robbers because you'll have better ways to spend your time than mix with the wrong crowd, to set yourself up for a fall and to commit crimes and land in jail.

If your elders screw up then they'll either give you crappy value programming or abuse you or throw you to the sharks or the piranhas and you'll find yourself getting abused. People who have been abused don't understand the clear boundaries of love.

A: And yet I have the highest regard for my father. Everything good about me, he taught me. I don't understand it, because, when he was alive, we didn't even have two words to say to each other. He was so not there for me.

X: Maybe you put him on a pedestal after he died?

A: Huh! That's a whole chapter!

X: The little girl inside you needs to have a fantasy father that was absolutely great so he can help you get through all this.

A: I'm the only one left of the whole family! Everybody else is dead. I don't want to be the head of the whole clan!

X: At some point everybody has to grow up.

A: I don't even know what I want to be when I grow up!

X: Even though you're a very competent woman, in many ways a large part of you is a little girl who is crying to have the childhood she didn't have. You also have to become your own parent in those cases where your real parents were inadequate.

A: There were none.

X: So you did your own do-it-yourself job and created this idealised father. The part of you that's brilliant created this fantasy father to help the scared little girl who was abused as a child and who confuses abuse with love. What happened is that you made a connection between really icky feelings and love.

A: How pathetic!

X: And abusive people are experts at finding abusees in order to perpetuate their own programming. We're all very good at getting our needs satisfied, even if those needs are warped. We're all very good at honing in on whomever will be 'willing' to play a role in our dramas.

A: But I'm just horrible then!

X: No you're not. You are a survivor. And you will heal, because other people have healed. Sixty percent of women have been abused. Sixty!

A: They just don't want to tell anyone. The worse part is I actually married a guy that did that to my kids. He treated me like shit and I said, 'You don't mean that. You don't mean that! You really love me!' He hated my guts!

X: For two reasons perhaps. You confused love with abuse, and he thought you were stupid because of that, and also because you let him abuse you.

A: And he hated me for that. It just went on and on. We'd break up, and then he'd come back and say, 'I love you, I love you.'

X: He had you trapped because you never knew when the good stuff would happen so you kept the relationship going through all this shit in the hope that if enough shit was spread around then something beautiful would grow. You were totally isolated.

If somebody had come in at some point and said, 'Hey, this is what's going on ...'

A: I didn't even know what my periods were. Please!

X: Because you're parents failed you—for whatever reason. They weren't there for you. You had to make it up. Of course you made mistakes! You didn't know any better!

A: I just thought, 'You're a good person, why shouldn't something good happen?' And then something even worse would happen!

X: That was another fundamental mistake you kept making. That's child logic. Child logic, which is not fully developed logic, makes that error. Children's boundaries aren't fully developed so they think like this:

Feeling good equals being good equals good things will happen to me because I deserve it. They also think: Feeling bad equals being bad equals bad things will happen to me because I deserve it.

Then reality hits you with experiences that confuse you. You feel bad, but you know you're good. That doesn't make sense to you so you conclude: I feel bad therefore I must be bad which is why bad things happen. If I become better and try harder I'll be good enough to deserve good experiences. So you can waste years trying harder to be good. 'If I'm good enough I won't feel worthless. If I can't be good I'll take drugs and feel good, for a while,' you think.

It's one vicious circle after another because then you start getting desperate and you end up doing something that gets you in trouble or in jail.

Bad things happen to good people because there is no connection between being good, and having good things happen to you. The trick is to realise that good things happen to people who make choices that lead them to good things, regardless of whether or not the people themselves are good or bad. Good things happen to bad people if bad people know how to make choices that will lead them to good experiences. All you've got to do is learn to make better choices.

A: I can't haul around this shit forever.

X: The biggest problem for me is that the shit is boring. Dysfunction is boring.

A: It is! And you have to retrain yourself because people can get really attached to their shit.

X: People use their shit as a way of filling in time, getting affirmation, getting attention and making friends. Men, the hunters, tend to focus on external processes: 'We're in this shit together, if we didn't keep setting up shitty projects we wouldn't be friends because we wouldn't have a common 'enemy'.'

Women tend to focus on relationships: 'Oh, we're friends because we have the same shit, and if we didn't have the shit we wouldn't be friends anymore! Or we wouldn't be able to play, 'My turd is bigger than your turd'.' Both men and women conclude: 'I can't give up all these shitty feelings and situations and friendships for something I don't know about!' And people have trouble giving up the 'in crime' dynamic because giving it up would be scary. What else would you fill your life with?

A: I'm onto that. I just want to get on with my life. Why haven't I been able to?

X: The adult part of you was too busy trying to keep you alive to examine why the little girl was getting into all this trouble.

A: It slipped right past.

X: The adult woman part of you was just too exhausted surviving the mess the little girl part of you was getting you into. You couldn't help it. You were cast adrift when you were too young.

A: I don't come from anywhere.

X: Like so many people of Indigenous background, and so many of non-Indigenous background too, you were displaced. There was no place you could call home. Cast adrift in a leaky boat, and you were too busy bailing the water out, with a leaky bucket, to know where you were going. Even if you had known, nobody taught you how to navigate, that's why you kept bumping into pirates. You've got to be on to the holes in the bucket. Then you've got to attend to the holes in the boat. Once you're not exhausted from bailing, you can attend to where you want to go.

A: But will I want to moor at just any marina?

X: No, because once you've plugged the holes you can relax for a moment and work out where you want to go.

A: That is just such a weird concept.

X: Of course. It's not familiar. You've never been there. You've spent your life plugging holes and bailing the boat while pirates shoot more holes in the boat and the sharks and piranhas smell weakness and are waiting to go for the kill.

A: And being a good person only works for about five minutes and then shit happens.

———

At the beginning of this book I asked a question: Are these women, these 'criminal' women mad (that is, crazy) or bad (that is, evil). I think you know the answer by now. Some are mad, but only a very few. Some are bad, but only a very fewer still.

Most women in crime are neither mad or bad. But most of them are sad. Most of them are depressed into violent desperation or compulsive drug taking because they are trying desperately to make their shitty lives work, and they don't know any other way out.

16   LAST WORDS—WHY SHOULD YOU CARE?

The process of criminalisation, the process of turning an innocent child into a guilty woman is a little like a play in which a woman in the main role sits at the head of a table speaking a language that no one else understands, a language that sometimes she hardly understands. The play is broken up into little acts. Bit players sit on either side of the table; they don't all necessarily see the woman or hear her. As the story progresses the bit players play their parts, one by one, down one side of the table and up the other. In each act, the bit players get to have their say, but like guests at a table in a dinner party they tend to speak only to the people on either side of them, and maybe the people sitting opposite to them. They're all overworked, because the play was written by a committee of the players' ancestors in yet another language, now extinct, so parts of the play no longer make any sense, but no one seems to have the time or the energy to rewrite the play because they're too busy being in it. And anyway, some of the bit players like the way the play is written. It gives them the opportunity to make a living being perverse and sadistic, or being helpful and supportive. A part may be small, but at least it's theirs.

And as the play progresses you realise an even weirder thing. The bit players all have more power than the lead. What's worse, nearly all the bit players think they know the whole story. Unfortunately the story comes to them in pieces, one—by one, down one side of the table and up the other. If you've ever played Chinese whispers, you'll know what I'm talking about. The woman in the lead listens intently to every word, but some people are sitting too far away, and she can't hear it all, and not all of it makes sense. This makes her crazy and confused. If she gets any relief at all it's that occasionally she can take another swig of wine. Or she can get out of her chair and sit at another table and be a bit player in someone else's play for a little while. Then she can experience helping along someone's damnation, or downfall.

As a reviewer, it would have been nice to have seen a complete performance, so I could give you a really good review and all the inside juicy goss. But the play never ends, it's like some nightmare version of *The Mousetrap* meets *The Trial*— 10 000 variations written by Agatha Christie and Franz Kafka while they were both high on LSD. And it's running in too many theatres all over the country, all over the world. I haven't seen the whole play myself, I'm not allowed to. Some of the bit players won't let me see the whole production. I could only really get an idea of what was going on during the intermissions. Some of the bit players get very testy about 'outsiders' who can 'never understand'. But some of the bit players let me sneak a peek here and there, in spite of the other bit players, or the theatre managers that fund the whole production. Some of the leads didn't want to talk about their roles either. It's too distressing, or they're too scared, or angry, or miserable about the whole deal. I don't blame them. The monsters, the sharks, the piranhas aren't entirely in their heads alone. There are other hungry players in the wings, ready to hurt them even more than they've already been hurt.

I think the play should close, myself. It's cliché-ridden, overly melodramatic, tragic and stupid. The plot is a mish-mash of trite, worn-out themes and we really have heard it all before. How many more stories can we take about physical, psychological, emotional and sexual abuse? How many more tales of wasted lives and ugly deaths do we really need? And I feel sorry for the leads, and the bit players.

Couldn't their agents have gotten them a better gig?

But the general public, who've seen even less of the play than I have, seem to want the play to go on. They get to read about the gory highlights and the icky bits. Sometimes though, the play spills off the stage and the icky bits stick to the audience, or someone in the audience gets hurt. Then the patrons get mad. That's when they want to hurt someone back. That's when they insist on getting their money back. But the management doesn't give refunds. In fact, the management builds another theatre and puts on another play, and the ticket price goes up. The patrons seem to want that.

I have a confession to make. Drug addicts are boring. Victims of abuse are boring. Thieves are boring. Murderers are boring. I know because I've met them.

After a while the crimes all begin to seem the same. After a while all the stories begin to sound the same. After a while the statistics are just a bunch of numbers. That's because 'drug addict', 'victim', 'thief' and 'murderer' are labels. And labels are thin pieces of paper that are even less interesting than stamps. And statistics are just a bunch of numbers that might help you decide how to push other numbers around, but that's about all.

Do you want to know what's interesting? The people behind the labels are interesting. When you peel the labels off you suddenly realise, 'Wow! There's a real person down there! They're enough like me so we can talk, but they're different enough so we can explore new possibilities together.'

When I was talking to people for this book, a small part of my mind was thinking 'Okay, so she almost killed him with a kitchen knife' or 'Okay, so her old man treated her like a sexual toilet' but another part of me was feeling the energy, sensing something physical and tangible and three dimensional, the wholeness of a human being in front of me who was letting me share, for one brief moment, a small glimpse of the infinity inside them. And there wasn't one moment when I didn't wish that their lives hadn't been different. They didn't need this, I thought. Nobody needs this. No matter how melodramatic the story (and I'm a writer, I love stories) there wasn't a moment that some part of me wasn't thinking, IT'S NOT WORTH IT.

The story isn't worth the suffering that went into making the story. The sleazy years that the underdogs go through are too high a price to pay for the feeling of superiority you get when you decide that someone else is inferior because they're just a piece of druggie trash. The years of torment are too high a price to pay for the few paragraphs of drama and vicarious thrills that someone will get reading yet another newspaper article about a life gone wrong. The entire life was too high a price to pay for the momentary, delicious chill of being close, but not too close to someone else's demon.

It's all just too expensive. We can't afford it.

If someone steals from me, I don't want them put in jail. I want them to give me my stuff back, as good as new. I want them to take responsibility for what they've done and then get placed into a state of mind where they won't ever want to steal from anyone ever again.

If someone takes drugs I don't want them put in jail. I want to know what hurts so bad that they have to anaesthetise themselves just to get through life, or why they're so bored they need expensive, cheap, chemical thrills. Then I want them to learn a way of being in the world that doesn't rely on screwing with their synapses.

If someone rapes a child I want a guarantee that they won't do it again. If that means jail then so be it, but if there are alternatives I want to explore them. I also want him to pay the child's and the family's therapy bills.

If someone kills someone, I want to know why that was an option. Only if someone committed murder because they thought it would be fun, or because they were greedy, thoughtlessly negligent or because they're so damaged that they think everyone's life is equally worthless, do I want them in jail, to protect us from them, and preferably to be re-educated, if it's at all possible.

And I don't want to wait years for the justice system to do something about it while the accused, many of whom are innocent, rot on remand. Innocent people don't deserve to be exposed to the sadism of the unredeemable.

I don't want to pay the ticket price for this farce anymore.

From what I was able to find out, I don't think that prison helps. Most of the women I spoke to should have been offered better, less expensive alternatives than prison. When a woman is in prison, she isn't helping to 'repay her debt to society', she's an expensive indulgence of our society's need for punishment and revenge. She's serving time, but who is she serving? More than $150 of taxpayers' money per day is a little expensive for clean headsets for my aeroplane trips.

WHY SHOULD YOU CARE WHAT HAPPENS TO A BUNCH OF CRIMS?

About 0.5% of the adult population of Australia are either in jail or in community-based correction at any one time. This costs the taxpayer approximately:

- $2000 million per year for police.
- $1000 million per year for the courts
- $1368 750 000 per year for prisoners in jails (25 000 prisoners— average daily population x 365 days x $150 per day)

Feel free to quibble with these figures, I'm estimating, but I don't think I'm far off in real terms. Rounding down in order to be really conservative we're looking at $4000 million or $200 per year for every man woman and child in Australia. If you're married with three children it costs you $1 000 per year from your family tax bill to police, process and imprison people—$70 per year for the 7% of women prisoners.

I haven't even bothered to estimate how much you spend on locks, security systems or insurance to protect yourself from this 0.5%. I haven't bothered to estimate the cost of hidden or unreported crime. Also, I haven't bothered to estimate what living with this less-than-perfect state of affairs is costing you in terms of peace of mind, or the impact of job-related stress of the professionals involved. What's the divorce rate among police officers or prison officers? Would it surprise you if you learned that it was significantly higher than the national average? I don't know what it is, but it would be interesting to find out. Here's an interesting bit of 'costing':

> Justice Action quoted recent research by the Rand Foundation in the US which showed that $1 million spent annually on providing cash and other incentives for disadvantaged young people to graduate from high school would result in a reduction of 258 crimes per year; $1 million spent on training for parents and family therapy for families with 'difficult' children would result in a reduction of 160 crimes per year; and $1 million spent on prisons would prevent only 60 crimes a year.[16]

Who knows how much crime really costs the community, in real terms, if you cost everything, including lost human potential? I'd rather some of that $200 a year per capita be directed toward prevention, rather than 'punishment', which, in many cases, does nothing but destroy people further. I don't need to have another conversation with someone who hates me just for existing, because I represent everything that she hates, although I treasure the conversations I had with women who survived whole, or broken but later mended, and I look forward to more of them. But more than anything I look forward to the day when there'll be no need for, or market for, a book about women in crime.

CODA   THE GOD MOMENTS

Given that most criminals are not insane I had to ask the question:

X: Have you ever met any woman who was insane?

Collette: I've met people who the authorities considered mentally ill.

X: What makes the difference?

C: From what I can tell, they're not in reality.

X: How do you deal with someone who is not in reality?

C: You can't, unless they come back. The two I met in prisons were in cells on their own. I had to stand away from them, which I hated. I couldn't even give them a cuddle.

X: Is there a touch taboo in prisons?

C: Only in particular areas. But in these cases corrective services deemed that these women were not safe.

X: If you'd been allowed to do something do you think you might have been able to save them?

C: I don't know. They were so heavily drugged that I don't know if they knew what day it was, or if it was morning or night.

X: Of the thousands of women you have met in prisons, all of them are sane? All of them have made rational decisions?

C: There's a handful, though, that are there simply because there's nowhere else for them to go on the outside. They shouldn't be in jail but there's no mental institution for them. But sometimes prison isn't what people make it out to be. Sometimes prison, regardless of what it is, can be the person finding their soul, and their inner being, and they can come out, with a quality life.

X: So, while prison may be a bad thing, sometimes God works in mysterious ways?

C: Big things happen in jail, and if you're open to the possibility of change ... I have seen some women who have completely changed their life, and their outlook on life, while they've been in prison and have continued to live a decent life on the outside. Quality of life for these women has become the most important thing. And if a woman comes to jail with an attitude that she is going to sort herself out then, lo and behold, she's going to.

X: Do you think that people sort themselves out in prison because of prison, or in spite of it?

C: It's a lot of things. Prison will either make you or break you. There is so much in the daily rigmarole of just living in a prison that it can get to you. That's what some of us are there for, so you can offload, so that a woman to get rid of the junk, and to see the sun shining for the first time in her life ... it's that look on their face when they realise what they've got to do ... when they get tired of the petty life they have, that's when you know it's permanent. That look on their face stays there. There are those who you know aren't going to make it, but there are those you know who are. Their attitude changes. It's a massive decision, it happens immediately, instantly, and you know that when they get out they're going to get a flat, and they're going to get their life around and you can see them holding a job. For those women, if they had never been to jail, that option might never have been there for them. They would have continued eking out an existence. All of a sudden you can see that they've grabbed hold of it and they're running with it. All the money in the world will not pay for what you see on that woman's face. That's why some people are meant to have gone to jail. They are meant to have gone there to sort themselves out.

X: Many people who work in prisons, or who work with ex-prisoners, like you, come from a religious, especially a Christian background. You must have worked with and talked to prison chaplains. I wonder how they sell the idea of God the Father to people whose experiences of fathers are often so profoundly negative?

C: I once heard someone describe it something like this. Imagine the feeling of sunlight on your face on a warm autumn day. It's light. It's gentle and it's not tough. Feel that gentle kiss of light. If you can feel that light touch around your heart, that's God.

X: Regardless of whether you call God 'Father' or 'Mother' or anything else?

C: God is not a person that you can see. God is that loving touch that has no words. The gentle kiss of sunlight comes close to explaining that feeling that's around your heart, when you feel close to God, or you feel God moving in you. God's there all the time, ministering. All you need to do is acknowledge it.

X: Do you lead by example?

C: In my role I'm a professional, but I'm also a spiritual being, we all are. In that way I have to answer yes, I do what I can to lead by example, but not in such a rigid example that I can't come to their level and feel their pain and cry with them. I never want to lose the ability to cry and feel their pain and let them know that I care. Whatever my job description might be, in any situation my real work is about bringing people a greater understanding of themselves, to love themselves, to be able to say 'I'm O.K.' and then to have a strong relationship with God. Everyone is called to love their neighbour.

X: Do you think people commit crimes and are in prison because of a lack of love?

C: Some. But some have also come from very loving homes and have still chosen to do things that land them in prison.

X: Why?

C: Temptation. Drug traffickers, for example, want a lot of money fast. A woman once asked me, 'What do I need to do to find God again?' I said, 'That's easy, just sit with me and pray.' So we sat. I said a prayer. I asked the Lord to come into her heart. Then she said a prayer and then I said another prayer to finish off. Then she turned to me and grabbed hold of my hands. 'I needed that,' she said. 'I needed that too,' I said. Anyone can do this with anyone else. You just have to be there for them.

X: What does finding God mean to someone? Does finding God mean discovering that they're loved?

C: It's not only that they are loved, it's finding that inner strength. Sometimes through all the rules and regulations that all people have to abide by, not just prisoners, anybody, they lose themselves. Having the strength to cope ... some of the women have gone so deep. For me I couldn't cope working inside a women's prison if I weren't walking hand in hand with God or heart-to-heart with God. Without God you'd be doing this work on your own strength, and your own strength would run out about lunchtime.

There are just so many challenges that people who go to prison have to face. It can get a little overwhelming to someone who takes their freedom for granted—and that's the whole point.

This book isn't ultimately about criminals and prison. It's about freedom. I've spent my life doing everything I could to keep my freedom, and to let it fly—especially my freedom of speech, my freedom of opinion, my freedom of expression. Yet in spite of all the months I spent with the contributors of this book I didn't really appreciate what some of these people had lost. As I writer this last story touched me in the deepest way any story could. I hope none of you reading this ever take your freedom for granted, or anyone else's for that matter. Freedom is all you have, and it's worth everything.

Terry: You're dealing with people who are sharing houses when they've never shared with that many people before. You've got all these different attitudes. You've got that time of the month. You've got educated people. You've got non-educated people. You've got people there who can't even read and write.

I met a woman there who couldn't read or write. All I did was sit down with her and showed her the alphabet.

She was so excited she said she wanted to write a letter. Then I asked her who she'd write a letter to. She said her son. So I said, 'Talk to me as if you were talking to your son.' So I write the letter and I get her to copy what I've written. And I help her with all the letters she needed and at the end she even signs off 'All my love, mum.'

That was the first letter that woman had ever written.

She was forty-two.

APPENDIX 1 RESOURCES—AID AND COMMUNITY ORGANISATIONS

The following is a list of resources available to women who have had to deal with the Criminal Justice System. Some support is also available to their families and friends. If you need their help, but live too far away or in the wrong area, call them anyway and they may be able to refer you.

This list is by no means exhaustive, but the following organisations are a good place to start and the information below is current at the time of writing. A great many of these organisations are run by dedicated but often poorly resourced professionals and volunteers and their services are either free or very low cost. Feel free to make a donation or to volunteer to give whatever help you can. TTY numbers are for people who are hearing impaired.

AUSTRALIAN CAPITAL TERRITORY
Women's Information and Referral Centre (WIRC)
    Level 6, Eclipse House, 197 London Circuit Canberra City ACT 2600
    Ph: (02) 6205 1075. Wb: *www.wirc.act.gov.au/index.html*

NEW SOUTH WALES
Action Break Theatre Incorporated
    A theatre group for women caught up in the justice system. Female ex-prisoners are especially welcome to join these fine, extraordinary women and can explore their creative talents in a non-judgmental and productive environment, free of charge. Taaleah Jezierski, President & Artistic Director Pine Street Creative Arts Centre, 64 Pine Street, Chippendale NSW 2008. Mb: 0402 884 382, Em: *tkjez@optushome.com.au*

SHINE for Kids
    Holker Street Silverwater NSW 2128 PO Box 67 Ermington NSW 1700
    Ph: (02) 9714 3000, (02) 9714 3020, Fx: 02 9714 3030. Em: *admin@copsg.com*
    PO Box 2105 Bathurst NSW 2795. Em: *copsg@lisp.com.au*

Drug and Alcohol Treatment Accesss Line (Corella Drug Treatment Service)
    Treatment for people with drug or alcohol related problems in Fairfield and South West Sydney. Ph: (02) 9616 8586.

Community Restorative Centre (CRC)
    A community organisation established to helping prisoners, ex-prisoners

and their families and friends. They do great work and they also provide a CD (free!) to families explaining what happens to prisoners once they go into jail. It's interesting to compare the 'official' line on the CD to what some of the women reported as actually happening to them. Sydney Office 174 Broadway (corner of Shepherd Street) Broadway NSW 2007 Ph: (02) 9288 8700 Fx: 02 9211 6518 Em: info@crcnsw.org.au Wb: www.crcnsw.org.au

Newcastle Office
McKenzie Day Centre 16 Wood Street Newcastle West NSW 2300
PO Box 749 Hamilton NSW 2303

Women's Legal Services NSW Domestic Violence Advocacy Service
A free and completely confidential legal service for women.
Domestic Violence Advocacy Advice (02) 8745 6999
Women's Advice Line (02) 9749 5533
Hours 9.30am-12.30pm, 1.30pm-4.30pm M-F except Weds afternoon.
Indigenous Women's Program Advice Line
1800 639 784
Hours 10am-12.30pm, 2pm-4.30pm M-F except Weds afternoon.
PO Box H154 Harris Park NSW 2150
Administration ph: (02) 9637 5020
Fx: 02 9682 3844 Freecall: 1800 810 784 TTY: 1800 626 267

Inner City Legal Centre (ICLC)
Free and confidential legal advice, referrals and information on a wide range of issues including criminal matters and discrimination.
Room 31-32, 2nd Floor 94 Oxford Street Darlinghurst NSW 2010.
Ph: (02) 9332 1966 Wb: www.ICLC.org.au

Jailbreak Specialist community radio program dealing with prisoners and prison issues.
6:00 pm to 6:30 pm Tuesday evenings on 2SER FM 107.3.
Call 2SER for schedule changes—(02) 9514 9514.

Kairos Prison Ministry
Kairos Prison Ministry is an interdenominational ministry that conducts programs in prisons. Kairos aims to change the lives of prison inmates, particularly those who have the greatest potential to lead or influence others within a prison. PO Box 73, Northmead NSW 2152 Ph: (02) 9683 0286 Em: info@kairos.org.au

LifeLinks Community Support Services
Run by Baptist Community Services for individuals at risk of homelessness.
Baptist Community Services—NSW & ACT PO Box 655 Epping NSW 1710
28A Cambridge St Epping NSW 2121 Ph: (02) 9023 2500
Fx: (02) 9023 2501
Wb: www.bcs.org.au Em: corporate@bcs.org.au

Parent Line
Confidential help for parents, 13 2055

Prisoners Aid Association
174 Broadway (Cnr Shepherd Street) Broadway 2007 NSW
Ph: (02) 9281 8863 Fx: (02) 9211 6518

The Prison Fellowship
PO Box 411 Toongabbie, NSW 2146, Ph: 02 9896 1255
Em: pfansw@bigpond.com

Salvation Army Personal Support Program
273 Illawarra Road Marrickville NSW 2620 Ph: (02) 8585 2000

Stepping Out
Medium-term accommodation and support for women survivors of child
sexual assault, with or without children. PO Box 507 Leichhardt NSW 2040
Ph: (02) 9550 9398 Fx: (02) 9560 6549 TTY: (02) 9560 3464
Em: info@steppingout.org.au Web: ww.steepingout.org.au

Sydney Sexual Health
Centre 3rd Floor, Nightingale Wing Sydney Hospital and Sydney Eye
Hospital Macquarie Street Sydney NSW 2000

Ted Noffs Foundation
Provides a wide range of services and programs for marginalised youth and
young people at risk of offending. PO Box 120 Randwick NSW 2031.
Ph: (02) 9310 0133 Fx: (02) 9310 0020 Em: noffs@noffs.org.au

WorkVentures Connect@Waterloo
A low-cost Internet and email access service. Neighbourhood Technology
Centre Shop 2, 95 Wellington Street Waterloo NSW
Ph: (02) 9699 9201

NORTHERN TERRITORY
Offenders Aid and Rehabilitation Services
NT Inc Unit 13, 12 Charlton Court Stuart Park 0820 NT
PO Box 1028 Parap 0804 NT
Ph: (08) 8981 0487 Fx: 08 8981 1727 Em: *oars@oarsnt.org.au* Wb: *www.oarsnt.org.au*

QUEENSLAND
FNQ Families and Prisoners Support Inc
125 Abbott Street Cairns QLD 4870 Ph: (07) 4051 4485 Fx: (07) 4051 4485

Sisters Inside
PO Box 3407 South Brisbane QLD 4101 Ph: (07) 3844 5066
Fx: (07) 3844 2788 Em: *admin@sistersinside.com.au*

SOUTH AUSTRALIA
OARS SA (Offenders Aid and Rehabilitation Services Inc) Prison and
Community Services 234 Sturt Street ADELAIDE 5000 SA
Ph: (08) 8210 0811 Fx: (08) 8212 5515 WB: *www.oars.org.au*

TASMANIA
See Department of Justice, Prison Service.
Ph: (03) 6216 8180. WB: *www.justice.tas.gov.au/prisonservice*

VICTORIA
ACSO (Australian Community Support Organisation)
Ground Floor/357a Spencer Street West Melbourne VIC 3003
Ph: (03) 9320 4000 Fx: (03) 9328 4077 Em: *acso@acso.com.au*

Somebody's Daughter Theatre Company
Similar in mission to Action Break Theatre but longer established, having
begun in Fairlea Women's Prison in 1980. For further information contact
Maud Clark. Ph: (03) 9699 5961

VACRO (Victorian Association for the Care & Resettlement of Offenders)
Level 1, 116 Hardware Street Melbourne VIC 3000 Ph: (03) 9602 1366
Fx: (03) 9602 2355 Em: *enquiries@vacro.org.au*

WESTERN AUSTRALIA
Outcare Inc, 27 Moore Street EAST PERTH 6004 WA Ph: (08) 6263 8622
Fx: (08) 8263 8611 Em: *outcare@outcare.com.au*

APPENDIX 2 CORRECTIONAL FACILITIES FOR WOMEN IN AUSTRALIA

For a complete list of all correctional facilities in Australia, refer to the Australian Institute of Criminology Website
www.aic.gov.au/research/corrections/facilities/

AUSTRALIAN CAPITAL TERRITORY
Belconnen Remand Centre Rae St, Belconnen ACT 2617 Ph: (02) 6207 0733
The ACT's remand centre.

Periodic Detention Centre
Mugga Lane, Symonston ACT 2609
Ph: (02) 6207 2759 A periodic detention centre operating both during the week and on weekends.
The ACT has no current long-term correctional facilities for women. Prisoners are 'exported' to NSW, although there are plans to build some sort of facility in the future.

NEW SOUTH WALES
For further information about New South Wales Prisons see:
www.dcs.nsw.gov.au/ and *www.dcs.nsw.gov.au/sitemap.asp*

Berrima Correctional Centre
PO Box 250, Berrima NSW 2577 Argyle St, Berrima NSW 2577
Ph: (02) 4860 2555
Classification: Medium/Minimum.
The correctional centre is also responsible for the administration of periodic detention centres at Wollongong and Campbelltown.
Capacity: 70

Broken Hill Correctional Centre
109 Gossan St, Broken Hill NSW 2880 PO Box 403, Broken Hill NSW 2880
Ph: (08) 8087 3025
Classification: Medium (Male and Female);
Periodic detention centre, a reception prison. It holds a mixture of sentenced and remand inmates.
Capacity: 50 (45 males and 5 females)

Cooma Correctional Centre
   1 Vale St, Cooma NSW 2630 Ph: (02) 6455 0333
   Classification: Minimum/Medium (Males and Females)
   Capacity: 140

Dillwynia Women's Correctional Centre
   Part of the John Morony Correctional Complex, The Northern Rd, Windsor
   NSW 2756 Ph: (02) 4582 2509
   Classification: Minimum/Medium (Females)
   Dillwynia is the first prison in NSW built specifically for women. Some
   consider it to be somewhat of a showpiece of enlightened prison manage-
   ment and it has a strong focus on rehabilitation, reintegration and restora-
   tion. The facility has a wide variety of employment and education programs
   available to help empower prisoners.
   Capacity: 200

Emu Plains Correctional Centre
   Old Bathurst Rd, Emu Plains NSW 2750 Ph: (02) 4735 0200
   Classification: Minimum (Female)
   Emu Plains has a farm that provides the NSW prison system with produce. It
   also contains facilities and programs for mothers who have custody of their
   children below the age of five.
   Capacity: 118

Grafton Correctional Centre
   170 Hoof St, Grafton NSW 2460 PO Box 656, Grafton NSW 2460
   Ph: (02) 6642 0300
   Classification: Medium/minimum (males and females) A reception prison
   for northern NSW that also accommodates sentenced offenders.
   Capacity: Medium—154; Minimum—120

Long Bay Correctional Complex
   Anzac Parade, Matraville NSW 2036 PO Box 13 Matraville NSW 2036
   Ph: (02) 8304 2000
   Classification: Long Bay actually comprises five separate institutions: four
   maximum, one minimum security (males and females). Of relevance to
   women is Long Bay Hospital (maximum security) that holds a total of 120
   inmate patients in four wards—one medical ward and three for long-term
   and short-term psychiatric cases. The Department of Corrective Services and
   the NSW Department of Health jointly administer the hospital. The Metro-

politan Medical Transit Centre (maximum) holds discharged inmates of Long Bay Hospital as well as inmates awaiting medical appointments.

Mannus Correctional Complex

Linden Roth Drive, Mannus via Tumbarumba NSW 2653

Classification: Minimum (Male); Periodic detention centre (males and females). The PDC operates at weekends, employing detainees on community projects.

Capacity: Minimum—164; Periodic detention centre—24 males and six females. Ph: (02) 6941 0333

Mulawa Correctional Centre

Holker Street, Silverwater NSW 2128 Locked Bag 130, Australia Business Centre Silverwater NSW 1811 Ph: (02) 9289 5399

Classification: Maximum/medium/minimum (females) Principal correctional centre for women in NSW and is the first stop for many women prisoners in NSW. Mulawa comprises twelve living units, a protection/segregation area, induction unit and a hospital annexe. Remand prisoners, unsentenced and sentenced prisoners find themselves staying for various lengths of time in the three levels of detention at Mulawa.

Capacity: 235

Parramatta Correctional Centre

Locked Mail Bag 2 North Parramatta NSW 1750 Ph: (02) 9683 0300

Classification: PCC houses prisoners at various classifications for short-term stays until longer-term stays can be arranged at other centres depending on the nature of the individual case.

NORTHERN TERRITORY

For further information about Northern Territory Prisons see:

www.nt.gov.au/justice/graphpages/corrservs/index.shtml and
www.nt.gov.au/justice/graphpages/corrservs/contacts.shtml

Alice Springs Correctional Centre

Stuart Highway, Alice Springs NT 0870 PO Box 56, Alice Springs NT 0871 Ph: (08) 8951 8911

Classification: Maximum/Medium/Minimum (Male and Female) Main maximum security facility in the Northern Territory. Services most of the southern regions of the Northern Territory.

Capacity: 316 (main centre); 84 (low/open cottages outside main complex)

Darwin Correctional Centre
  Tivendale Rd, Berrimah NT 0828 GPO Box 1407, Darwin NT 0801
  Ph: (08) 8922 0111
  Classification: Maximum/Medium/Minimum (Male and Female). The Northern Territory's main reception prison services the northern part of the Territory.
  It also holds illegal immigrants and/or those subject to deportation.
  Capacity: 400

QUEENSLAND
  For further information about Queensland prisons see:
  www.dcs.qld.gov.au/index.html and
  www.dcs.qld.gov.au/contact.shtml

Brisbane Women's Correctional Centre
  PO Box 8025, Woolloongabba QLD 4102 Ph: (07) 3271 9000 Classification: Maximum/Medium/Minimum (Female).
  Secure facility for female prisoners in Queensland. Capacity: 270

Numinbah Correctional Centre
  Private Mail Bag 1, Nerang QLD 4211 Ph: (07) 5533 4131 Classification: Minimum Male and Female Prison Farm.
  Capacity: Male—104; Female—25

Townsville Correctional Centre (Farm and Main)
  PO Box 5574 MSO, Townsville QLD 4810 Ph: (07) 4799 8444
  Classification: Medium (Male); Maximum/Medium/Minimum (Female)
  Caters for all levels and mid-northern region of Queensland.
  Capacity: Main—399; Farm—95

SOUTH AUSTRALIA
  For further information about South Australian Prisons see:
  www.corrections.sa.gov.au/prisons/default.htm and
  www.corrections.sa.gov.au/contact/

Adelaide Women's Prison
  Grand Junction Road Northfield, SA 5085
  PO Box 2042 Regency Park SA 5010 Ph: (08) 8343 0100
  Classification: Maximum/Medium/Minimum (Female and remand)
  The prison has two main sections—mainstream, which accommodates high,

medium and low security and remand prisoners, and the Living Skills Unit for low security women.
Capacity: 71

James Nash House
140 Hilltop Drive C/- Hillcrest Hospital (Just off Fosters Road) Gilles Plains SA 5086 PO Box 94 Greenacres 5086 Ph: (08) 8266 9600
Classification: Maximum (Male and Female). Attached to the Adelaide Pre-release Centre JNH is a high-security unit for psychologically disturbed people.
Capacity: 30

Port Augusta Prison
Stirling North SA 5700 PO Box 6, Port Augusta SA 5700 Ph: (08) 8648 5400
Classification: Medium/Minimum (Male and Female) On account of its high population of Aboriginal inmates Port Augusta provides programs aimed at rehabilitation and reintegration. The Mobile Outback Work Camp scheme engages low security prisoners to help develop facilities in national parks and outback communities.
Capacity: 280

Yatala Labour Prison
Peter Brown Drive, Northfield SA 5085 Ph: (08) 8262 2421.
Like Long Bay in NSW Yatala also comprises distinct units including G-Division, the state's highest security facility.
Capacity: 406

TASMANIA
For further information regarding Tasmanian Prisons see:
www.justice.tas.gov.au/cc/ps_hp.htm

Hobart Remand Centre
27 Liverpool St, Hobart TAS 7250 Ph: 08 6233 4188
Capacity: 50

Launceston Remand Centre
Cimitere St, Launceston TAS 7250 Ph: 03 6336 3942
Classification: All security levels (Male and Female) Capacity: 33

Risdon Women's Prison
East Derwent Highway, Risdon TAS 7016 Ph: 03 6216 8180

Classification: Maximum/Medium/Minimum (Female). Risdon is the only facility in Tasmania specifically for women.
Capacity: 23

VICTORIA
Dame Phyllis Frost Centre
Riding-Boundary Road, Deer Park VIC 3023 Ph: (03) 9217 8400
Classification: Maximum/Medium/Minimum (Female). DPFC is the only secure facility for women in Victoria.
Capacity: 260

Tarrengower Prison
Cnr Baringhap and Nuggety Roads, Maldon VIC 3463
Classification: Minimum (Female) An 'Open Prison' with an emphasis on release preparation and community integration. Ph: (03) 5475 2011
Capacity: 54

WESTERN AUSTRALIA
For further information on Western Australian Prisons visit:
www.justice.wa.gov.au/portal/server.pt

Bandyup Women's Prison
Middle Swan Road, Middle Swan 6056 Ph: (08) 9374 8700
Classification: Maximum/Medium/Minimum (Female). Bandyup is the only secure facility in WA specifically for women.
Capacity: 164

Boronia Pre-release Centre for Women
14 Hayman Road, Bentley WA 6102 Ph: (08) 9212 3600
Classification: Minimum (Female) Boronia is a sort of combined prison / halfway house with accommodation for up to seventy women and their children with a main focus of reintegrating women offenders back into the community.

Broome Regional Prison
Hamersley St, Broome WA 6725 Ph: (08) 9193 8500
Classification: Minimum (Male and Female); Medium (short time only and remands). Broome is the only prison in the vast Kimberly region of Australia. Like Townsville, its existence reflects this country's huge geography and sparse non-urban population.
Capacity: 89

Eastern Goldfields Regional Prison
  Vivian St, Boulder WA 6432 Ph: (08) 9093 5100
  Classification: Minimum (Male and Female); very short term holding capacity for higher security prisoners.
  Principally a low-security facility with some remand functions.
  Capacity: 96

Greenough Regional Prison
  Narngulu Road, Greenough via Geraldton WA 6530 Ph: 1 800 680 807
  Classification: Medium/Minimum (Male and Female); Maximum (remand).
  Capacity: 246

Roebourne Regional Prison
  Sampson Road, Roebourne WA 6718 Ph: (08) 9182 0100
  Classification: Medium/Minimum (Male and Female); Maximum (short term). Roebourne is a facility in which all prisoners are required to work or study.
  Capacity: 163

JUVENILE JUSTICE CENTRES/DETENTION CENTRES FOR GIRLS

AUSTRALIAN CAPITAL TERRITORY
Quamby Youth Detention Centre
  Mugga Lane Symonston ACT 2609 Ph: (02) 6207 0792

NEW SOUTH WALES
Yasmar, 185 Parramatta Road, Haberfield NSW 2045
  Ph: (02) 9797 3000

NORTHERN TERRITORY
Alice Springs Juvenile Holding Centre Aranda House
  9 Kemp St Alice Springs 0870 Ph: (08) 8953 5934
  Designed for use as a short-term holding/remand centre for up to four days.

Don Dale Juvenile Detention Centre
  Berrimah, adjacent to the Darwin Correctional Centre Ph: 08 8922 0400
  Classification: Maximum/Medium (Male and Female).
  Main centre for the detention of juveniles within the Northern Territory.

QUEENSLAND
Brisbane Youth Detention Centre
 Cnr Aveyron and Wolston Roads
 Wacol QLD 4076 Ph: (07) 3271 0777

SOUTH AUSTRALIA
Cavan, 1 Jonal Drive Cavan SA 5094 Ph: (08) 8200 6400

TASMANIA
Ashley Youth Detention Centre
 PO Box 126 Deloraine TAS 7304 Ph: 03 6362 2311

VICTORIA
Parkville Youth Residential Centre
 930 Park Street Parkville VIC 3052 Ph: 03 9389 4400

WESTERN AUSTRALIA
Banksia Juvenile Detention Centre
 PO Box 1512 Canning Vale WA 6155 Ph: 08 9333 2222

Rangeview Remand Centre
 PO Box 149 Willetton WA 6155 Ph: 08 9333 9100

APPENDIX 3 PRISON POPULATIONS THROUGHOUT AUSTRALIA AS AT 2003-04

For an in-depth statistical overview of criminality in Australia I recommend the Australian Institute of Criminology's website, in particular relating to prison statistics: *www.aic.gov.au/publications/facts/2003/part5.html*.

According to the Steering Committee for the Review of Commonwealth State Service Provision 2004, 'Report on government services, volume 1: education, justice, emergency management', Productivity Commission, Canberra (which can be found at *www.pc.gov.au/gsp/reports/rogs/2004/index.html*) out of all offenders throughout Australia 69% are dealt with by community programs. Only 31% of all offenders end up serving time in prisons. Males make up approximately 93% of the prison population. So if you've got 25 000 people serving time in jails, then there's about another 55 000 who offend but who don't spend time in jails. This means that about 80 000 Australians have dealings with the criminal justice system every year. A population equivalent to a city the size of Ballarat is either in jail or doing some other form of penance every year in Australia.

According to the Australian Bureau of Statistics 2004, *Prisoners in Australia* 2003, cat. no. 4517.0, ABS, Canberra:

A total of 23 555 people were in prison on 30 June 2003. The growth over ten years from 1993 to 2003 was 50%; the adult population increase in this time was 15%. The Northern Territory recorded the highest imprisonment rate of 513 prisoners per 100 000 adult population: three times the national rate. Victoria recorded the lowest imprisonment rate of 94 prisoners per 100 000 adult population. The highest imprisonment rate increases between 2003 and 2004 were in the Australian Capital Territory (11%) and Western Australia (8%). The highest imprisonment rate decreases between 2003 and 2004 were in Tasmania and Victoria (a decrease of 3% and 2% respectively). Between 1995 and 2004, all states and territories (with the exception of South Australia) recorded an increase in imprisonment rates. There were 5048 Indigenous prisoners in Australia (21% of the prisoner population) at 30 June 2004. The crude imprisonment rate for the Indigenous population was 1852 prisoners per 100 000 population. After adjusting for age differences between the Indigenous and non-Indigenous populations, *Indigenous people were 11 times more likely than non-Indigenous people to be imprisoned* (age-standardised imprisonment ratio). There were 22 499 male prisoners at 30 June 2004 (93% of the prisoner population) and 1672 female prisoners (7% of the prisoner population). The proportion of prisoners who were female ranged from 2% in Northern Territory to 8% in Western Australia. The imprison-ment rate for males was 297 per 100 000 adult male population and for females it was 21 per 100 000 adult female population. While males were 14 times more likely than females to be in prison, over the past 10 years the female prisoner population has increased at a faster rate than the male prisoner population. Between 1994 and 2004, *the female prisoner population has increased by 101%, in comparison to a 40% increase in the male prisoner population.*

Just over half of all prisoners were males aged between 20 and 34 years. The 25–29 year age group had the highest imprisonment rates for both males and females, with 641 male prisoners per 100 000 adult males aged 25–29, and 49 female prisoners per 100 000 adult females aged 25–29. In 2003 there were 1594 female prisoners compared with 380 in 1984.

Endnotes

1) Before the academics who are reading this book start ganging up on me and leaping on any lapse of pedantic semantics to undermine my credibility and for the interest of the general public let me make one thing clear: The word history comes from the Latin *historia*, meaning, well, history, and is ultimately derived from the Greek *histor*, 'one who knows or sees'. There's no connection between history and the Old English/Germanic 'his'. Nevertheless this linguistic coincidence has allowed more than one writer to note that, for the most part, it is men who write 'his story'—history.

2) The law is unconstitutional anyway. It violates Chapter 5 section 116 of the Commonwealth of Australia Constitution Act. You can follow almost the whole stupid saga on the Pagan Awareness Network website. It's a little out of date but it gives you an idea of what a media circus the Watts case was, and how a woman's life can be messed up because of stupid and archaic laws.

3) Daniels, K., *Convict Women*, Allen and Unwin, Sydney, , 1998, p. 51.

4) Ibid. p. 91.

5) Lloyd, A., *Doubly Deviant, Doubly Damned—Society's Treatment of Violent Women*, Penguin Books,1995. pp. ix, x.

6) Source: Australian Institute of Criminology Website.

7) Kelleher, M.D. and Kelleher, C.L., *Murder Most Rare—The Female Serial Killer*, Praeger, Wesport, Connecticut, 1998, V 162.

8) This is true, for the most part, however, according to the *Encyclopaedia of Aboriginal Australia* (Aboriginal Studies Press for the Australian Institute of Aboriginal and Torres Strait Islander Studies, 1994) Aboriginal people very seldom indulged in mood-altering substances and drugs played an almost non-existent role in Aboriginal cultures before 1788.

9) Of course, these figures don't exactly make sense. If ATSI women are 25 times more likely to end up in jail than non-ATSI women then they should be 50% of the prison population, since 2% times 25 is 50. Would someone please make sense of this? No wonder people don't trust statistics. Either way ATSI women are highly over-represented in prisons.

10) Brahm, A., *Opening the Door to Your Heart*, Lothian, Melbourne, 2004 pp. 77–79.

11) Davenport-Hines, R., *The Pursuit of Oblivion*, Phoenix Press, Orion Books, London, 2001.

12) Australian Bureau of Statistics 2004, *Prisoners in Australia* 2003, cat. no. 4517.0, ABS, Canberra.

13) For a full treatment of Lonnie Athens' provocative theory of violentisation read Rhodes, R., *Why They Kill*, Vintage Books, Random House, New York, 1999.

14) Hardly surprising considering our society's education system: 'When you finish your education, you will not remember much of the course content, but the habits of passivity, hierarchy and obedience will be deeply ingrained.' Sign on Ray Jackson's wall he attributed to a 'Marxist saying'.

15) Poster, The People Justice Alliance, PO Box 1567, Collingwood, 3066.

16) *Green Left Weekly*, Online edition, 1999, 355, p. 2.

Index

More true crime titles

- **Twelve Crimes that Shocked the Nation**— *Alan Whiticker*

- **You Be The Judge** — *Craig Jensen*

- **Australian Crime** — *Malcolm Brown*

- **Bombs, Guns & Knives** — *Malcolm Brown*

- **Life Behind Bars** — *Neer Korn*

- **Milperra** — *Ron Stephenson*

- **Scent of a Crime** — *Ron Stephenson*

- **To Protect and To Serve**— *Tim Priest and Richard Basham*

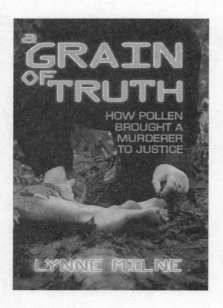

- **A Grain of Truth** — *Lynne Milne*

Published by New Holland: www.newholland.com.au

- **Halfway to Justice** — Ken Turner and Lesley Turner

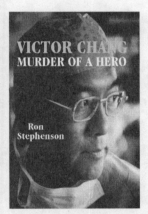

- **Victor Chang, Murder of a Hero** — Ron Stephenson

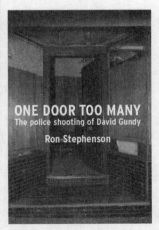

- **One Door Too Many** — Ron Stephenson